The Growth of American Constitutional Law

The Growth of American CONSTITUTIONAL LAW

BENJAMIN F. WRIGHT

Associate Professor of Government
in Harvard University

HENRY HOLT AND COMPANY
NEW YORK

December, 1946

PRINTED IN THE UNITED STATES OF AMERICA

For

Janet and David

Preface

IN THIS BOOK I have attempted to give a brief account of the work of the Supreme Court of the United States in passing upon the constitutionality of legislation. The institution of judicial review of legislation has long seemed to me to be one of the American institutions of which it is essential to have some understanding in order to comprehend the course of American history or the character of American political life. It is a more peculiar feature of American history than, for example, the frontier movement, or immigration, or the growth of cities. It resembles less the constitutional laws and practices of other states than do the systems of checks and balances, or federalism, or adult suffrage, all of which have sometimes been spoken of as uniquely American.

Since the present book deals only with those decisions of the Supreme Court which consider the constitutionality of state or Congressional legislation it does not deal with the entire body of constitutional law, if that term be used in its broader sense. It does not, that is to say, deal with doctrines expressed in cases interpreting the meaning of statutes (except for a few deviations for the purpose of illustration), nor with decisions reviewing the findings of lower courts where the validity of legislation was not involved, nor with the review of administrative officers and commissions. It is concerned with constitutional law in its narrower sense, with what James Bradley Thayer, in his classic essay, called "The American Doctrine of Constitutional Law." Even within the bounds of "constitutionality" law it can, of course, make no pretence of complete coverage or of thorough analysis. It is offered only as a general survey and interpretation of this aspect of American development. This is said not in apology, but in explanation. The notes will indicate some of the articles and books which deal more intensively with portions of the subject. And of such intensive work there has been an abundance. The four thick volumes of *Selected Essays on Constitutional Law* published in 1938 under the auspices of the Association of American Law Schools contain a collection which is invaluable to one who desires a closer acquaintance with the history and principles of American constitutional law up to the time of the Court struggle of 1937. But, although this mass of periodical literature has been supplemented in recent years by a number of very useful monographs, there have been few attempts to survey the entire story.

Although this book does not attempt to deal even sketchily with all the problems of constitutional law, it was based upon a survey of all Supreme Court decisions, and it is an attempt to present an organized picture of the results of that study. The comprehensiveness of this survey was made possible by the assistance of Professor Earl G. Latham, Mr. A. W. Warner, and Miss Eleanor Poland who laid the groundwork for it by digesting and rechecking some thousands of opinions. I am very gateful to them, and to the Committee on Research in the Social Sciences of Harvard University for a grant which made it possible for me to secure their services. Professor Harvey Mansfield of Yale University read the manuscript and made a number of suggestions which were of value in its revision. Mr. Robert A. Horn checked citations for me and made many useful criticisms of both form and substance. Mr. Louis Hartz helped me to clarify my ideas about the nature of judicial review and its relation to other aspects of American history.

Leverett House, B. F. W.
Cambridge, Massachusetts,
January 28, 1942.

Contents

The Growth of American Constitutional Law

Chapter I

CONSTITUTIONAL DEMOCRACY AND THE COURTS

JUDGED by the objective criteria the American is one of the most rigid of modern constitutions. It is composed of a body of rules which are denominated "the supreme law of the land." It cannot be altered by vote of Congress even though the Congress be one elected but a few weeks earlier, though its vote be unanimous, and though the President enthusiastically concur. For the American constitutional system is based upon the principle that once the fundamental law, or constitution, is established, it is not to be altered by any simple process of majority vote. The Constitution does contain that great modern invention, of which William Penn was apparently the originator, an amending clause. It makes possible change by legal, constitutional means. It assumes neither everlasting perfection nor improvement only through extra-constitutional, possibly revolutionary, channels. But though constitutional amendment is possible, it is very difficult. Not so difficult, to be sure, as in the predecessor of the present Constitution, the Articles of Confederation, where unanimous consent of the states was required. The change from unanimous consent to a three-fourths majority was one of the great achievements of the Federal Convention, but it did not go far enough to make for frequent amendment, or for what would be described as a flexible constitution.

Yet if the American Constitution is relatively inflexible, it is also the oldest of national constitutions. It has outlived all of those which were less rigid, which seemed to make orderly growth an easier and a more normal part of the procedure of government. Only the Constitution of Massachusetts, adopted in 1780, is older than that of the United States, and while the former has been so many times amended that the original document has been largely obscured, the latter has had few formal changes made in it. The first ten amendments were adopted as a kind of explanatory guarantee or appendix immediately after the Constitution went into effect. In the one hundred and fifty years since those amendments were adopted only eleven additional amendments have been added. Two were added early, in 1798 and in 1804, and were not so much additions to, as technical corrections of, the clauses providing for the jurisdiction of the federal courts and the election of the President. Of the remaining nine amendments two, the Eighteenth and Twenty-first, dealing with the prohibition of intoxicating beverages, cancel out and leave the Constitution where it was before the Eighteenth was adopted. The remaining seven amendments provide for alterations of some substantive importance. During Reconstruction three amendments dealing with the rights of Negroes were adopted. The Sixteenth and Seventeenth came in 1913. The first provides for income taxes, the second for direct election of Senators. By the Nineteenth, adopted in 1920, suffrage discrimination against women is prohibited, and the Twentieth, adopted in 1933, alters slightly the time at which Congress shall meet and the President take office.

This combination of longevity and of an absence of numerous radical amendments indicates that there is something wrong in the classification of the Constitution as a rigid document. In a purely formal sense it is not flexible. But when it has continued, for over a century and a half, to serve as the instrument of government for a country in which the settled area has more than quadrupled, the population has multiplied by more than thirty times, the way of life has changed from a rural, agricultural pattern to a predominantly urbanized industrialism, and remains the fundamental law for a country which has experienced invasion, a fierce civil war, several adventures in imperialism, and basic alterations in its racial composition, that Constitution has, by any meaningful standard, been an adaptable, as well as a successful one.

It is in the history of the Constitution's interpretation that we find the chief clue to the successful adaptation of that instrument's provisions to the multiple transformations of American life. Formal amendments are not to be neglected. Certainly the possibility of official, legally sanctioned change has always been an essential presupposition of American constitutionalism. It is true, nevertheless, that most of the development of the constitutional system is not accounted for by these amendments.

American constitutional history is not lacking in paradoxes. Not the least of them is to be found in the combination of the greatest and most enduring reverence for written constitutions of which modern history at least gives any record with the fact that many of the most significant changes in our constitutional system have come without any legal sanction. Of these usages or customs perhaps the most striking are those which have proceeded from the growth of political parties. The founding fathers neither desired nor anticipated parties as we know them. The Constitution makes no provision for them. Yet our government is of parties, by parties, and, at times, for parties. The party system has altered the method of electing the President far more than did the Twelfth Amendment, just as it has conditioned the relationship of President and Congress well beyond the regulations of the Constitution.

This book is not concerned with those extra-legal usages of the Constitution of which the party system is such a notable example. It is concerned with the development through law and judicial interpretation. The great influence of the non-legal changes is freely granted, but it remains true that the central course of American constitutional development has been legal. Our tradition is heavily legalistic. A century ago Alexis de Tocqueville, the most perspicacious of foreign commentators upon American institutions, wrote that "If I were asked where I place the American aristocracy, I should reply, without hesitation, that it is not among the rich, who are united by no common tie, but that it occupies the judicial bench and bar." [1] Even at that time it was becoming apparent how great was to be the control exercised by the exponents of a legal tradition upon American institutional development.

Not all of the legalistic interpretation of the Constitution has emanated from the courts. Ordinarily the Congress initiates the process of interpretation when it enacts a statute. As the President's leadership in the legislative process has grown he has increasingly participated in constitutional interpretation through his advocacy and initiation of legislation. At any rate it is in the acts passed by Congress that one finds the greatest bulk of constitutional interpretation. In England a statute of Parliament is subject to judicial interpretation but not to judicial review. Its meaning is determined by the courts but the judges may not hold it to be unconstitutional, even though it may, like the Act of Settlement of 1701 or the Parliament Act of 1911, fundamentally alter what is called the British Constitution. Under the American system of judicial review the final decision, short of constitutional amendment, rests with the judiciary. By simple majority vote the members of the Supreme Court might conceivably override the unanimous vote of the Congress to which had been added the approval of the President. Thus decisions on the meaning of the Constitution are determined not by majority

---

[1] *Democracy in America,* I, ch. XVI (ed. by Francis Bowen, 1862, p. 355).

vote of the people or of the Congress but by majority vote of the Supreme Court.

No other state has ever entrusted to its courts a power of this magnitude. Some countries, notably certain of the British Dominions, have imitated the American system in part but none has gone the whole way. The institution of judicial review may, indeed, be termed our most unique and most characteristic institution. Since 1789 federalism of the sort devised by the Federal Convention has ceased to be as peculiar to the United States as it originally was. Our separation between the legislative and executive departments has been copied by many Latin American countries. Only in part has judicial review been an export commodity.

Because it has been both a uniquely American institution and a powerful force in American life and thought an understanding of its history and its results is essential to an appreciation of the character of American democracy. Certainly the story of American democracy is not any simple narrative of successive movements for broadening the bases of privilege and of power. The story is much more complex than that, for the democratic tradition in America is a tradition of constitutionalism as well as of increasingly popular government. Indeed, the period in which the greatest strides toward a more popular government were being made, the period to which the name Jacksonian democracy is usually given, was also the era in which judicial review was expanding most rapidly. It is, I believe, entirely incorrect to see in these two tendencies a basic antagonism, as if judicial review were the product of a group or groups opposed to the growth of a democratic polity. Both of these developments, like others not here under consideration, were the resultants of powerful urges in American thought, just as written constitutions were no less characteristic of the American Revolution than was the Declaration of Independence. Not all of the democratic reformers were supporters of the growing power of the

courts, but the majority of those who, in the constitutional conventions of the first half of the nineteenth century, voted for a broader suffrage and for the popular election of members of the executive and judicial departments, were also sympathetic to the judicial interpretation of the documents they were writing. It is frequently assumed that judicial review either originated in or was first developed by the Supreme Court of the United States. This assumption is incorrect. As will be indicated in the next chapter, the earliest instances of judicial review came in the state courts before the present national Constitution was written. The expansion of the judicial power did not proceed at a uniform rate in all of the states, but neither was it confined to any particular state or group of states. It has been a national phenomenon in more senses than one.

Although constitutional exegesis has long been the supreme occupation of the American judiciary, it does not follow that other and less final sources of constitutional interpretation have been of slight significance. I have already pointed out that most constitutional interpretation originates with the President or Congress and ordinarily takes the form of statutes. Just what proportion of Congressional acts are tested for constitutionality in the courts I do not know, but I should suppose that it is a minority. Even though nearly all of those statutes which represent important interpretations of the Constitution are subject to judicial review, it is probable that scores, and more likely hundreds, of statutes which add their small bit to the ever-growing constitutional structure are not so tested. If this statement is true it does not detract from the importance of judicial review, for the decisive point is that when there is doubt regarding the constitutionality of an act it is the courts which resolve that doubt.

The power of judicial review has sometimes been labeled a veto power, but this characterization is not entirely accu-

rate. In one sense the courts do confine their decisions of invalidity to saying, "this may not be done." They do not initiate legislation, and, with rare exceptions, they do not suggest possible substitutes for statutes declared unconstitutional. Their power is closely related to the legislative power, but they do not legislate. They do not legislate, that is, when passing upon the validity of an act. When they are interpreting its meaning and applying it to particular situations they do exercise a function which may be called one of legislation. But this function is not peculiar to American courts. It has frequently been pointed out that English courts may amend the meaning of statutes under the guise of interpreting them. American courts have been known to do the same thing. But to say, as many have said, that when a court nullifies ar act it is legislating is a misuse of terms. The result of t judicial veto is not legislation but an absence of legislatio It may mean that legislation on the subject of the statute impossible, short of a constitutional amendment. The con stitutional interpretation upon which the decision of invalidity was based may not be well founded, whether considered in terms of the original meaning of the Constitution, the purposes for which it was established, or the meaning given in earlier judicial opinions. Such an opinion might, were it not for the awkwardness of the term, be called constitutionalizing, but it cannot be called legislating.

Since judicial review, as here discussed, has consisted of passing upon the constitutionality of statutes already enacted, how may it be said that the courts have contributed materially to the growth of the Constitution? It might seem that theirs has been an exclusively negative contribution, and consequently one of minor, not major, significance. When the courts declare an act invalid they may be preventing a violation of the Constitution. When they sustain it they but approve of what Congress has done. This is true, but it is not the whole truth. Judicial review has not been limited to saying yes or no. For the courts have in sustaining laws done more than give to those laws an authoritative stamp. They have also added to them a reasoned justification. By virtue of the persuasive reasoning which it has added to the new interpretations or adaptations of the Constitution the judiciary has created an ideology or opinion or "myth" which the public can unite in accepting.

This rational reconciliation of a fixed constitution with continuous growth and change has been one of the really essential elements in both the permanence and the flexibility of the Constitution. Where the President's approval or veto has ordinarily been exercised in terms of policy, the courts have expressed their approval or disapproval in terms of constitutional principles. And though the Americans have not been a philosophical people, they have been constitution-minded. Constitutionalism has been one of the most persistent and pervasive characteristics of American democracy. A very large proportion, perhaps the greater part, of American political thought since 1789 might as well be called constitutional theory. It has proceeded upon the assumptions contained in, or derived from, the written Constitution. Because this has been the basis for most political thought, justification of change in terms of constitutional principles has given a vitality and a sanction to constitutional expansion which could have been obtained in no other way. Because the Supreme Court has been the final interpreter of the Constitution that Court has come to be a major symbol of constitutionalism, which is to say that it has been the great symbol of stability and security. The way in which the Court attained this position and the uses it has made of its great power are the subjects of the present book.

Chapter II

THE BEGINNINGS OF JUDICIAL REVIEW

THE power of the courts to pass upon the constitutionality of legislation was not invented by the founding fathers in 1787, and it was not copied from the experience of any other country. That much is certain. It is also clear that the ultimate origins of this institution are part of that seamless web of history which Maitland found when he came to deal with the earliest period of English legal history. We cannot hope to unravel and then to reweave into a pattern understandable to modern minds all of the strands of that web, but some elements of the design can be deciphered.

THEORIES OF HIGHER LAW

For one thing it is evident that judicial review as we know it would be an impossibility without a long antecedent history of legalism, of a high regard for law and for the interpreters of the law. The growth of the common law is an essential part of the picture. But long before the time of Bracton one can find expressions of the attitude which, two thousand years later, was to help to place the courts of the United States in a position of power unknown to the ancient world. *The Republic* is the greatest of arguments in support of the doctrine that there are fundamental principles superior to any man-made rules. And *The Laws* gives ample evidence of Plato's faith in the efficacy of constitutions and codes. "The law," said Aristotle, "is reason unaffected by desire." [1] "Surely the ruler cannot dispense with the general principle which exists in law," for "the rule of law is preferable to that of any individual." [2] It was Greek philosophy which the Roman jurists wove into the great body of law which governed the world long after the fall of the Empire. And in the legal and political thought of Europe such doctrines persisted throughout the changes of rulers, of social systems, and of principles of government. In its most prevalent form this concept was that of a law of nature. The law of nature was made by no man or group of men. It is behind and superior to human rules. Man cannot alter, but he should conform to the principles which are of eternal validity. The quality of justice inheres in the laws of men only as those laws reflect the laws of nature. It follows that if the rules of men do express the natural law they are thereby endowed with a fundamental character, and they are, therefore, not lightly to be altered.

During the sixteenth and seventeenth centuries this ancient doctrine of natural law gave birth to a conception of natural rights which was in turn to be one of the most useful weapons in the modern armory of revolution. In the English Civil War and Glorious Revolution it was expressed and reiterated as against the Stuart ideal of divine right. Defended eloquently by Milton, given a martyr's sanction by Sydney, and stated in heavy but impressive terms by Locke, it filtered into the American colonies during the first half of the eighteenth century, and became the principal dogma of the Revolution.[3] The rights of self-government, of taxation

[1] *Politics,* Book III, ch. 16. [2] *Ibid.,* ch. 15.

[3] Edward S. Corwin, "The 'Higher Law' background of American Constitutional Law," 42 *Harvard Law Review,* 149, 365 (1928-1929), also in *Selected Essays on Constitutional Law* (1938), I, 1; C. G. Haines, *The Revival of Natural Law Concepts* (1930), Part I; B. F. Wright, *American Interpretations of Natural Law* (1931), ch. IV.

by their own representatives, and of judicial procedure for which the Americans at first argued and later fought were set forth as the rights guaranteed by the British constitution and the laws of nature. When the British constitution proved to offer no sanctuary, they placed sole reliance upon the "laws of nature and of nature's God." These rights were "self-evident" truths, because they were derived from a source of universal authority.

But the resort to nature was not the whole of the theory of fundamental law. Beginning with the early charters as a basis the colonists had shown themselves to have a fondness for written statements of their basic political laws.[4] This practice was not copied from the experience of England for, except for a few months in 1653, the mother country never had a written constitution. These Englishmen on a distant continent carried the principle of Magna Charta, and of many other medieval compacts of the kind, to what seemed to them a reasonable conclusion—the formulation of written constitutions. From the day in 1639 when the settlers in Connecticut gave to the modern world its first constitution adopted by popular authority, it gradually became increasingly clear that in this country the theory and practice of written constitutions was to occupy a position of importance, the like of which no country had previously known. When the Revolution came it was natural for the colonists to prepare and adopt written statements of the rules under which they were to be governed. These constitutions were fundamental laws as distinguished from legislative statutes. But not one of them made any provision for judicial review.

If factors essential to the development of judicial review are to be found in the history of fundamental law, unwritten and written, the exercise of that power by the courts is not accounted for by it alone, as, indeed, it can not be accounted

[4] B. F. Wright, "The Early History of Written Constitutions in America," *Essays in History and Political Theory* (1936), 344.

for by any single source or example. Another factor of great importance is to be found in the common law tradition that is embodied in the great constitutional documents and expressed by many a judge. Akin to the doctrine of natural law it holds that certain fundamental rules of the law are above the power of Parliament to alter. It was stated in its most extreme form by Sir Edward Coke in Bonham's Case where Coke said: "And it appears in our books, that in many cases, the common law will controul acts of parliament, and sometimes adjudge them to be utterly void: for when an act of parliament is against common right and reason, or repugnant, or impossible to be performed, the common law will controul it, and adjudge such act to be void." [5]

In England the tradition of the supremacy of the common law survived, but the practice whereby that supremacy was given expression in decrees of the courts was never established. There is, in all English history, no authenticated instance of a decision setting aside an act of Parliament. But if Coke lost his cause in England he won it in America. For when the colonists began to protest against the tax and regulatory acts of Parliament they turned to the theory of constitutionality. The most famous instance of its expression is that reported by John Adams, a spectator of the trial in which James Otis declaimed against the Writs of Assistance. "Reason and the constitution," said Otis, "are both against this writ . . . had this writ been in any book whatever, it would have been illegal. All precedents are under the control of principles of law. . . . No acts of Parliament can establish such a writ; though it should be made in the very words of the petition, it would be void. An act against the constitution is void." [6] In his famous pamphlet published three years later

[5] 8 Co. 118a (1610). Cf. Theodore F. T. Plucknett, "Bonham's Case and Judicial Review," 40 *Harvard Law Review*, 30 (1926), *Selected Essays on Constitutional Law*, I, 67. [6] John Adams, *Works*, II, 525.

he declared that "if the supreme legislative errs, it is informed by the supreme executive in the King's courts of law." [7]

COLONIAL INSTITUTIONS

Talk of constitutionality was much in the air, even though England had no single written constitution, partly because of the doctrine of a higher law, partly because of the existence in many of the colonies of a charter or a proprietary frame of government which, in some measure, served as a constitution, and partly because the colonists were not unaccustomed to seeing their statutes reviewed by a higher authority. The review of colonial legislation by the Privy Council was not judicial review.[8] It was nearer to our executive veto, except that it was exercised by a superior, not a coordinate or equal authority. Judicial procedure was not observed and decision was not on the basis of constitutionality. It was, however, of importance in habituating the colonists to the conception of a higher standard of legality than legislative will.

Nor were the courts in the colonies courts of final resort. Appeals were taken in some 265 cases from them to the Judicial Committee of the Privy Council.[9] In all except three of these cases the validity of colonial statutes was apparently not involved. One case resulted in a decision contrary to the validity of a statute, but that was subsequently overruled, nor does there seem to have been any general conception of this practice as one involving constitutional issues.

---

[7] *The Rights of the British Colonies Asserted and Proved* (1764), 71.

[8] E. B. Russell, *The Review of American Colonial Legislation by the King in Council* (1915); L. W. Labaree, *Royal Government in America* (1930), ch. VI.

[9] A. M. Schlesinger, "Colonial Appeals to the Privy Council," *Political Science Quarterly*, XXVIII, 279, 433 (1913).

STATE PRECEDENTS AND CONSTITUTIONS

Throughout the colonial period there was no instance in which a colonial court authoritatively set aside a colonial statute.[10] There may have been such cases but, if there were, there were no published court reports in which they could be discovered or to which citation could be made. In spite, however, of lack of precedent and of absence of provision in the early state constitutions, there are some seven cases in which state courts declared state legislation invalid between 1778 and 1787. Again, there may have been other such decisions, but if so, they have been lost for lack of official published reports. The decisions of invalidity were apparently not effective in all of these cases.[11] As judicial precedents they are frail reeds upon which to lean. Their importance lies not in their legal effect, or lack thereof, but rather in that they give evidence of a widespread trend toward judicial safeguarding of the fundamental law. That it was remarkably widespread is shown by the fact that the seven "cases" are from seven states and the states are scattered from Connecticut to North Carolina.

If none of the early state constitutions provided for judicial review, three contained provisions for institutional devices intended to achieve somewhat similar purposes. Under the New York Constitution of 1777 a Council of Revision, consisting of the governor and members of the judiciary, was established. This council was given a qualified negative over legislative acts. This was not judicial review; it was a veto shared by the executive and judges. This veto, which could be overridden by a two-thirds vote in the legislature, was to be exercised for the prevention of "laws inconsistent with the spirit of this constitution, or with the public good." In

---

[10] But cf. C. G. Haines, *The American Doctrine of Judicial Supremacy* (2d ed., 1932), 57, for the interesting statement of a local magistrate in Giddings v. Brown (1657). [11] Haines, *op. cit.*, ch. V.

short, the council was charged with checking laws which were unwise, harmful, or contrary to the general principles, as well as the letter, of the constitution. A proposal to establish such a system for the federal government was strongly supported in the Convention of 1787, but it was rejected by the majority.

In the ingenious but unpopular and short-lived Pennsylvania Constitution of 1776, section 46 provides for the establishment of a Council of Censors, whose duty was to preserve the constitution, to pass public censures, to order impeachments, to recommend the repealing of harmful or unconstitutional laws, and to recommend constitutional amendments. Almost from its first day this body, which was elective, was in difficulties, largely because it was as much involved in the partisan politics of the time as was the legislature itself. With the adoption of a new constitution in 1790 the system was dropped. It lingered on in Vermont until 1869. The Vermont Constitution of 1777 copied the Pennsylvania Council of Censors section as it did most of the other provisions of that constitution. Largely because the Vermont council was less ambitious than that of Pennsylvania, it continued to exist long after it had ceased to be a factor of great importance in Vermont's affairs. Indeed, its chief contribution appears to have been its influence in slowing up the introduction of judicial review in Vermont.[12]

THE FEDERAL CONVENTION

When the Federal Convention met in 1787 there were a few rather shaky precedents for judicial review, though none of them was published in a law report, but no existing constitution made any provision for the exercise of such a power by the courts. It is clear that the federal Constitution includes no clause expressly conferring this power upon the

[12] Haines, *op. cit.*, 80, 82.

federal courts.[13] There is, nevertheless, evidence adequately demonstrating that a number of the framers assumed that the power of review would be exercised by federal, as well as state courts, and over congressional as well as state legislation. The number is not large and many of the statements relied upon as evidence of a belief in judicial review are of an equivocal character.[14] But the very fact that such views were expressed, and only very rarely questioned, even though no motion to incorporate a provision for judicial review by the federal courts was ever made in the Convention, is indicative of the existence of a belief that no express constitutional sanction would be needed for the exercise of that power. The important question is what kind of judicial review the framers, and those who took part in the ratification controversy of 1787-1788, apparently had in mind. Judicial review is not definable in terms of yards or pounds or any other precise standard of measure. It has not always meant the same thing, even though the same term has been used. The evidence supports the conclusion that although a number of the founding fathers—variously estimated at from seven to seventeen—favored judicial review, or, more frequently, simply assumed that the courts would pass upon the validity of legislation, they did not anticipate that judicial review would have the scope or the importance that it came to have during the nineteenth century.

In the Virginia Plan, submitted to the Convention on

[13] The supreme law clause (Art. VI, cl. 2) so frequently cited in defence of the opposite proposition provides that "the Judges in every State shall be bound" by the national Constitution, laws, and treaties. Nothing is said of the federal courts. It seems only accurate, therefore, to say that the framers provided for review of state laws and constitutions by state courts, but made no such explicit provision for review by the federal courts of either state or national legislation.

[14] The figures presented in Charles A. Beard, *The Supreme Court and the Constitution* (1913) need correction. Cf. Edward S. Corwin's review in *American Political Science Review,* VII, 330 (1913), and the same author's discussion of this point in *Court over Constitution* (1938), pp. 26 *et seq.*

May 29th, the eighth article or resolution provided that "the executive and a convenient number of the National Judiciary, ought to compose a council of revision with authority to examine every act of the National Legislature before it shall operate, and every act of a particular Legislature before a negative thereon shall be final; and that the dissent of the said council shall amount to a rejection, unless the Act of the National Legislature be again passed, or that of a particular Legislature be again negatived by [left blank] of the members of each branch."[15] Now this is as near as the Convention ever came to a proposal to incorporate a provision for judicial review by the national courts. It is obviously far nearer to an executive veto than to judicial review. The decision would be taken before the provision went into effect; it would be reached without any recourse to the forms of legal procedure; it would be based upon considerations of policy as well as, perhaps exclusive of, constitutionality; and it could be set aside by a special vote of the national legislature. This proposal was rejected by the Convention each time it was considered, but it was in connection with its discussion that most of the utterances concerning judicial review were made. The earliest of these was that of Elbridge Gerry who, on June 4th, doubted whether the judges should form a part of a council of revision,

> as they will have a sufficient check against encroachments on their own department by their exposition of the laws, which involved a power of deciding on their constitutionality. In some states the Judges had actually set aside laws as against the Constitution. This was done too with general approbation. It was quite foreign from the nature of the office to make them judges of the policy of public measures.[16]

Gerry was later to oppose ratification, but in this statement he was very probably expressing a view as nearly representa-

[15] Farrand, *Records of the Federal Convention* (1911), I, 21.
[16] *Ibid.*, 97-98.

tive of the attitude of the Convention as can be found. He assumed that judicial review would exist without benefit of special provision. He was familiar, at least by hearsay, with the exercise of the power in "some States." He does not make clear precisely how broad is the scope of judicial review, but it includes protection of the powers of the courts and probably some other subjects as well, since the state court decisions of which he had evidently heard were not exclusively of this category.[17] It does not and should not extend to "the policy of public measures."

It is this final point which seems to me to be of great, and contemporary, importance. Gerry conceived of judicial review as an institution of limited scope and usefulness, as being sharply distinguished from decisions on the policy or wisdom of statutes. And Gerry is not alone in this, for the same point of view is expressed by almost every man who says anything at all on this subject in the Convention and in the ratification controversy. This is true whether like Gerry, King,[18] Martin,[19] Sherman,[20] and Gorham [21] they disapproved of a council of revision, or like Wilson,[22] Mason,[23] and Madison,[24] they favored it. Consider, to take two ex-

---

[17] Haines, *op. cit.,* ch. V. [18] Farrand, *op. cit.,* I, 109. [19] *Ibid.,* II, 76. [20] *Ibid.,* 300. [21] *Ibid.,* 73. [22] *Ibid.,* 73. [23] *Ibid.,* 78.

[24] It is not certain that Madison was, in the Convention, one of those who assumed that the courts would have the power to pass upon the constitutionality of statutes, although it is probable that he did have a conception of judicial review which would confine the power of the courts within narrow limits. In arguing for a council of revision he does say that this would give the judiciary "an additional opportunity of defending itself against legislative encroachments." *Ibid.,* 74. Certainly the implication of this speech is that even if the courts do have the power of *judicial* review they will lack the power to check "those unwise and unjust measures which constituted so great a portion of our calamities." *Ibid.* Five weeks later, when the Convention was discussing the jurisdiction of the courts, Madison opposed extending the courts' authority to cases arising under the Constitution, on the ground that it should be limited to "cases of a Judiciary nature. The right of expounding the Constitution in cases not of this nature ought not to be given to that Department." *Ibid.,* 430. The Convention then accepted the clause Madison had questioned, "it being generally supposed," notes Madison, "that the jurisdiction given was constructively limited to cases of a Judiciary nature." There is

amples, the speeches of Wilson and Mason, the first, one of the strong nationalists of the Convention, the second, a stalwart defender of the rights of the states, and later an Anti-Federalist. Both favored the council of revision. Both apparently assumed that the judges would in the future exercise the power of judicial review. Neither thought this adequate, without participation in the council of revision. Said Wilson: "Laws may be unjust, may be unwise, may be dangerous, may be destructive; and yet not be so unconstitutional as to justify the Judges in refusing to give them effect." [25] A little later Mason used almost the same words:

> It had been said (by Mr. L. Martin) that if the Judges were joined in this check on the laws, they would have a double negative, since in their expository capacity of Judges they would have one negative. He would reply that in this capacity they could impede in one case only, the operation of laws. They could declare an unconstitutional law void. But with regard to every law however unjust, oppressive, or pernicious, which did not come plainly under this description, they would be under the necessity as Judges to give it a free course.[26]

There is, in this speech by the author of the first American bill of rights, no suggestion of a judicial review which incorporates the general principles of the Declaration of Independence or of other laws of nature and of nature's God into the law of the Constitution. Some of the fathers, at least, expressed the view that the courts would not accept as law "a direct violation of the Constitution," [27] but there is no evidence that, in their opinion, the judges would be warranted in passing upon the policy or wisdom or even

---

room to differ as to Madison's meaning of "judiciary nature" here, but at least it would appear to represent a theory of judicial review which did not recognize the courts as the exclusive or final interpreters of all parts of the Constitution.

[25] Farrand, *op. cit.* I, 73. [26] *Ibid.*, 78. [27] *Ibid.*, 299 (Gouverneur Morris).

the justice of measures, unless those measures were in clear conflict with the words of the Constitution.[28]

THE STRUGGLE OVER RATIFICATION

With two exceptions the theories of judicial review expressed in the ratification controversy reflect those of the Convention. The usual attitude of the proponents of the Constitution was that the courts would protect against the usurpation of undelegated powers by the Congress. "If the United States go beyond their powers," said Oliver Ellsworth in Connecticut, "if they make a law which the Constitution does not authorize, it is void; and the judicial power, the national judges, who to secure their impartiality, are to be made independent, will declare it to be void." [29] John Marshall, in the Virginia convention, employed almost the same words,[30] as did Grayson,[31] Randolph,[32] and Pendleton.[33] James Wilson [34] in Pennsylvania and William Davie [35] in North Carolina, both, like Ellsworth, members of the Federal Convention, likewise defended the proposed constitution on this ground. In none of these speeches or writings is there any suggestion that judicial review will or should go beyond safeguarding the specific provisions of the Constitution.

Among the Anti-Federalists, it was customary to express grave fears that the national judiciary would swallow up the

---

[28] Mercer and Dickinson expressed themselves as being opposed to judicial review (Farrand, *op. cit.* I, 298, 299) and Franklin was probably of that point of view. *Ibid.*, I, 98-99, 109. For further discussion of the attitudes of the framers see Corwin, *Court over Constitution*, 26-33. [29] *Ibid.*, III, 240-241.

[30] "If they [the national government] were to make a law not warranted by any of the powers enumerated, it would be considered by the judges as an infringement of the Constitution which they are to guard. They would not consider such a law as coming under their jurisdiction. They would declare it void." Elliot, *Debates* (2d ed.), III, 553.

[31] *Ibid.*, 567. [32] *Ibid.*, 205. [33] *Ibid.*, 548.

[34] McMaster and Stone, *Pennsylvania and the Federal Constitution* (1888), 304, 340, 354. [35] Elliot, *Debates*, III, 155-157.

state courts. This fear did not spring from an expectation that the scope of judicial review would be expanded until the state governments were supervised by the national courts. Rather did they fear the taking of jurisdiction in private law cases from the state courts. Indeed almost all of the Anti-Federalists who said anything about judicial review by the federal courts approved of it, but thought that it was an inadequate basis of protection. Patrick Henry, than whom there was no more bitter opponent of the Constitution, and of Article III in particular, had the highest praise for the review of state legislation by state courts and doubted whether the federal courts would afford such protection against oppressive acts of Congress, except those touching the courts themselves.[36] It is not the possibility or expectation of judicial review which bothers him but rather its inadequacy, at least as concerns its review of the acts of Congress.[37]

There are two essays of the ratification controversy which remain to be considered, those of Robert Yates and Alexander Hamilton. Both were New Yorkers, both had been in the Convention, although neither had held views in that body at all representative of the majority attitude, and neither had been present during the greater part of the proceedings.[38] Yates, in opposing ratification, expressed a point of view almost the opposite of that stated a few weeks later by Patrick Henry. He believed that the clause giving equity jurisdiction to the federal courts would empower them

[36] "I take it as the highest encomium on this country, that the acts of the legislature, if unconstitutional, are liable to be opposed by the judiciary." Elliot, *Debates,* III, 325. Also *ibid.,* at 539-541.

[37] Cf. the speech of Luther Martin of Maryland in Elliot, *Debates,* I, 380.

[38] Yates, along with his fellow delegate from New York, John Lansing, left the Convention before the middle of July and did not return. Under the instructions of the New York legislature Hamilton, the third New York delegate, was unable to cast the vote of that state in the Convention. Because of this and of business in New York he was present during only a small portion of the remaining two months of the Convention.

> to explain the constitution according to the reasoning spirit of it, without being confined to the words or letter.
>
> They will give the sense of every article of the constitution, that may from time to time come before them. And in their decisions they will not confine themselves to any fixed or established rules, but will determine, according to what appears to them, the reason and spirit of the constitution. The opinions of the supreme court, whatever they may be, will have the force of law; because there is no power provided in the constitution, that can correct their errors, or controul their adjudications.[39]

Yates then expressed the fear that the judicial power will tend to restrict the limits of state jurisdiction and that the federal structure as interpreted by the federal courts will result in "an entire subversion of the legislative, executive and judicial powers of the individual states." [40] In this respect his views were representative of a large segment of Anti-Federalist thought, but, so far as has been discovered, no one before him, either in the Convention, or in the ratification controversy, had entertained the idea that the courts would have so broad and inclusive a power of interpretation. The various speeches in the Convention were all based upon the assumption that the courts would have the authority to declare legislation void only when it was in conflict with the letter of the Constitution. The conception of construction according to the "reason and spirit" of the Constitution was not a product of the Convention's debates nor was it expressed by one of the principal authors of the Constitution.

The letter from which these quotations are taken was published in the *New York Journal and Weekly Register* for January 31, 1788. It was probably in answer to this argument that Hamilton wrote the 78th and 81st numbers of the *Federalist*. The preceding seventy-seven numbers will be

---

[39] The "Letters of Brutus," as reprinted in Corwin, *Court over Constitution*, 236-237. [40] *Ibid.*, 238.

searched in vain for more than a bare mention of judicial review. This is surprising since there are several places where some discussion of this institution would seem to have been entirely relevant. To be sure, in Number 39 Madison had remarked that "in controversies relating to the boundary between the two jurisdictions, the tribunal which is ultimately to decide is to be established under the general government."[41] This might be taken as an unequivocal acceptance of judicial review were it not that in the numbers concerned with the separation of powers the check of judicial review is not mentioned. Thus in the 49th he says that "The several departments being perfectly co-ordinate by the terms of their common commission, none of them, it is evident, can pretend to an exclusive or superior right of settling the boundaries between their respective powers." [42] And in the 51st he finds that the only remedy for the evil of republican government—that "the legislative authority necessarily predominates"—is bicameralism.[43]

THE CONTRIBUTION OF HAMILTON

Madison's lack of clarity on judicial review in the *Federalist* is reflective of his equivocal position in the Convention and his later criticism of judicial review as it was developed by the Supreme Court under Marshall. It is not so easy to explain Hamilton's attitude in the earlier numbers of the *Federalist,* for Hamilton, more than any other single man, is the author of judicial review as the nineteenth century was to know it. In Number 16 there is a reference to the power of the judges, presumably in the state courts, to check the legislatures and thus assist in preserving "the supreme law of the land." [44] In the 33rd *Federalist,* however, Hamilton answered the question, "Who is to judge of the *necessity* and *propriety* of the laws to be passed for executing the pow-

---

[41] Ford ed., 251. [42] *Ibid.,* 335. [43] *Ibid.,* 345. [44] *Ibid.,* 102.

ers of the Union?" with the statement that "the national government, like every other, must judge, in the first instance, of the proper exercise of its powers, and its constituents in the last."[45] Except for the reference to the final powers of the people, this is consistent with Hamilton's views as expressed in the Convention. For the plan which he presented on June 18th contained little of democracy and less of federalism.[46] Instead of judicial review it provided for an absolute executive veto of both national and state legislation, the latter to be exercised by governors appointed by "the General Government." [47] He advocated an executive, elected for life, and given an unqualified veto power over all acts of the national congress. He obviously desired strong-man government, and in such a system there would be little more room for judicial review than in a totalitarian government of the twentieth century.

If Hamilton was late in accepting judicial review, when he did do so he went beyond any other advocate of ratification in foreseeing its possibilities. In Number 78 he is not content with a brief statement that the courts would declare acts contrary to the Constitution void. He sets forth the principle of fundamental law in such fashion as to make of it the voice of the people with the judges as its only true guardians. The elected representatives of the people, the President and Congress, would have no authority, or at least no final authority, to interpret the meaning of the Constitution. Only the judges can give a final interpretation of its meaning; only they can determine the limits of power assigned to the various branches of the government. Anything else would be to subvert "the intention of the people to the intention of their agents." [48]

Under the influence of Hamilton's great follower, Mar-

---

[45] Ford ed., 203. [46] Farrand, *Records,* I, 282 *et. seq.* [47] *Ibid.,* 292-293.

[48] Ford ed., 521. See also the paraphrase of Yates' arguments and Hamilton's reply thereto in Number 81. *Ibid.,* 523.

shall, we so much take the doctrine of the 78th *Federalist* for granted that it is today difficult to see how profound was the change of emphasis here made. The courts under this doctrine do not simply declare void instances of "direct violation" of the Constitution. They become the guardians of the "manifest tenor of the Constitution," the spokesmen for "the intentions of the people," while the President and Congress are reduced to the position of being always potential enemies of the Constitution and of the reserved rights of the people, and even the people are to be protected against themselves by the judges.[49] Hamilton has taken the fears of Yates and made of them an extraordinarily effective substitute for the highly centralized, undemocratic plan which he had proposed in the Convention. For if judicial review as he now described it lacked the positive powers of the government he had earlier advocated, it would afford an almost equally effective substitute against the excesses of popular majorities.

That Hamilton was far more concerned with security of property rights than with the protection of civil liberties is clear from his speeches in the Convention. On June 18, in defending his plan for a strong-man government and a senate with life terms, he had said that all communities may be divided into the "few and the many. The first are the rich and well-born, the other the mass of the people." The voice of the people, he continued, is not the voice of God for the people "are turbulent and changing; they seldom judge or determine right." The rich and well-born should be given a "distinct, permanent share in government." Since they do not stand to gain by change they will provide a check on the unsteadiness of the masses. "Nothing but a

[49] "This independence of the judges is equally requisite to guard the Constitution and the rights of individuals from the effects of those ill humors which the arts of designing men or the influence of particular conjunctures sometimes disseminate among the people themselves." Ford ed., 523.

permanent body can check the imprudence of democracy."[50] A week later "he acknowledged himself not to think favorably of Republican Government."[51] The same attitude is exhibited both in the ill-fated Letters of Caesar[52] and also in the *Federalist,* Number 84, where he deals with the absence of a bill of rights in the proposed Constitution. He here echoes the usual Federalist argument,[53] that such guarantees are not needed in the Constitution. Beyond that his contempt for the state declarations and bills of rights slips out when he speaks of "those aphorisms which make the principal figure in several of our State bills of rights, and which would sound much better in a treatise of ethics than in a constitution of government."[54]

THE FIRST CONGRESS

This was not Madison's attitude, even though he had shared the almost unanimous view of the Convention that a bill of rights was not needed for the central government, since the state bills would remain in effect. After the great mass of opposition in the ratification controversy had shown the desirability of attaching a bill of rights in the form of a series of amendments, Madison introduced into the first Congress the proposals which became the first ten Amendments to the Constitution. When he did so he said that the courts would "consider themselves in a peculiar manner the guard-

---

[50] Farrand, *op. cit.,* I, 299. [51] *Ibid.,* 424.

[52] Writing for the purpose of convincing the voters that they should elect delegates to the New York ratifying convention who would favor the proposed Constitution, Hamilton said: "I am not one of those who gain an influence by cajoling the unthinking mass (tho' I pity their delusions), and ringing in their ears the gracious sound of their *absolute sovereignty. . . .* For my part, I am not much attached to the *majesty of the multitude. . . .* I consider them in general as very ill qualified to judge for themselves what government will best suit their peculiar situations. . . ." P. L. Ford (ed.), *Essays on the Constitution* (1892), 287.

[53] B. F. Wright, *American Interpretations of Natural Law* (1931), 130-148.

[54] Ford ed., 573.

ians of those rights; they would be an impenetrable bulwark against every assumption of power in the Legislative or executive; they will be naturally led to resist every encroachment upon rights expressly stipulated for in the Constitution by the declaration of rights." [55] It is reasonably clear that Madison had come to have a somewhat clearer belief in judicial review, at least to the extent of seeing in it a means of protection against encroachments on civil liberties. It may be here remarked, however, that he had not then accepted and he never accepted the theory of judicial review expressed by Yates and Hamilton and later written into our basic law by Marshall. Indeed he apparently never accepted the principle that the courts, and the courts alone, had a final, authoritative power to interpret the Constitution. This power, he held, the courts shared with Congress and the executive.[56]

Madison's statement of the power of the courts to serve as the guardians of the rights to be guaranteed in the amendments to the Constitution is not the only evidence from the proceedings of the first Congress. One of the most important statutes then enacted was the great Judiciary Act of 1789.[57] Section 25 empowered the Supreme Court to review decisions of state courts "where is drawn in question the validity of a treaty or statute of, or an authority exercised under the United States, and the decision is against their validity," or where a state act had been questioned on the ground of its violation of the national constitution, statute, or treaty, and the state act sustained. This provision would seem to be clear evidence that the members of the first Congress assumed that both state and federal courts would exercise the power to review statutes on grounds of constitutionality. That Congress contained many members who had served, two years

---

[55] 1 *Annals of Congress*, 439. Cf. the statement of Hugh Williamson in the Convention when speaking of the *ex post facto* clause. It may do good, he said, because "the Judges can take hold of it." Farrand, *Records*, II, 376.

[56] E. M. Burns, James Madison, *Philosopher of the Constitution* (1938), 156-161. [57] 1 *Statutes*, 73, 85-86.

before, in the Federal Convention, among them four of the seven members of the Senate Judiciary Committee which drafted the bill. Neither among the former advocates of ratification nor among the Anti-Federalists who were present in the Congress of 1789 was there any openly expressed opposition to the assumption that the power of judicial review was a proper function of the courts.

COURT DECISIONS IN THE FEDERALIST PERIOD

To say that the practice of judicial review was firmly established in the states by 1803 would be to exaggerate the weight of the ten cases, more or less, in which state courts between 1789 and 1803 either held legislative acts unconstitutional or asserted that they had the power to do so when the legislature transgressed the provisions of the Constitution or of the principles of right and reason.[58] The dogma of Coke and the theory of the *Federalist* were undoubtedly being disseminated through the medium of judicial opinions. Only a few of these opinions were, however, published at this time, and the period is rather one of preparation than of maturity. There is, that is to say, evidence that the state judges were gradually but generally coming to accept not only the principle that "the legislature have not power to change the fundamental laws," but also that "the judiciary may and ought to adjudge a law unconstitutional and void, if it be plainly repugnant to the letter of the Constitution, or the fundamental principles thereof." [59] The same judges were, moreover, beginning to exercise this authority, but it was still the exception when they did so, and most of them were self-consciously on the defensive. The constitutions, after all, did not confer this power upon them, and although they could cite the mighty

---

[58] Haines, *op. cit.*, ch. VII.

[59] Roane, J. in Kamper v. Hawkins, 1 *Va. Cases,* 30, 32 (1793) quoted in Haines, *op. cit.*, 154.

Coke and the almost sanctified *Federalist* in their support, authoritative judicial precedents were still lacking.

During the same period the beginnings of judicial review of state legislation by the federal courts are discoverable. They are only beginnings; but the circuit courts held state acts to be contrary to the federal Constitution in some five cases.[60] With one or two exceptions those decisions were not published. The one significant exception is the case of Vanhorne's Lessee v. Dorrance.[61] Here the circuit court, consisting of Justice Paterson and District Judge Peters, held an act of the Pennsylvania legislature to be contrary to the obligations of the contract clause. With the merits of the controversy we are not here concerned, but Paterson's statement of the theory of judicial review, and its relation to the principle of a written constitution is of significance.

> The Constitution is certain and fixed; it contains the permanent will of the people, and is the supreme law of the land; it is paramount to the power of the Legislature, and can be revoked or altered only by the authority that made it. . . . What are Legislatures? Creatures of the Constitution. . . .
>
> I take it to be a clear position; that if a legislative act oppugns a constitutional principle, the former must give way, and be rejected on the score of repugnance. I hold it to be a position equally clear and sound, that, in such case, it will be the duty of the Court to adhere to the Constitution, and to declare the act null and void.[62]

There is here no emphasis, as there had been in the Convention, upon clear or direct violation of the words of the Constitution. The black letter constitution gives way to "the permanent will of the people," and it becomes the function of the courts to protect constitutional "principles." Paterson, who had expressed no such theory in the Convention of 1787, is giving evidence of the influence of Hamilton's 78th and

[60] Charles Warren, *The Supreme Court in United States History,* (1922), I, 65 *et. seq.* [61] 2 Dall. 304 (1795). [62] *Ibid.,* 308-309.

81st *Federalist* papers, as he is helping to lay the foundations for the work of John Marshall.

There is no equally clear instance during this period in which the Supreme Court set aside a state statute, although it certainly took jurisdiction of several cases involving the constitutionality of such acts. In Calder v. Bull [63] a Connecticut statute challenged as being in conflict with the *ex post facto* clause was sustained, but the language of the opinions, particularly that of Justice Chase, is conclusive evidence that the Court believed that it had the authority to hold legislation void. In Ware v. Hylton [64] the Court upheld the supremacy of the treaty of peace as against state statutes in conflict therewith. It is a fact of some interest, although of no particular importance, that John Marshall, who appeared as counsel for Virginia, asserted that the legislative authority of a country can be restrained only by its own constitution. "This is a principle," he continued, "that springs from the very nature of society; and the judicial authority can have no right to question the validity of a law, unless such a jurisdiction is expressly given by the constitution." [65]

Four years before the Ware case the Supreme Court had exhibited some of the hesitation which the point of view expressed in Marshall's plea of 1796, although not in his speech in the Virginia convention in 1788, would be expected to produce. An act of Congress providing that the circuit courts should pass upon the claims of invalid pensioners was believed by most, if not all, of the justices to be in conflict with the separation of powers principle.[66] A formal decision of un-

---

[63] 3 Dall. 386 (1798). See also Cooper v. Telfair, 4 Dall. 14 (1800).

[64] 3 Dall. 199 (1796). The same ruling was handed down the next year in Clerke v. Harwood, 3 Dall. 342 (1797), a case involving a Maryland statute. According to Mr. Charles Warren there were three similar decisions which were unreported by Dallas. See Warren, "The First Decade of the Supreme Court of the United States," *University of Chicago Law Review,* VII, 631, 650 (1940). [65] *Ibid.,* 211.

[66] Hayburn's Case, 2 Dall. 409 (1792). On this curious "case" see Max Farrand, "The First Hayburn Case," *American Historical Review,* XIII, 281

constitutionality was probably never handed down,[67] partly because the justices, all Federalists, were sympathetic with the attempts of the new government to get under way, partly because Congress altered the provisions of the act. But just before the Ware case the Court had taken jurisdiction of a case involving the constitutionality of an act of Congress. In this case, Hylton v. U.S.,[68] the statute was sustained, but only after a careful consideration of the issue of possible conflict with the Constitution. It did so, furthermore, without any discernible opposition to the practice of reviewing acts of Congress.

The final prelude to the drama of John Marshall was staged not by the Court but in Congress. After the Republican victory of 1800 the Federalists enacted the Judiciary Act of 1801. This product of a lame-duck Congress had several desirable features, particularly in that it relieved the members of the Supreme Court of the burdensome duty of riding circuit, a duty which made a seat on the Court an honor of dubious value. But the act also provided for sixteen new circuit court judgeships, a number much larger than was then necessary. Before he left office President Adams filled all of the new vacancies—with Federalists. "The Federalists," Jefferson later wrote, having been defeated at the polls, "have retired into the judiciary as a stronghold . . . and from that battery all the works of republicanism are to be beaten down and erased." [69]

The Jeffersonians were not content to protest against the statute. In 1802 a heated controversy in Congress resulted in

---

(1908) and Warren, *Supreme Court in United States History,* I, 69 *et seq.* In view of the attention given to the separation of powers issue in the Hayburn case it is interesting that no question seems to have been raised concerning the validity of the requirement that the Chief Justice be one of the Commissioners of the Sinking Fund. 1 Statutes, 186, 282.

[67] See, however, U.S. v. Yale Todd, 13 How. 52 (1851).

[68] 3 Dall. 171 (1796).

[69] Jefferson to Dickinson, Dec. 19, 1801. *Writings* (Washington ed.), IV, 424.

the repeal of the Act of 1801.[70] In the course of the debate the principle of judicial review was discussed repeatedly and at length. "All the reasons for the opinion which John Marshall, exactly one year later, pronounced in Marbury v. Madison were given during this debate." [71] The authority of Coke, of the *Federalist,* and of all the decisions in which state or federal courts were known to have held statutes unconstitutional was appealed to. After decades, if not centuries, of preparation the stage was finally set. The debate in Congress served as a curtain raiser, for the hero (or to the Jeffersonians, the villain) of the piece was already in his place and anxious to begin. His appointment to the Chief Justiceship had been one of the last acts of President Adams.

---

[70] The story is admirably told in A. J. Beveridge, *Life of John Marshall* (1919), III, ch. II. [71] *Ibid.*, 75.

Chapter III

THE ESTABLISHMENT OF JUDICIAL SUPERVISION

During its first decade the Supreme Court had not established itself as a part of the governmental machinery comparable in importance to the executive or legislative departments. No act of Congress had been declared unconstitutional, although, to be sure, the Court had assumed that it had the power to make such decisions. Two, perhaps more, acts of the state legislatures had been held to violate the Treaty of 1783, but these rulings seemingly attracted little attention. The Court's principal decision against a state had gone unenforced, and its assertion of jurisdiction in the case had been set aside by the Eleventh Amendment. Membership on the Court was not much sought after. Two associate justices, Rutledge and Harrison, had resigned to accept state judicial offices, and even the Chief Justiceship had been refused by Patrick Henry, by William Cushing, and by Alexander Hamilton. John Jay, who had resigned from that position in 1795 to serve as Governor of New York, declined a second appointment in 1800. It is not difficult to understand why the architect who designed the national capitol made no provision for a room for the Supreme Court. "When the seat of government was transferred to Washington, the Court crept into an humble apartment in the basement." [1]

[1] Beveridge, *op. cit.*, III, 120n.

There can, nevertheless, be little doubt but that the foundations for judicial review had been laid. What would be built upon those foundations had not been determined. Had circumstance given the appointment of the new Chief Justice to Jefferson, rather than to Adams, it is almost certain that the Supreme Court would have, sooner or later, exercised the power to review the constitutionality of both state and national legislation. It seems probable, however, that this review would have been less comprehensive in scope, as well as somewhat different in doctrinal results.

John Marshall was a distant cousin of Jefferson, and both were Virginians. Beyond that there is little of similarity and much of contrast. The first was an ardent Federalist who had served in Congress and as Adams' Secretary of State, an office which he continued to hold for a short time after his nomination as Chief Justice was confirmed. The latter was the leader of the opposition party who had been elected to the Presidency before Marshall was appointed to the Chief Justiceship. Marshall was a "supreme conservative"; Jefferson was a life-long reformer who believed that neither property rights nor constitutions should stand in the way of statutes seeking a more equitable distribution of property.[2] Marshall, a nationalist since Valley Forge, faced Jefferson, who, although not a doctrinaire states-righter, as the acts of his administration showed, was opposed to the exercise of powers of doubtful constitutionality by the Federalists, including the Federalist judges, when they were used for purposes he thought harmful to the public good. While Jefferson was far more learned in the history and system of the common law than Marshall, he had little liking for the contentiousness or the precedent-matching of legal practice. It may finally be remarked, although not by way of contrast to Jefferson, that Marshall had neither judicial experience nor what is usually

[2] C. M. Wiltsie, *The Jeffersonian Tradition in American Democracy* (1935), 136-140.

understood by that elusive phrase, the judicial temperament. He was a partisan. More than that he was a partisan who dominated his colleagues.

THE CLASSIC STATEMENT OF JUDICIAL REVIEW

That Marshall was a superb strategist, as well as a strong leader who sought to write his theory into the law of the land, is clearly evident from his first great case, Marbury v. Madison.[3] The facts of the case are only partially told in the reports. There it is set forth that William Marbury had been nominated to one of the new justiceships of the peace for the District of Columbia and that his nomination had been confirmed by the Senate and the commission signed and the seal affixed to it by the Secretary of State. We are further informed that the commission had not been delivered when Adams went out of office, and that the new Secretary of State, Madison, refused to deliver the document. That the negligence of the former Secretary of State, Marshall, or of someone in his office, was responsible for its original non-delivery is one of the curious aspects of the story which the reports do not record. Nor do they tell of how little value was the office which was to be the excuse for this great case. Just why Marbury sought a writ of *mandamus* from the Supreme Court to require Madison to deliver the commission is not clear, for the case seemed at first to be one of very doubtful value from the point of view of the Federalists. If the Court issued the writ it would almost certainly be ignored by the administration. If it acknowledged its inability to compel the administration to obey the order of the Court, the prestige of the Court would suffer.

The dilemma seemed inescapable, except to Marshall. He it was who conceived the plan of lecturing the administration as to its duties, then escaping a showdown by denying juris-

---

[3] 1 Cranch 137 (1803).

diction and, in doing so, declaring section 13 of the Judiciary Act of 1789, under which the writ was sought, unconstitutional. The excuse for the decision was that Congress had sought to add to the original jurisdiction of the Court. Now this act was drafted by Ellsworth, a member of the Federal Convention and Marshall's predecessor as Chief Justice. It was approved by a Congress containing many of those who had helped to frame the Constitution, and signed by a President who had presided over the Convention. No one, before Marshall conceived his brilliant tactical maneuver, had ever suspected that it was unconstitutional to vest the power to issue writs of *mandamus* in the Supreme Court.[4] Marshall did not quote the entire sentence of Article III, section 2, which he found to be applicable. He quoted "In all the other Cases before mentioned, the Supreme Court shall have appellate Jurisdiction," but omitted from consideration: "both as to law and fact, with such Exceptions, and under such Regulations as the Congress shall make."[5] Nor did he follow the principle so to construe the act as to find it constitutional, for section 13 could have been held to give authority to issue the writ only where the court had jurisdiction over the cause. He wanted, as Beveridge has said, both a way out of the dilemma, and an opportunity to declare an act of Congress invalid. He wanted, that is to say, an opportunity to expand the authority of his Court.

The outcry against the Court's action was directed not against the holding of unconstitutionality. Section 13 was of interest to few save the judges themselves. Marshall's statement of the theory of judicial review met with little criti-

[4] Section 13 authorized the Supreme Court to issue "writs of mandamus, in cases warranted by the principles and usages of law, to any courts appointed, or persons holding office, under the authority of the United States."

[5] Marshall does not here discuss the meaning of the term "exception." It may be noted, however, that in the Virginia convention he had said that it applied only to an alteration which was a diminution and not an extension of jurisdiction. Elliot's *Debates,* III, 559-560. He was, at least, consistent.

cism. By 1803 the principle of judicial review was generally accepted, although few who accepted it understood it to include as much as did Marshall. At any rate not one of the thirty-nine members of the Federal Convention who was alive at the time expressed publicly any opposition to the exercise of the power of review. The opposition centered about Marshall's nine thousand word *obiter dictum* which preceded his very brief finding that section 13 was unconstitutional and his relatively brief statement of the theory of judicial review. In this long partisan essay he considered the merits of the cause before holding that the Court did not have jurisdiction to discuss the merits of the cause, a violation of the principles of judicial procedure. His castigation was of the practices of Jefferson and Madison, but his holding, paradoxically, was that a section of the Federalist Judiciary Act of 1789 was invalid.

In the long-run view the significant part of the opinion is not in the partisan censure of the administration, nor yet in the finding that an unimportant section of a Congressional act was invalid. It is in the assertion of a theory of judicial review which follows the doctrine of Hamilton, not the Hamilton of the Convention but the Hamilton of the later numbers of the *Federalist*. It is a theory of the judges as the only true guardians of the permanent will of the people which is incorporated in the Constitution. The assumption throughout is that the Congress and President cannot be trusted to interpret that will. It is assumed that if the Court believes that an act is not in harmony with the Constitution then it is most certainly inconsistent with that document.

It is an enlightening commentary upon this theory that in this first case in which a Congressional statute was held to violate the Constitution, the statute was written by men who helped to write the Constitution while the decision was that of a man who had not taken part in that historic process. Yet

Marshall, rather than Ellsworth, or Madison, or Washington, or any other former member of the Convention who was in the Congress of 1789, knew the true meaning of Article III, section 2. What we actually have in this most famous of constitutional decisions is not protection of the original Constitution but a judicial revision of its meaning. And, too, we have the formal assertion that in the Court is vested the power of determining the meaning of the Constitution.

During the remaining thirty-one years of Marshall's period there were fourteen cases in which the Court considered the validity of acts of Congress, but in no other instance was a statute held to be unconstitutional. Marshall was a nationalist, as well as an exponent of the judicial power, and, having once asserted the supremacy of the Court, he was content to exercise the power as a means of keeping the states within bounds.

THE POWER OF THE FEDERAL COURTS

One doctrine essential to the upholding of national authority was the constitutionality of section 25 of the Judiciary Act of 1789. This section, it will be remembered, provides for review by the Supreme Court of decisions in state courts denying some right or claim under the national Constitution, or a statute or treaty. The constitutional validity of this right of appeal from the state courts to the Supreme Court was challenged in the Congressional debates of 1789 and it was repeatedly challenged in the Marshall period. Marshall's own state of Virginia was probably the most vigorous opponent of the federal judiciary, as Judge Spencer Roane and John Taylor of Caroline were the outstanding leaders among the judicial and the pamphleteering critics. It should not be assumed, however, that this opposition to the Supreme Court's right of review was confined to this state, or to the South. In 1824, when the Ohio Bank case reached the Court, "seven states were formally in revolt against the National Judiciary, and others were hostile." [6]

Indeed the first challenge to the power of the Supreme Court under section 25 came from Pennsylvania, a state which was, upon several occasions during the first thirty years of the new government, a strong opponent of the national government. The case of U.S. v. Peters [7] involved ultimately the power of the Continental Prize Court of Revolutionary times and more immediately the power of the federal district courts to enforce a decree of that court as against the opposition of the Pennsylvania legislature, governor, and judiciary. The Supreme Court won out, in part at least, because President Madison upheld its authority and rebuked Pennsylvania. That state's legislature passed a set of resolutions inviting the other states to join in favoring an amendment to establish an "impartial tribunal to determine disputes between the General and State Governments." This proposal makes the same assumption found in the Kentucky and Virginia resolutions of 1798. Now as then that proposition met with little favor. Ten states passed resolutions of disapproval, and among them were Kentucky and Virginia, now as nationalistic as was President Madison who, in 1798, had been the proponent of the Virginia resolutions. In the Virginia resolutions of 1810, it is even declared that "a tribunal is already provided by the Constitution of the United States (to wit: the Supreme Court) more eminently qualified to decide the disputes aforesaid in an enlightened and impartial manner than any other tribunal which could be created." [8]

Virginia was not always to take this attitude toward the power of the Supreme Court. In the famous case of Martin v. Hunter's Lessee [9] a Revolutionary issue was again involved—the title to lands in Virginia declared confiscated

[6] Beveridge, *op. cit.*, IV, 384.
[7] 5 Cranch 115 (1809).
[8] Warren, *Supreme Court in United States History*, I, 389n.
[9] 1 Wheaton 304 (1816).

before 1783, but under acts not put into effect until after the Treaty of Peace. Here there was, as in the Peters case, controversy not only concerning title to property but also as to the authority of the Supreme Court to review a decision of the Virginia courts. Over the emphatic assertion of the Virginia Court of Appeals that it had the final right of decision, the Supreme Court asserted and maintained its superior authority on the grounds that the cause involved the application of a treaty.

Five years later in Cohens v. Virginia,[10] a case involving an issue so trivial that the Quarterly Session Court of Norfolk was the highest state court having jurisdiction, was appealed to the Supreme Court. Once more the Virginians denied the constitutionality of the Supreme Court's right to pass upon the issue, even though a Congressional statute was involved. The Supreme Court was successful in maintaining its supervisory authority here, as it had been in the earlier cases, and as it was in all subsequent cases coming up from the state courts, with one exception. In Worcester v. Georgia [11] a ruling that the state of Georgia had violated federal treaties and statutes in its dealings with the Indians went unenforced. The reason is simple. President Jackson sympathized with Georgia, not with the decision of the Court. Whether he made the remark attributed to him, "John Marshall has made his decision, now let him enforce it," is not certain. What is certain is that he concurred in the nullification by Georgia of federal treaties, statutes, and a Supreme Court decision. This was in the same year that South Carolina attempted to nullify a Congressional act and failed because the same President upheld federal authority.

[10] 6 Wheaton 264 (1821). [11] 6 Peters 515 (1832).

THE CONTRACT CLAUSE AND VESTED RIGHTS

Thus far in this chapter the discussion has concerned the Marshall Court's assertion and defense of its power to review the constitutionality of Congressional statutes and the merits of state court decisions. That is only one part of the story, an essential part to be sure, but it does not tell us what that Court did with its power. For that we must turn to the interpretation of particular clauses of the Constitution. The first group of cases concerns the contract clause. They are first chronologically, and they are also first in that they illustrate as does no other group of cases before the closing years of the century, the possibilities inherent in the Hamiltonian theory of judicial review.

Originally the provision of Article I, section 10, prohibiting the states from passing any law "impairing the obligation of contracts" was understood to apply only to private contractual arrangements, that is, to contracts between persons. Certainly the discussion in the Convention and in the ratification controversy affords no evidence to support the view that it was intended to have a broader meaning.[12] Rather was it intended to prevent future legislative interferences with private contracts, of which there had been so many in the years preceding the Convention. Between 1789 and 1810 there were, however, several utterances which suggest the possibility of a broader interpretation. In the case of Vanhorne's Lessee Justice Paterson apparently assumed that the clause gave protection to a contract between a state and private purchasers of lands.[13] He did not attempt to defend or explain the assumption.

A year later Alexander Hamilton, at the time a lawyer in private practice in New York, gave an opinion on the validity of Georgia's repeal of the notorious Yazoo land sale. The

[12] B. F. Wright, *The Contract Clause of the Constitution* (1938), 3-16.
[13] Vanhorne's Lessee v. Dorrance, 2 Dallas 304, 320 (1795).

revocation of such a land grant, made for a valuable consideration, is, he wrote, contrary to the "first principles of natural justice and social policy." In addition it is contrary to the contract clause of the Constitution. This opinion was printed in a pamphlet dealing with the problem.[14] And in the Congressional debates over appropriating a sum to reimburse the purchasers of these lands statements similar to that of Hamilton were made by several speakers, apparently without contradiction.[15]

It is obvious that Marshall was not the first to see in the contract clause a wider sphere of usefulness than that envisaged by the framers. Not before the great case of Fletcher v. Peck [16] in 1810, however, did the Supreme Court pass upon the meaning of the clause. In this case the Court ruled that the Georgia repeal act was invalid. The opinion of Marshall is hardly more than an expanded version of Hamilton's opinion which had been published eleven years before. Marshall cites neither Hamilton's opinion nor Paterson's, nor does he refer to the debates in Congress. That he understood the reasons for the inclusion of the clause in the Constitution—legislative interferences with private debtor-creditor relationships—is made clear years later in another of his opinions,[17] but here he was anxious to give to the clause a broader meaning than was warranted by that knowledge of the prohibition's origins. Nevertheless it is apparent from his opinion, and especially from his concluding paragraph, that he was not entirely certain whether the Constitution alone could sustain this interpretation. The "general principles" of society and of government are brought in

[14] The pamphlet was the work of Robert Goodloe Harper and was entitled *The Case of the Georgia Sales on the Mississippi, with a Reference to Law Authorities and Public Acts* (Philadelphia, 1799). The opinion of Hamilton is at pp. 88-89, and the immediately relevant portion thereof is reprinted in Wright, *op. cit.*, p. 22.

[15] *Annals of Congress,* 8th Cong. 2d. Sess. 1083, 1096, 1143.

[16] 6 Cranch 87 (1810).

[17] Cf. Ogden v. Saunders, 12 Wheat. 213, 354-355 (1827).

for support, even as Hamilton had employed them. The Hamilton-Marshall theory of natural law was, to this extent, written into the Constitution. Thus began the process of extending by tenfold the protection of the contract clause. This protection was, of course, to the rights of property. It is in 1810, therefore, that, as Professor Corwin has put it, the doctrine of vested rights became the basic doctrine of American constitutional law. Until the rise of due process toward the end of the century the principal clause employed by the Court for the protection of the interests of the propertied was the contract clause.

Having once held, with the aid of the principles of natural justice, that the contract clause applied to agreements to which states were parties, the two great subsequent extensions of the clause were comparatively easy. They were also of major importance in the economic history of the century. A doctrine not anticipated by Hamilton was set forth in New Jersey v. Wilson.[18] Here an exemption from taxation was brought under the protection of the contract clause. Although this doctrine is highly dubious as a matter of governmental policy, and is entirely lacking in historical justification, there seems to have been no opposition on the Court to Marshall's ruling. And in the most famous of contract cases the Court held that a corporate charter is a contract.[19] There was some doubt among the Justices whether Dartmouth College was a public or a private institution. The total lack of resemblance between the granting of a charter by the Crown and the making of a private contract of the sort envisaged by the fathers apparently bothered them very little. This particular case involved the charter of an educational institution, but in the vast majority of cases in the future where the Court passed upon the validity of a charter, a business rather than an educational or charitable corpo-

[18] 7 Cranch 164 (1812).

[19] Dartmouth College v. Woodward, 4 Wheaton 518 (1819).

ration was involved. In 1819 there were still relatively few industrial or financial corporations. That form of enterprise was in its infancy. Thanks to the Supreme Court's construction of the contract clause the corporate form of industry was to enjoy, during its years of growth, a kind and degree of protection against legislative regulation which has been given it in no other country.

If the Court made its most important interpretation of the contract clause in the Dartmouth College case, its least important came in the Kentucky land case four years later.[20] This holding that the clause protected interstate compacts had repercussions in the contemporary political opposition to the Court, but its legal effect was short-lived. Subsequent cases were dealt with, as this one should have been, under the clause permitting interstate compacts with the consent of Congress.

Only in the bankruptcy cases[21] is there any discernible relation between the Court's rulings and the intent of the framers, and here the historical justification is tenuous. There is no evidence that the men of the Convention were opposed to legislation of this kind. On the contrary they provided that Congress might pass "uniform laws on the subject of bankruptcies throughout the United States." The inclusion of "uniform" might well be understood to mean that state laws on the subject would be valid until Congress saw fit to occupy the field. But, at least the statutes did affect the debtor-creditor relationship. There is a good logical, although a slight historical, justification for finding *retrospective* bankruptcy statutes to be contrary to the contract clause. When in Ogden v. Saunders,[22] Marshall attempted to extend this prohibition to include legislation

[20] Green v. Biddle, 8 Wheat. 1 (1823).

[21] Sturges v. Crowninshield, 4 Wheat. 122 (1819); M'Millan v. M'Neill, 4 Wheat. 209 (1819), Farmers and Mechanics Bank v. Smith, 6 Wheat. 131 (1821). [22] 12 Wheat. 213 (1827).

applying to future contracts, to agreements not yet entered into, he was unable to carry with him a majority of his Court. It is his one known failure to expand the scope of the judicial power and it was as ambitious an attempt as it was a significant failure. Had he succeeded, the contract clause would have become almost as flexible a limitation upon legislation as was the due process clause after 1890. That the framers were thinking of retrospective legislation is clear. Marshall's attempt to convert a relatively specific limitation into one of almost unlimited application failed for lack of one additional vote in the Court. Even with this failure, there were eight cases in the Marshall era in which the contract clause was the justification for holding state legislation invalid. Not one of them deals with the subject matter mentioned when the clause was debated in the Federal Convention and in the state ratifying conventions. Marshall was successful in transforming a specific limitation upon the states into a comprehensive restriction, but he was unable to extend it until it became as comprehensive as it was undefinable.

THE MARSHALL COURT AS FEDERAL UMPIRE

During his reign of thirty-four years there were no less than thirteen cases in which state laws were set aside as being contrary to the principles of federalism.[23] In them the nationalism of Marshall, and of Hamilton, is apparent, but virtually all of them do bear a relation to the intent of at least many of the fathers. In a number of instances an op-

[23] Wilson v. Mason, 1 Cranch 45 (1801); Hopkirk v. Bell, 3 Cranch 454 (1806); The U.S. v. Judge Peters, 5 Cranch 115 (1809); Fairfax's Devisee v. Hunter's Lessee, 7 Cranch 603 (1813); Chirac v. Chirac, 2 Wheat. 259 (1817); Burton's Lessee v. Williams, 3 Wheat. 529 (1818); McCulloch v. Md., 4 Wheat. 316 (1819); Gibbons v. Ogden, 9 Wheat. 1 (1824); Osborn v. Bank, 9 Wheat. 738 (1824); Brown v. Md., 12 Wheat. 419 (1827); Weston v. Charleston, 2 Peters 449 (1829); Carver v. Jackson, 4 Peters 1 (1830); Worcester v. Ga., 6 Peters 515 (1832).

posite conclusion could have been reached and the authority of some members of the Convention or of the state conventions cited in support. It is nevertheless reasonable to say that whatever may have been the opposition in Marshall's day, his broad interpretation of the judiciary, treaty, commerce, and financial clauses of the Constitution does not, with one exception, exceed the elasticity essential in the construction of a brief and general constitution; not, that is, if the constitution is to be an effective instrument of government.

The cases in which Marshall fought for the Supreme Court's power to review the decisions of state courts where federal questions were raised were considered earlier in this chapter. He was victorious in that controversy, although his opponents did not concede his success, and even though in one of the last cases of his career his decision against Georgia went unenforced. Throughout his long term as Chief Justice he sought to secure for the Supreme Court the role of umpire-in-chief for the federal system. The review of state court decisions was only one step in this program. There was nothing petty about his ambition. Nor was the issue a complex one. To him it was simple. The Constitution is the highest law. The Supreme Court is the final court. The final court gives the authoritative interpretation of the law. Unlike Hamilton in the 33d *Federalist* Marshall never, at least after 1801, thought that "the national government" in the first instance, and the voters, in the second, would judge whether Congress had exceeded its powers. Not the government in general, but the judicial branch of that government would exercise the power to mark off the boundaries.

Of the many cases in which the Marshall Court did act as umpire none is of greater interest or of more strategic importance than McCulloch v. Maryland,[24] and none produced so intense and prolonged a controversy. Now in the

[24] 4 Wheaton 316 (1819).

simplest terms all that the Court did here was to sustain the validity of the Congressional act chartering the second Bank of the United States, and hold that the state of Maryland could not tax the notes issued by that bank. There is nothing in the Constitution about banks, nor is Congress empowered to grant charters of incorporation. The states, furthermore, were not forbidden to tax bank notes. Indeed, under the Tenth Amendment not only this power to tax bank notes, but also the power to establish and to regulate banks was apparently reserved to the states. Had the majority on the Court been inclined toward strict construction there would have been no difficulty in finding that Jefferson's opinion on the constitutionality of the original bank charter, rather than Hamilton's, was in accord with the Constitution. Here, as elsewhere, Marshall followed Hamilton.

If the national government was granted no powers with regard to banks it was empowered to raise money by taxes and by borrowing, and to coin money. It was also empowered "to make all laws which shall be necessary and proper for carrying into execution the foregoing powers." The problem, therefore, is very largely to determine the meaning of "necessary." It was clear that the government would exist without the Bank. This it had done between 1811 and 1816. If "necessary" meant "indispensable" or "absolutely essential" the constitutional justification was doubtful. But if "necessary" meant "desirable," or "highly useful," then the difficulty was slight. As early as 1804 Marshall had asserted that "congress must possess the choice of means, and must be empowered to use any means which are in fact conducive to the exercise of a power granted by the Constitution." [25] "It would," he wrote, "be incorrect, and would produce endless difficulties, if the opinion should be maintained that no law was authorised which was not indispensably necessary to give effect to a specified power."

[25] U.S. v. Fisher, 2 Cranch 358, 396 (1804).

Like most Federalists Marshall had opposed Madison's nationalism in the War of 1812. He took no part in the ill-fated Hartford Convention, that New England precursor of Southern attempts at nullification and secession, but he was "as bitterly opposed" to the war policy as were the leaders of that movement.[26] But his nationalism was put to no such test in the matter of the Bank. Here it was not the agrarian interests of the South and West which favored the act of Congress, but the financial and mercantile groups of the East. And in the defense of this Hamiltonian principle of government aid and encouragement to these interests Marshall enunciated his classic theory of broad construction.

> We admit, as all must admit, that the powers of the government are limited, and that its limits are not to be transcended. But we think the sound construction of the constitution must allow to the national legislature that discretion, with respect to the means by which the powers it confers are to be carried into execution, which will enable that body to perform the high duties assigned to it, in the manner most beneficial to the people. Let the end be legitimate, let it be within the scope of the constitution, and all means which are appropriate, which are plainly adapted to that end, which are not prohibited, but consist with the letter and spirit of the constitution, are constitutional.[27]

Thus in the same term of Court which saw Marshall extending the limitations of the contract clause as against state legislation interfering with property rights, the effectiveness of the Tenth Amendment as a limitation upon Congress, when Congress was legislating in support of property rights, was greatly reduced. There was some justification for Jefferson's characterization of the Court as "the subtle corps of sappers and miners constantly working under ground to undermine the foundations of our confederated fabric." [28] The book of John Taylor of Caroline, *Construction Con-*

[26] Beveridge, *op. cit.*, IV, 55. [27] 4 Wheaton, 316, 421 (1819).

[28] Letter to Thomas Ritchie, Dec. 25, 1820, *Writings* (Ford ed.), X, 170.

strued and Constitutions Vindicated (1820) develops at length and with partisan bitterness the same theme. But the future, in this respect at least, was to be on Marshall's side, and the Court has not often departed from his theory of interpretation. When it has done so, more often than not, it has encountered criticism as scathing as that of Jefferson and Taylor. It has been rare that the Court has, in its capacity of federal umpire, been able to please everyone, but that has not weakened the Court's determination to retain that power.

In the second part of the McCulloch opinion the Court held that the Maryland tax levied on the Bank's notes was invalid. It has been pointed out that neither in Article I, section 10, nor elsewhere in the Constitution is there such a limitation upon the states. But it is also true that the tax was both a highly discriminatory and a destructive tax. If the tax had stood the note-issuing function of the Bank would probably have been extinguished in Maryland, and in any other state which chose to follow her example. Marshall's platitude, "the power to tax involves the power to destroy," is generally true but has little to do with the issue of constitutionality, for the question was whether the state had the power to tax. He held that the tax was contrary to the principles of the federal system, for the Bank was employed as an agency of the national government. As such it was to be protected against destruction by the states. "A power to create implies a power to preserve." As is so frequent in Court opinions we are faced with a list of terrible, although imaginary, possibilities were this doctrine not to be accepted. The states might tax, and destroy, the mail, the mint, patent rights, the papers of the customhouse, the judicial process, "all the means employed by the government." "This was not intended by the American people." And, in all fairness, it should be added that it was not being attempted by the states. The tax was levied on the notes issued by a Bank which may have been constitutionally chartered but which was certainly not comparable in status to the functions and public offices that he lists.

In the McCulloch case [29] Marshall follows his usual penchant for the principle of absoluteness. If, he said, a state may tax at all, it may tax in any amount. The economic harmfulness of that principle begins to be apparent in Weston v. Charleston.[30] Here Marshall, over the dissent of Johnson and Thompson, applied the McCulloch rule against state taxation of a national agency or instrumentality. There, be it remembered, the tax was discriminatory and destructive. If we accept Marshall's argument that the notes were instrumentalities of the national government his conclusion is easy to accept, although his doctrine is questionable. But in the Weston case the tax was certainly not destructive and it was apparently not discriminatory. The tax amounted to twenty-five cents on every hundred dollars and was levied upon "all personal estate, consisting of bonds, notes, insurance stock, six and seven per cent. stock of the United States, or other obligations upon which interest has been or will be received during the year, over and above the interest which has been paid," excepting the stock of the state itself, of banks chartered by the state, and of the Bank of the United States.

To Justice Johnson this was a "clumsily worded" form of income tax. In his view the six and seven per cent. federal securities were specified, not in order to submit them to discriminatory taxation, but to avoid taxation of the three and four per cent. federal stock.[31] Certainly the stock, or bonds, as we should call such securities, of the federal government was not the only form of obligation subjected to the tax, and the rate of the tax was very low indeed. A tax of one quarter of one per cent. is far removed from oppressiveness, especially for securities bearing six and seven per

[29] 4 Wheaton, 316, 432 (1819). [30] 2 Peters 449 (1829).
[31] *Ibid.*, 472-473. See also the argument of Thompson, J. at 475-476.

cent. interest. Nor does Marshall rest his finding of unconstitutionality upon either the rate of the tax or its selectiveness. Any tax upon an instrumentality employed by the government is invalid as a violation of the principles of American federalism.

Many of the absurdities, fluctuations, and economically undesirable results of the doctrine of immunity from taxation of governmental instrumentalities might have been avoided if Marshall had not been obsessed with his absolutist concept of federalism. For, to his way of thinking, the central government and the states were always rivals and ordinarily opponents. At times he seemed to believe that there was a fixed quantum of power, so that if the states exercised a power, the central government of necessity lost out by that amount. Or possibly he was again under the spell of Hamilton, whose extraordinary work as Secretary of the Treasury left a legacy of sectional jealousies as well as of financial solvency. In his famous Report on the Public Credit in 1795 Hamilton had argued against any taxation of government securities.[32] He probably had in mind only national taxation of national securities but his point of view is easily transferable to state taxation of those securities. The principle was, at any rate, applied. It mattered not that the tax was a very light one, that it was not discriminatory (for Marshall did not argue that it was), and that the securities were owned by private persons who would have had to pay the tax. Under these circumstances the Charleston ordinance seems far removed from a threat to national finance. But Marshall's thinking was still conditioned by the troubled days of the Confederation, and he did not hesitate to use the power of the Court to check any possibilities of state attacks upon the national security. That, in this case, he went far beyond what was either necessary or desirable, the financial history of the past half century has made apparent.

[32] *Works* (Lodge ed.), III, 24-26.

THE COMMERCE POWER

It is a striking commentary upon the success of the Constitution in checking some of the greatest evils of the Confederation that the Supreme Court did not decide a case under the commerce clause until 1824. The interstate trade barriers and retaliations which did so much to bring about the Convention of 1787 apparently disappeared before the Court had an opportunity to declare them invalid. And the first commerce case, which produced one of the greatest, as well as the most popular, of Marshall's opinions sprang out of circumstances not in existence in 1787. For Gibbons v. Ogden [33] was a product of the age of invention. New York attempted to secure for itself and its grantees the exclusive right of navigation in the waters of the state for all vessels propelled by steam. This was clearly in violation of the intentions of those who wrote the commerce clause and the opinion in the case could have been a short and simple one. Instead it is long and complex. Marshall was not content to find that the commerce clause had been violated. He began the long and never finished task by which the Court passes upon the relative powers of the national government and the states under the commerce power. After several times suggesting, but never quite saying, that the Congressional power over commerce is exclusive, he went on to find that a federal coasting license act had been violated. It was unnecessary to bring in this act, which was of dubious applicability, if the power of Congress was exclusive. Why he was so wary in this case is not clear. It may, as Mr. Justice Frankfurter has suggested, have been a matter of strategy,[34] but Marshall was not ordinarily so hesitant in making broad assertions of national power. The long-run effect of combining a bold definition of "commerce among the several states"

[33] 9 Wheaton 1 (1824).

[34] *The Commerce Clause under Marshall, Taney and Waite* (1937), 25.

with a cautious use of a Congressional statute placed on the books long before the steamboat was a commercial factor, was to increase the work and the authority of the Court. Although the formula which was to make apparent this enlargement of the Court's discretionary power was not enunciated until 1851, it may be that Marshall foresaw this possibility, even though he never quite made it explicit.

Some indication of the scope of the Court's discretion under the decision in Gibbons v. Ogden is seen in Willson v. Blackbird Creek Marsh Company.[35] Here a very brief opinion suffices to sustain the constitutionality of a Delaware statute permitting the building of a dam across a small but navigable tidal stream. The stream was navigable to coasting vessels and the dam blocked their passage, but Marshall found that Congress had not acted, and that the state act could not be "considered as repugnant to the power to regulate commerce in its dormant state." [36] One of the curious but relevant facts of the case is that the vessel whose voyage was impeded was enrolled and licensed under the federal navigation acts. Marshall held, nevertheless, that Congress had not intended to deal with local matters of the sort here involved. Had it done so the act of Congress would have been a valid exercise of the commerce power, but until that power was exercised the states continued to have the authority to regulate.

Marshall had but three commerce cases to deal with during his thirty-four years, but, taken together, they illustrate admirably his conception of the Court as federal umpire. For if in the Willson case he sustained a local regulation which affected commerce among the states in a remote and insubstantial manner, in Brown v. Maryland [37] the nationalism of Gibbons v. Ogden is again apparent. A discriminatory license fee imposed upon the wholesalers of imported goods was dealt with as though it were non-discriminatory. It was not

[35] 2 Peters 245 (1829). [36] *Ibid.*, 252. [37] 12 Wheaton 419 (1827).

..fficient for him to find that the license fee was contrary to the prohibition against import and export duties. He attempted to lay the basis for a limitation upon the states' power to tax all original packages whether brought in from sister states or imported from abroad. The act was, furthermore, held contrary to the commerce clause. But the dormant commerce power, as in the Gibbons case, is insufficient, and "the act of Congress which authorizes importation" was found to have been violated by this tax. If the single example of the Willson case is a legitimate basis for generalization, Marshall was not opposed to state regulation of commerce, provided it in no way threatened the freedom of commercial intercourse among the states and with foreign nations. If there was even a remote possibility that the states' action would tend toward a restoration of "the oppressed and degraded state of commerce previous to the adoption of the Constitution," then the statute should be declared void. The nationalism of his theory should not obscure the magnitude of the role reserved for the Supreme Court. It, and it alone, is to serve as umpire of the federal system. A holding that Congress had the exclusive power to regulate commerce with foreign nations and among the several states would have been a more nationalistic one than the less clear and positive rule in his three opinions, but it would have left less for the Court to do.

Chapter IV

JACKSONIAN JUDGES AND THE JUDICIAL POWER

When Marshall died in 1835 there died the last of the Justices appointed by Federalist Presidents. Bushrod Washington, also appointed by John Adams, had gone five years earlier. To be sure Story remained, and although he was appointed as a Democratic-Republican by Madison, he was a Federalist in principles from the time he first came under Marshall's influence until he left the Court in 1845. Not all of those appointed by Jefferson and his successors became such wholehearted supporters of the Chief Justice, even though he did maintain control of his Court to a remarkable degree, at least until about 1827. After that there is more wavering, and there are fewer extensions of doctrine. Beginning with McLean in 1829 every one of the fourteen men who took a seat upon the Supreme Court between that time and the Civil War was a Democrat, save only for Curtis, a Whig. And Taney, the new Chief Justice, had, like Marshall before him, served in the Cabinet, but not as a judge of another court. He was a Jacksonian partisan, as Marshall had been a good Federalist.

Given these facts it is not difficult to conclude that the Taney period (1836-1864) is one in which the Court repudiated, or at least greatly modified, the Federalist constitutional law of Marshall. It is easy, if only one confines one's examination of decisions to those which point that way. A more comprehensive survey will produce doubts. For the traditional view of this era has apparently been based upon the simple conception of Taney as Jackson's puppet in removing the deposits from the Bank of the United States, upon the Dred Scott decision, and only one side of that, and upon the three important decisions of Taney's first term. The Dred Scott case may be reserved for later consideration, but a brief consideration of the other factors in this equation is in order here.

THE DEMOCRACY OF THE JACKSONIAN DEMOCRATS

As acting Secretary of the Treasury, Taney did remove the deposits, but he was no rubber stamp. He was only carrying out a policy he had been urging upon Jackson for months.[1] Taney had supported the Bank in Maryland until he came to distrust it because of its activities there. If he subsequently fought it, it does not follow that he was opposed to all banks. He came from the planter aristocracy, and he had been an active Federalist in Maryland as long as there was a Federalist party. It was not until 1824 that, his old party being extinct, he gave his allegiance to the Jackson wing of the Democrats.

When he did so he did not cease to have a strong sense of the sanctity of property rights, nor did he cease to regard courts as the true interpreters of the laws of property and of the Constitution of the United States. Like Jackson he remained essentially a conservative. So much has been written about Jackson as the man of the people, the frontiersman, and the opponent of the Bank, that it is easy to forget that he was, from early manhood, a cotton planter and slaveowner, whose favorite sport was horse racing, not bear hunting, who fought duels with pistols in the manner of a gentleman, not with fists in the manner of a backwoodsman.[2] For a very large part

[1] Carl B. Swisher, *Roger B. Taney* (1935), chs. VIII-XII.

[2] Cf. the article on Jackson by Thomas P. Abernethy in the *Dictionary of American Biography*, IX, 529, and the same author's *From Frontier to Plantation in Tennessee* (1932).

of the movement which is called Jacksonian democracy he had little sympathy, and, indeed, little understanding. Neither Taney nor the other Democrats appointed to the Court by Jackson and his successors were leaders in the great movements of the age for the broader distribution of power and property. They were successful men of affairs who were very far from being adherents to the programs of Robert Owen or Seth Luther. Some were less extreme in their economic conservatism than Marshall or Story or Kent, but the difference is rarely a great one. Most were less nationalistic, partly because of the growing sectionalism, partly because they had not been young men during the Revolution or the Confederation. But it is remarkable how slight was the effect upon Supreme Court decisions of the sectional and states' rights controversies of the age. For the purpose of this book the most significant fact is that all were lawyers and all held it as a cardinal principle of politics that the Court was the final arbitral authority.

In Taney's first term there were important cases involving the commerce, the bills of credit, and the contract clauses.[3] In each the Court apparently went against the Marshall doctrines, or so Justice Story, who dissented in all three, asserted. If we were to base an assessment of the twenty-eight year Taney period upon an estimate of the change in doctrinal emphasis indicated in these three decisions of his first year we might come out with a conclusion of clear and simple contours, although it may be doubted whether a dispassionate examination would justify the feeling of Story that the columns had been torn down. These are, however, but three out of scores of constitutional decisions in this long period, and, taken alone, they are only a little less inaccurate as indica-

[3] Mayor of New York v. Miln, 11 Peters 102 (1837), Briscoe v. Bank of Kentucky, 11 Peters 257 (1837), Charles River Bridge v. Warren Bridge, 11 Peters 420 (1837).

tions of the nature of the Court's work than a conclusion based solely upon the Dred Scott decision.

JURISDICTION OF THE FEDERAL COURTS

Mr. Charles Warren made one of his important contributions to a better understanding of the Court's place in history when he pointed out that the Taney Court extended the jurisdiction of the federal courts.[4] It was in this period that the Court first took jurisdiction of a suit by one state against another and involving a disputed boundary line.[5] In the century since that decision there have been many cases in which the Court dealt with this problem which has been so productive of wars between nations. Taney dissented in the case on the theory that Rhode Island was attempting to secure a ruling on a political rather than a properly judicial question. Had the rights of property, rather than the rights of sovereignty, been involved the Court would, he agreed, have had jurisdiction to determine the true boundary.[6] He was outvoted in this case, but he wrote the opinion in Luther v. Borden[7] ten years later, the famous decision in which the Court refused to pass upon a "political" question. The issue presented in this case concerned the disputed control of the government of Rhode Island during that curious episode called Dorr's Rebellion. On the basis of an action for trespass the Court was asked to determine whether the old constitution or the "Peoples Constitution" was in effect, and whether the government under the old or the reformed constitution

[4] In *The Supreme Court in United States History*, ch. XXI, *et seq.* I am, however, unable to understand Mr. Warren's characterization of the difference between Marshall and Taney. "Marshall's interests," he writes, "were largely in the constitutional aspects of the cases before him; Taney's were largely economic and social." II, 308. This does not seem to agree with many of the demonstrable facts, among them, as Mr. Warren well says, that Marshall's leading doctrine was "vested rights." *Ibid.*

[5] Rhode Island v. Massachusetts, 12 Peters 657 (1838).

[6] *Ibid.*, 752-754. [7] 7 Howard 1 (1849).

was legitimately in office. The Court wisely held that such a question was not, to use the phrase of Madison in the Federal Convention, "of a judiciary nature." It was a political question to be determined by the political departments. The President, upon application of the governor under the old constitution, did recognize him as "the executive power of the state, and took measures to call out the militia to support his authority if it should be found necessary." That, the Chief Justice asserted, is a decision which any court in the United States must accept.

In considering the attitude of the Taney Court to the power of the courts there are several reasons why an unadorned citation of Luther v. Borden is misleading. For one thing this case dealt with a situation of rare occurrence and the doctrine of the case was not applied in another important case during the Taney era, nor, for that matter, has it since been given a wide application.[8] This doctrine, furthermore, was supported by two of Marshall's opinions.[9] And, finally, the Taney Court not only followed in general Marshall's conception of the Supreme Court's authority, it went even further than he had done in expanding the scope of that power. In at least two cases the Democratic Justices actually overruled Marshall's narrower conception of the federal judicial power.

Since 1809 it had been the accepted principle that a corporation had, for purposes of jurisdiction, no citizenship other than that of the various members or shareholders of the corporation.[10] Such a ruling greatly restricted the judicial business of the federal courts, since it made it impossible in most instances to get a corporation case into the federal co[illegible]s under the clause giving to those courts jurisdiction of ca[illegible]es

[8] Charles G. Post, Jr., *The Supreme Court and Political Questions* (1936).

[9] Martin v. Mott, 12 Wheaton 19 (1827), Foster v. Neilson, 2 Peters 253 (1829). Cf. also Marshall's remark in Marbury v. Madison, "Questions in their nature political . . . can never be made in this Court." 1 Cranch at 170.

[10] Bank of the United States v. Deveaux, 5 Cranch 61 (1809).

involving "citizens of different states." In 1844 the Court unanimously overruled this doctrine and held that for purposes of a suit in the federal courts brought on the ground of diversity of citizenship, a corporation was presumed to be a citizen of the state by which it was chartered.[11] The result was greatly to increase the number of cases involving corporations which could and were tried in the federal courts.

Justice Story had spoken for a unanimous Court when, in 1825, he had held that the admiralty jurisdiction of the federal courts extended only upon the seas or within the limits of the tidal ebb and flow.[12] Congress provided in an act of 1845 that the admiralty jurisdiction of the district courts should extend to the Great Lakes and the waters connecting them. This act was sustained in an opinion given by Taney six years later.[13] The earlier decision, he said, was given "when the great importance of the question as it now presents itself could not be foreseen. . . . For the decision was made in 1825, when the commerce on the rivers of the west and on the lakes was in its infancy." [14] He points out that the old rule was based upon English practice. In that country navigation ceased with tide water; here navigation was possible for hundreds, even thousands, of miles beyond tide water, and there is no admissible reason why the tidal line should mark the end of the admiralty power of the national government. The result here, as in the Letson case, has been considerably to augment the business, and the authority, of the federal courts.[15]

Another illustration of the willingness of the Taney Court to extend its authority is to be found in Story's opinion in Swift v. Tyson.[16] Before this decision section 34 of the Judi-

[11] Louisville, etc. R.R. v. Letson, 2 Howard 497 (1844).

[12] The Thomas Jefferson, 10 Wheaton 428 (1825).

[13] The Propeller Genesee Chief v. Fitzhugh, 12 Howard 443 (1851).

[14] *Ibid.*, 456.

[15] In Steamboat New World v. King, 16 Howard 469 (1853) the same ruling was applied to the navigable rivers beyond the tidal flow.

[16] 16 Peters 1 (1842).

ciary Act of 1789, which provides "that the laws of the several States, except where the Constitution, treaties, or statutes of the United States shall otherwise require or provide, shall be regarded as rules of decision in trials at common law in the courts of the United States, in cases where they apply," had been understood to include the decisions of the state courts as well as state statutes. But, said Story, the law regarding bills of exchange, the subject of this case, which is enforced in the New York courts need not necessarily be followed by the Supreme Court. On subjects of this kind the principles of general commercial law may be applied by that Court. This decision did not add to the jurisdiction of the federal courts but it did add to the range of their discretion.

These decisions in which the Court added to its jurisdiction or to its freedom of action are far from an adequate survey of the uses of judicial review during this period. Here, as in the study of the Marshall period, we need to know something of the issues presented to the Court, and of the decisions upon those issues, before drawing any reliable conclusions concerning the character of judicial review.

BILLS OF CREDIT

That the three constitutional decisions of Taney's first term as Chief Justice gave Story some reasons for his fears there can be little doubt. Two of them deal respectively with the contract and commerce clauses and will be considered not as single and final instances of constitutional interpretation but as the first cases of the long series interpreting those clauses. Briscoe v. Bank of Kentucky[17] stands alone. Here a majority of the Court sustained a Kentucky act establishing a state-owned and state-controlled bank and providing for the issuance by that bank of paper notes or currency. According to Story, who dissented, this act violated the prohibition

[17] 11 Peters 257 (1837).

against emitting bills of credit, and the case was adequately covered by Craig v. Missouri.[18] But to Justice McLean, who had been one of the three dissenters in the Craig case, the notes of the Bank of Kentucky were not issued by the state and they were not bills of credit. They were issued by a bank which could sue and be sued. They were not on the credit of the state, but were redeemable by the bank and a fund had been established for that purpose.

It is possible to agree with Story that the old majority of Marshall's Court would have found this act to be unconstitutional without agreeing that this decision overrules the Craig case. The antique Federalism which saw in the Bank of the United States the only remedy for the monetary evils of the Revolution and Confederation did not approve of the issuance of paper notes by a state-owned and controlled bank, although it seems reasonably clear that such a bank is not on quite the same constitutional footing as a state loan office. The former is what is familiar to us as a public corporation; the latter was a department of the state. But, whatever the distinction, it is also evident that the bare majority of 1830, for the Craig case was carried by a vote of four to three, no longer controlled the Court. A generation which had not had personal experience of the financial troubles of the early years of the Republic had come to power.

PROPERTY RIGHTS AND CONTRACT

If the Briscoe case reflects a point of view somewhat different from, possibly inconsistent with, that of the Craig case, it cannot be cited as the first of a group in which the old doctrines of constitutional law were reinterpreted. Since, moreover, not even Marshall and Story appeared to find that private banks chartered by the states could not issue paper notes, it may be questioned whether what may be called the

[18] 4 Peters 410 (1830).

constitutional economy of the country was greatly affected by the Briscoe ruling. A case of much greater economic importance, and one much more frequently cited as proof of the Jacksonian revolution on the Court is Charles River Bridge v. Warren Bridge.[19] This decision was, in chronological sequence, the third of the famous trio of 1837, and to Story it furnished the final and conclusive evidence that "the Constitution as we knew it has gone," to use a phrase reputedly uttered from the bench a century later.

This case involved the construction of a charter issued to the Charles River Bridge Company in 1785. While this Company's franchise was still in effect Massachusetts incorporated the Warren Bridge Company and authorized it to build another toll bridge within a few rods of the first. After a few years, it was stipulated, this bridge was to become a free bridge and the property of the Commonwealth. Against the plea that the contract in the first charter had been violated by the grant of the second, the Court held that the first grant was not an exclusive one, and that, therefore, it was no impairment of the obligation of contract to grant the franchise to the Warren Bridge Company. Grants, said the Chief Justice, are always to be construed strictly. Nothing passes by implication.

Since the effect of the second grant was greatly to reduce the value of the first, there were many Whigs, and not a few property-conscious Democrats, who joined in Mr. Justice Story's fears that the doctrines ensuring the sanctity of property rights, so carefully built up under Marshall, were all to be repudiated.[20] The next twenty-seven years were to show how unfounded were these lamentations. And, indeed, no new principle was expressed in the Bridge case. The rule of strict construction of public grants had been stated by Marshall,[21] and repeated in two cases where he was of the major-

---

[19] 11 Peters 420 (1837). [20] Warren, *op. cit.*, II, 302-303.

[21] Providence Bank v. Billings, 4 Peters 514 (1830).

ity.[22] What is even more important, in this case the validity of Marshall's two great contract clause doctrines, that a charter is a contract, and that an agreement to which a state is a party is to be protected under the contract clause, were not questioned. Except for the rule of the inalienability of the right of eminent domain,[23] a principle with which Marshall would almost certainly have agreed, there was no new doctrine enunciated in these years which had the effect of limiting the scope of the contract clause. There were, on the other hand, eighteen cases involving the clause in which state legislation was declared unconstitutional.[24]

Of these cases the group of greatest interest is that concerning debtors' relief legislation. In these the Court was, for the first time, dealing with statutes of the sort which the fathers apparently had in mind when they wrote the contract clause. For these acts altered the contractual relationships of private persons. And when such statutes were retroactive in their effect the Taney Court did not hesitate to declare them invalid, unless it was found that only the remedy, and not the obligation itself was affected. Marshall had held, in Sturges v. Crowninshield, that the remedy, the legal method of enforcing the contract, might be modified, so long as the obligation of contract remained unimpaired. In several cases of the Taney period the Court found it difficult to draw a clear distinction between the terms of the contract and the means of its enforcement, but in four cases statutes were held to alter the provisions of the contract. In Bronson v. Kinzie,[25] first and most famous of them, mortgagors were retrospectively given the privilege of redeeming property sold on foreclosure by repaying the purchase money together with

[22] Beaty v. Lessee of Knowler, 4 Peters 152 (1830), U.S. v. Arredondo, 6 Peters 691 (1832).

[23] West River Bridge Co. v. Dix, 6 Howard 507 (1848).

[24] See Wright, *op. cit.*, ch. III for a more complete discussion than is here possible. [25] 1 Howard 311 (1843).

interest at ten per cent. In another case [26] a statute prohibiting sales of foreclosed property at auction unless for two-thirds of the appraised value was set aside, when given a retrospective application. The other two cases [27] concerned statutes of very similar pattern. Together the group of cases demonstrates the entire willingness of the Democrats on the bench to give judicial protection to the vested rights of private property.

Nor does this solicitude for property rights stop with the debtors' relief legislation cases. In six cases the extreme principle of New Jersey v. Wilson was given effect and the doctrine of tax exemption applied. There was some hesitation in the earlier Taney years but in the Piqua Bank case [28] in 1853 the Court faced the issue and, with but a single dissenter, followed the Marshall ruling that a contract of tax exemption is protected by the contract clause. Indeed it is with this and the other cases of this kind during the Taney era that the tax exemption doctrine came to be accepted by the Court. And it was accepted after its implications had been faced and discussed, as they had never been faced in the Marshall era. Only as the consequences of generous grants of tax exemption, promoted by the optimism and exuberance of a rapidly expanding economy, began to be apparent could the issue of policy concealed by the simple logic of Marshall's opinion be faced. It is a significant commentary upon the economic conservatism of the Taney Court that, after confronting this situation, it followed the Marshall ruling.

The three decades between Jackson's veto of the charter for the Bank of the United States and the establishment of the national banking system during the Civil War were the period in which state chartered banks flourished. They flour-

[26] McCracken v. Hayward, 2 Howard 608 (1844).

[27] Lessee of Gantley v. Ewing, 3 Howard 707 (1845), Howard v. Bugbee, 24 Howard 461 (1861).

[28] Piqua Branch of the State Bank v. Knoop, 16 How. 369 (1853).

ished, that is to say, if number be the criterion, for many of them were less than a complete financial success. During these years there was much state legislation regulating the activities of the banks, for even then the practice of *laissez faire* was rapidly losing ground. Most of this legislation was not tested in the Supreme Court, but in three cases [29] the Court did find such regulatory statutes invalid under the contract clause, ordinarily because of a conflict between the terms of the original charter of incorporation and a subsequent statute.

A more unusual application of this clause was that in which the Court held that a contract between the United States government and a state is one which a state may not, consistently with the contract clause, subsequently alter or repudiate.[30] This is a distinct addition to the law of the Constitution. It is also a far cry from the objectives envisaged by the fathers in 1787.

An extension which was to be of more economic importance, as well as a source of a great deal of confusion in constitutional law, was made in the strange case of Gelpcke v. Dubuque,[31] a case decided in Taney's last term as Chief Justice. The effect of this none-too-clear decision was to hold unconstitutional a ruling by the Iowa Supreme Court which altered a previous decision of that court. By the earlier ruling a bond issue of the city of Dubuque was valid. Under the altered construction of the state constitution it was invalid and the bonds were worthless. The United States Supreme Court's holding that the change of decision by the Iowa court impaired the obligation of the contract contained in the bonds would be unexceptionable were it not for the wording of the contract clause in the federal Constitution. There it

---

[29] Planters' Bank v. Sharp, 6 Howard 301 (1848), Woodruff v. Trapnall, 10 Howard 190 (1851), Curran v. Arkansas, 15 Howard 304 (1853).

[30] Searight v. Stokes, 3 Howard 151 (1845), Neil, Moore & Co. v. Ohio, 3 Howard 720 (1845). Wright, *op. cit.*, 76-78, 214-216.

[31] 1 Wallace 175 (1864).

is stipulated that no state "shall pass any law impairing the obligation of contract." The clause is a limitation upon state legislatures, not upon the state courts. Over the vigorous denial of Mr. Justice Miller that there was here "any question of the obligation of contracts," [32] the Court employed the doctrine of the contract clause, even though it did not admit that it was basing its ruling upon that clause. As Mr. Justice Holmes remarked many years later, this is a decision "which it took the Court a good while to explain." [33]

FEDERALISM AND COMMERCE

Like the Marshall Court before it the Taney Court had to deal with many issues of federalism, of the relative powers of the states and the central government. Two eminent historians have repeated a frequent characterization of this work of the Court in these words: "For practical purposes they [the Justices of the Taney era] declared the states to be sovereign. So in 1860 the country stood in fundamental respects just where it did in 1787 under the Articles of Confederation." [34] This extravagant statement is evidently based upon the holding in the Dred Scott case that Congress lacked the power to abolish slavery in the territories, and that decision will be considered below. It could not have been based upon the cases dealing with the powers of the federal courts for, as has been shown, the tendency there is to strengthen, not weaken, the national power. Nor could it have been founded upon the construction of Marshall's rule against the taxation of federal instrumentalities. This rule was, seemingly without hesitation, applied in a case involving the taxation of United States government bonds in common with the securities held

[32] *Ibid.*, 210.

[33] Muhlker v. N.Y. & Harlem R.R. Co., 197 U.S. 544, 573 (1905). Cf. Wright, *op. cit.*, 79-82, ch. XI.

[34] Charles A. and Mary Beard, *The Rise of American Civilization* (1927), I, 689.

by a bank,[35] and also where a non-discriminatory tax was levied on the salary of an officer of the United States.[36]

The story is a more complicated one when we come to the commerce clause cases, although it can be shown that the deviation here amounts to no more than a slight change in emphasis. Too often a generalization about the commerce decisions of this period has been founded only on the first case of the eighteen in which the Taney Court dealt with the commerce clause, just as the Charles River Bridge case, decided in the same term, has sufficed for the contract cases. In the Mayor of New York v. Miln [37] the Court sustained a statute providing that the master of every ship arriving in New York should make a report to the mayor of the complete passenger list of the vessel, the report to give the name, age, last legal settlement, and occupation of each person. This was upheld as an exercise of the state's police power, an attempt to deal with the problem of indigence and disease produced by the increase in immigration, and no interference with, or even regulation of, commerce.

Story dissented, arguing that the statute was a regulation of commerce, and as such was invalid under the principles of the Gibbons and Brown cases. We may believe Story's contention that Marshall thought the act invalid and yet find the statute to be far less of an infringement of the Congressional power than that involved in Gibbons v. Ogden. Indeed, the infringement seems to be not so much in this statute, which placed no obstacle in the way of immigrants, but in the fears of Story and Marshall that it might be an entering wedge. It was not to be that.

There are two periods in the commerce clause story of the Taney Court, before and after 1851. For until the doctrine of selective exclusiveness was stated by Curtis in the Cooley case the Court was floundering in its attempt to deal with

[35] Bank of Commerce v. New York, 2 Black 620 (1863).
[36] Dobbins v. Erie County, 16 Peters 435 (1842). [37] 11 Peters 102 (1837).

the problem of the validity of state regulations of commerce when Congress had not legislated. The blame, if such a term is an appropriate one, is to be credited to Marshall as well as to the Jacksonian jurists. In his three commerce cases he had opened but not settled the question. In both the Gibbons and Brown cases he went out of his way to find that Congress had dealt with the subject. In the Blackbird Creek case he sustained a state act, which was a clearer interference with interstate commerce than the one involved in the Miln case, although indicating that Congress could so legislate as to render the act invalid.

The confusion over the dormant power of Congress under the commerce clause is most vividly illustrated in the License cases [38] and the Passenger cases.[39] In the first group statutes of three states regulating the sale of liquor imported from other states or from a foreign country were sustained. In the nine opinions written by six Justices there is not enough agreement to warrant a statement as to precisely what the Court decided, except that the statutes were not unconstitutional. There is clearly a growing tendency in the Court to make explicit what was implicit in the Blackbird Creek Marsh case, that is, that the states have some power to regulate interstate commerce unless and until Congress takes over. This is the position which Taney here stated [40] with emphasis and to which he afterward adhered. But it was not accepted by all of the Justices at this time and in the Passenger cases the diversity of view is even more apparent. Here, by a five to four decision, statutes of New York and Massachusetts were held to be unconstitutional regulations of commerce. Nine Justices wrote opinions. Of the majority, three held that the power of Congress to regulate commerce was exclusive. The four members of the minority said that it was not. The other two of the majority didn't decide on this basis.

[38] 5 Howard 504 (1847). [39] 7 Howard 283 (1849).
[40] 5 Howard at 579 *et seq.*

It should not be assumed that because the Court was, in these years, unable to come to a definite conclusion concerning the states' power over commerce that it was hesitant when it came to sustaining Congressional power. Only two acts of Congress came up under the commerce clause before 1851 and both were unanimously upheld. The first case involved a statute providing for the punishment of theft from vessels in distress even though the act was committed above the high-water mark.[41] Story, relying upon Gibbons v. Ogden, said that the power to regulate commerce does not stop at the boundary line of a state. "It extends to such acts, done on land, which interfere with, obstruct, or prevent the due exercise of the power to regulate commerce and navigation with foreign nations, and among the states." [42] In the second [43] the Court upheld Congress' power to punish those who brought counterfeit coin into the country, and declared that the power to regulate commerce included the power to prohibit certain articles from being imported. "Since the passage of the embargo and non-intercourse laws, and the repeated judicial sanctions those statutes have received, it can scarcely, at this day, be open to doubt, that every subject falling within the legitimate sphere of commercial regulation may be partially or wholly excluded, when either measure shall be demanded by the safety or by the important interests of the entire nation." [44]

A formula was badly needed then, not because of any hesitancy about sustaining Congressional legislation, but in order to deal with state regulation where Congress was silent. The formula was stated by the lone Whig on the Court, the newly appointed Justice Curtis, in the Cooley case.[45] Here a Pennsylvania act regulating pilots and pilotage in the port of Philadelphia, a measure which was clearly a regulation of

[41] U.S. v. Coombs, 12 Peters 72 (1838). [42] *Ibid.*, 78.
[43] U.S. v. Marigold, 9 Howard 560 (1850). [44] *Ibid.*, 566-567.
[45] Cooley v. Board of Wardens, 12 Howard 299 (1851).

interstate and foreign commerce, was sustained. The majority thus clearly rejected the theory that state power to regulate commerce among the states or with foreign nations was entirely destroyed by the constitutional grant to Congress. But, said the Court, there is a sphere within which the power of Congress is exclusive. Where a single uniform rule is required the states may not legislate even though Congress has not dealt with the subject.[46]

This formula of selective exclusiveness is not so nationalistic a doctrine as the one sometimes attributed to Marshall. It may be doubted, however, whether it is more than a deft combination of the Gibbons and the Blackbird Creek opinions. Marshall, after all, never held a state regulation of commerce invalid unless it conflicted with an act of Congress, even though he had to go out of his way to find the act. And in the Blackbird Creek case he sustained a state regulation on the theory that it was a matter of local concern with which Congress had not yet seen fit to deal. The Cooley formula, furthermore, is far from a self-denying ordinance, so far as the judicial power is concerned. It extended the discretionary power of the Court, more so than if the power of Congress had been held to be exclusive. It is the Court which must determine when a single uniform rule is necessary and when, therefore, state legislation is invalid as contrary to the dormant power of Congress. This decision is more than an important interpretation of the commerce clause. It is also a landmark in the growth of the power and scope of judicial review.

Between 1851 and 1864 the Court passed upon Congressional legislation under the commerce clause only in the Wheeling Bridge controversy.[47] After holding Virginia's

---

[46] See the interesting discussion in Frankfurter, *The Commerce Clause*, ch. II.

[47] Pennsylvania v. Wheeling, etc. Bridge Co., 13 Howard 518 (1851), Pennsylvania v. Wheeling etc. Bridge Co., 18 Howard 421 (1856).

grant of the right to erect a bridge over the Ohio River invalid as contrary to the Congressional power to regulate commerce, a power exercised in the coasting license acts, the Court had to find the grant valid after Congress passed an act approving the bridge and declaring it lawful. The outcome of the affair was, among other things, a vindication of Taney's dissent in the first case. There he had argued that the matter was one with which Congress should deal, that it had not done so under the acts cited by the majority, and that the courts could not secure adequate information or lay down general rules for bridges over navigable streams. "It is too near the confines of legislation, and I think the court ought not to assume it." [48]

In the Davenport cases [49] a statute requiring vessels coming into the port of Mobile to furnish information to local authorities was unanimously held contrary to Congressional legislation regulating the coasting trade. But in Hays v. Pacific Mail Steamship Company [50] it is not clear whether a state act taxing steamships touching at San Francisco was held invalid because of Congressional legislation providing for registration with the Collector of the home port, here New York, or whether the Court believed that the commerce clause served to render unconstitutional double taxation of vessels engaged in interstate commerce. The rule of selective exclusiveness is not explicitly invoked, although it seems to be the basis of the decision. In the other commerce cases of the period the point of view of the Blackbird Creek case is evident. This precedent is not always cited but its doctrine, which in this respect means also the doctrine of the Cooley case, is almost always present. The acts sustained, that is to say, were held to deal with matters of primarily local concern. On most, if not all, of the subjects Congress could

[48] 13 Howard at 592.

[49] Sinnot v. Davenport, 22 Howard 227 (1859), Foster v. Davenport, 22 Howard 244 (1859). [50] 17 Howard 596 (1855).

legislate, but until it did do so, the state regulations were valid.[51]

SLAVERY AND THE JUDICIARY

The most unfortunate single episode in the history of judicial review is the Court's handling of the slavery problem. This characterization is not applicable to every decision affecting slavery but it is apparent in more than the Dred Scott case. Even in the first case in which the Court passed on the merits of the controversy, Prigg v. Pennsylvania,[52] the majority was not content to hold unconstitutional a state statute interfering with the right of a slaveowner to recapture a fugitive slave. Justice Story's opinion went beyond that decision and asserted that the fugitive slave clause of the Constitution vested exclusive power over this subject in Congress, even though the clause is not so worded.[53] Three Justices dissented, arguing that Congress was not given exclusive power, and that, under the Constitutional provision, the free states were under obligation to cooperate in the recovery of fugitive slaves. That the majority's interpretation had aided in intensifying sectional bitterness became apparent when some free states passed "personal liberty laws" which instructed their officers of the law to give no aid to persons seeking to recover runaway slaves. The Southern states indignantly petitioned Congress for a stronger federal act. The Fugitive Slave Law of 1850 was stronger than that

[51] See, e.g., Veazie v. Moor, 14 Howard 568 (1852), Smith v. Maryland, 18 Howard 71 (1855), Withers v. Buckley, 20 Howard 84 (1858), The James Gray v. The John Fraser, 21 Howard 184 (1859). It is a curious fact that no commerce clause case of the period was concerned with railroad regulation, although there were several contract clause cases dealing with that subject.

[52] 16 Peters 539 (1842).

[53] "No person held to service or labour in one state, under the laws thereof, escaping into another, shall in consequence of any law or regulation therein, be discharged from such service or labor, but shall be delivered up on claim of the party to whom such service or labor may be due." Art. IV, sec. 2, par. 3.

of 1793, but it was scarcely designed to placate the sectional bias of the North.

Strader v. Graham [54] is the outstanding exception to the tendency of the Court to take an extreme stand when dealing with the slave problem. Here the Court unanimously refused to take jurisdiction when asked to determine the status of three negroes who had been held as slaves in Kentucky and who had escaped to Canada. The owner of the boat on which they had fled from Louisville to Cincinnati was, by the Kentucky courts, held liable for the payment of their value to the former master. When the unsuccessful defendant appealed to the Supreme Court and contended that the alleged slaves were actually free men because they had, from time to time, been taken by their owner into the free state of Ohio, Taney for the Court ruled that it was for the laws of Kentucky to determine the status of persons domiciled within its territory. The national Constitution would not, in this instance, control the law of Kentucky.

The situation in the Dred Scott case [55] was similar to that in Strader v. Graham, and it seems certain that seven members of the Court believed the earlier case to be controlling. Dred Scott sued for his freedom on the grounds that his master had taken him into the free state of Illinois, and into the Upper Louisiana Territory (now Minnesota) which was free under the Missouri Compromise Act of 1820.

Justice Nelson, who had the merit of coming from New York and not being suspect as a slaveowner or a sympathizer with slavery, was at first chosen to write the opinion of the Court. This he did and, as in the Strader case, refused jurisdiction on the ground that the state in which Dred Scott was domiciled, Missouri, must determine his status. But McLean and Curtis, the dissenters, were not content to discuss the issue on this ground. They wished to insert a defence

[54] 10 Howard 82 (1850).

[55] Dred Scott v. Sandford, 19 Howard 393 (1857).

of the constitutionality of the Missouri Compromise.[56] Except for Nelson, the members of the majority decided to accept that challenge, and to hold that Act invalid. According to the theory of Nelson's opinion it mattered not whether Congress had power to abolish slavery in the territories. Whether Dred Scott was in free or in slave territory during his stay in Upper Louisiana, he was a slave in Missouri if the laws of that state so provided. When the dissenters insisted upon discussing the power of Congress six members of the majority followed suit, possibly because they hoped thereby to take the burning issue of slavery in the territories out of the area of controversy. The result was, of course, to accentuate the controversy and to plunge the Court into the midst of it.[57]

The seven members of the majority required 132 pages for their opinions, while the dissenters produced two opinions totaling 105 pages. Nelson's twelve-page opinion is almost lost in the avalanche, and yet it is his which follows the unanimous decision of the Strader case, decided only seven years before. Of the majority opinions Taney's is the longest, most usually cited, and most influential. It is not, as the reporter has it, the opinion of the Court, but it was accepted by the majority on most counts. According to Taney Dred Scott could not bring an action in the federal courts because he was not a citizen within the meaning of Article III, section 2, providing for jurisdiction in cases "between citizens of different states." He was not a citizen because he was a negro and at the time the Constitution was adopted negroes were outside the citizenship pale. He was not a citizen, moreover, because he was a slave. His period of residence in the Louisiana Territory had no effect on his status, because Congress lacked the power to abolish slavery in the

[56] See Francis P. Weisenburger, *The Life of John McLean: A Politician on the United States Supreme Court* (1937), 199, 207, and G. T. Curtis, *The Life and Writings of Benjamin Robbins Curtis* (1879), I, 180, 206, 234, 235, 236. [57] Warren, *op. cit.*, ch. XXVI.

territories. The power to govern territories follows from the power to acquire them. Territories can be acquired only for the purpose of eventual admission to statehood. While they are being governed by Congress as trustee, they are the common possession of all of the states. Any citizen of any state is entitled to go into the territories and there to enjoy all of the rights guaranteed in the first nine amendments to the Constitution. They are entitled to take their property there and to have their rights of property, including their rights of property in slaves, protected by the law. An act of Congress depriving a citizen of his liberty or property in any territory of the United States "could hardly be dignified with the name of due process of law." [58]

It is Taney's theory that his entire argument is addressed to the question of jurisdiction, that is, to Dred Scott's right to bring a suit in the federal courts. It is not so certain as many writers have assumed that the part of the opinion asserting the unconstitutionality of the Missouri Compromise was *obiter dicta*.[59] As the final paragraph of Taney's opinion indicates, the argument as to the power of Congress to deal with slavery in the territories was intended to buttress the argument that negroes could not become citizens. What is evident is the folly of attempting to settle a burning issue in a court decision.

It is not sufficient, however, to characterize this decision as unfortunate. The case is more than a single instance of judicial recklessness. It is one of the major steps in the expansion of judicial power. As Marshall in Fletcher v. Peck transformed a specific limitation upon state legislatures into a general one, so the majority here attempted to transform the guarantees of civil liberties contained in the first eight amendments into positive protections to the rights of prop-

[58] 19 Howard 393, 450 (1857).

[59] Edward S. Corwin, *The Doctrine of Judicial Review* (1914), ch. IV.

erty in slaves. In arguing that the guarantees of these amendments restrict the discretionary power of Congress, Taney was making the first judicial assertion of a general supervisory jurisdiction over Congress. The Missouri Compromise Act was, furthermore, the first Congressional act of any general consequence which the Court held invalid. Temporarily the prestige of the Court suffered from the effects of the decision, but, as we look back over the history of the review of Congressional legislation, it is apparent, that, in a long-run sense, the case was a critical victory in the campaign for judicial control.

A SURVEY OF THE CLASSIC AGE

With the death of Taney we come to the approximate halfway mark in the Court's history. It was seventy-five years since the passage of the first Judiciary Act. In simple numerical terms the results of judicial review do not at first appear to be very great, not at least when compared with the figures for later periods. But even those statistics make it apparent that judicial review was very much an established and growing concern. The Supreme Court had ruled against the constitutionality of acts of Congress in two cases and against state legislation in sixty cases. Since there was no authenticated instance of such a decision before the Revolution, either in England or in the colonies, and only a shaky halfdozen in the states before 1789, sixty-two is a fairly impressive number of decisions of unconstitutionality to come from a single court.

Of more significance than the number is the character of these decisions. For one thing the institution of judicial review obviously did not develop out of a zeal for protection against legislative interference with civil liberties. In this entire period of seventy-five years there was just one case in which a civil right was protected against legislative action.[60] After Marshall held[61] that the first nine amendments did not limit the states, but only Congress, the possibilities for review on grounds of violation of civil rights were greatly reduced, but it is nevertheless an important fact that it was not in protection of such rights as freedom of speech or religion that the Supreme Court built up its power. Indeed, in one of the two most far-reaching decisions of the period, the guarantees of civil rights were transformed into guarantees of the rights of slave property in the territories.

During the first two decades of the Court most of the cases in which the judicial veto was exercised had to do with the conflict between federal treaties of the Revolutionary or post-Revolutionary years and state statutes, or with the establishment and jurisdiction of the federal courts. The first group produced few fireworks and resulted in the effective establishment of the principle of the supremacy of federal treaties which was set forth on paper in the supreme law clause. The jurisdictional cases produced frequent and prolonged bursts of oratorical fireworks, extending even to threats of nullification. Only Georgia, however, was successful in its attitude of defiance. Not only was the ruling in the Chisholm case set aside by the Eleventh Amendment, but the decision in Worcester v. Georgia went unenforced. But Pennsylvania, Virginia, Kentucky, Ohio, and the other states which challenged the authority of the Supreme Court, lost out. And in Marbury v. Madison Marshall's brilliant idea led to a slight tactical loss for the Court combined with a great strategical gain.

It is with Fletcher v. Peck that the unforeseen possibilities of judicial review begin to appear. Where there was a single

[60] Webster v. Reid, 11 Howard 437 (1851). Here an act of the Iowa territorial legislature providing that in certain instances the territorial court should decide matters of fact without a jury was held contrary to the Seventh Amendment.

[61] Barron v. Baltimore, 7 Peters 243 (1833).

decision of unconstitutionality before 1865 in which civil liberties received protection there were twenty-six protecting against the impairment of contracts. In not more than six of these cases was there any ascertainable relation to the intentions of the authors of the Constitution. Protection to the vested rights of property is not confined to the contract cases, although they illustrate the principle in its clearest form. And most of the cases having to do with the commerce clause are much more than essays in abstract federalism. Although the general course of those decisions is in harmony with the intentions of the founders and the needs of a growing country, it is just as apparent that their tendency, as summed up in the Cooley formula, is also toward the expansion of the judicial power. Nor is the rule against the taxation of governmental instrumentalities to be neglected when one is adding up the record of the Court's gains and considering its potential power in the future. Its original application in the McCulloch case was in support of an easily understood principle of federalism, but the Weston and Dobbins decisions suggest the possibility of a wider field of fire in the future.

So far as the history of the institution of judicial review is concerned perhaps the most significant of characteristics is its continuity. Changes of parties and administrations produced no break in the growth of the Court's power. The membership of the Court changed from Federalists to Republicans and from Republicans to Democrats, but the expansion of power and authority went on almost without interruption.

Chapter V

THE EMERGENCE OF MODERN CONSTITUTIONAL LAW

BETWEEN 1865 and 1937 there are no clear and definite breaks in the development of judicial review. There are changes of doctrine and there are variations in the kind and number of legislative acts which come before the Court, just as there are variations in the training, experience, and outlook of the Justices who took office during this period. But the process of judicial review continued without any basic interruption from wars, inventions, economic depressions, or changes of administration. The power of the Supreme Court to determine the constitutionality of legislation had become an accepted part of American life. There were, as will be pointed out, controversies over its power and its rulings, but none of those episodes is of sufficient stature to afford an excuse for a stopping point in a survey of Supreme Court history.

There being no natural break an artificial one must be made, if only because the bulk of material becomes so great that it cannot be well discussed in a single, uninterrupted sequence. Although the date is not signalized by any one episode or decision of outstanding importance, I think that the end of the year 1898 is a desirable point at which to pause and take stock. There are tendencies pointing toward an enlarged sphere for the judicial power which begin a few years after the Civil War and which reach maturity between 1890 and 1898. By the latter date virtually all of the doctrines which made of the Court so effective a censor of American life and legislation had been clearly expressed. Their multiple application followed.

THE COURT DURING WAR AND RECONSTRUCTION

During the Civil War, to take a brief look backward, the Court was relatively inactive. It very nearly held Lincoln's declaration of blockade invalid, but three new appointees turned what might have been a minority into a five to four majority.[1] It did not interfere with the limitations imposed upon civil liberties during the war,[2] and handed down no decisions, save that in the Gelpcke case, which extended appreciably the familiar doctrines.

Probably the most spectacular action of the Court during the reconstruction period was negative. In successive decisions[3] it refused to pass upon the constitutionality of the military reconstruction acts. If the Court's rulings in these years had been applied, particularly those holding that the Southern states had never been out of the Union,[4] and that military trials were not constitutionally justifiable where the civil courts were in operation,[5] the acts would probably have been declared invalid. But the Court had discovered in 1857 that some questions cannot be settled by judicial decision. It evaded this explosive issue and it was well advised in doing so. Had it held the acts invalid in 1868 or 1869 it would very probably have accomplished little save an intensification of the already bitter sectional feeling of the day. And cer-

[1] The Prize Cases, 2 Black 635 (1863). Three members of the majority, Swayne, Miller, and Davis, were appointed in 1862.

[2] J. G. Randall, *Constitutional Problems under Lincoln* (1926).

[3] Mississippi v. Johnson, 4 Wallace 475 (1867), Georgia v. Stanton, 6 Wallace 50 (1867), Ex parte McCardle, 7 Wallace 506 (1869).

[4] Texas v. White, 7 Wallace 700 (1869), White v. Hart, 13 Wallace 646 (1872).

[5] Ex parte Milligan, 4 Wallace 2 (1866).

tainly such a decision, like that in Dred Scott, would have resulted in a storm of criticism against the Court. Doubtless most persons would today agree that military reconstruction did little more for the social and economic equality of the negroes than it did for the cause of the Republican Party in the South. But, whatever may have been the quality of statesmanship behind the acts, the Court wisely refrained from interfering in a controversy which could not be resolved by appeal to doctrines of constitutional law.

Because the Court evaded ruling upon this most prominent of questions, it might be assumed that the inactivity and acquiescence of the war years is carried into the reconstruction period. This is not in accordance with the facts, for the Court under Chief Justice Chase (1865-1873) was more vigorous in its condemnation of state legislation than at any time since Marshall's most active years,[6] and in no fewer than ten cases it held congressional legislation to be unconstitutional. This activity is not accounted for by the new amendments; they do not begin to serve as the justification for such decisions until after 1873. Rather are the old provisions applied with renewed intensity. There is no extension of the contract clause but there were many cases under this clause and the statutory mortality rate in them is extraordinarily high.[7]

In its interpretation of the commerce clause the Court developed no doctrine materially altering the principles previously set forth. It unanimously applied the old Gibbons rule to federal control of navigation on a river entirely within a single state,[8] but, where Congress had not acted, its holdings were less uniform. In one decision [9] a majority

---

[6] There were 46 cases in which the Court ruled against state laws, 23 of them involving issues of federalism, 20 the contract clause, 2 civil liberties, and 1 a state constitutional provision. [7] Wright, *op. cit.*, 92-93.

[8] The Daniel Ball, 10 Wallace 557 (1871).

[9] Crandall v. Nevada, 6 Wallace 35 (1868).

relied upon a vague conception of the national rights of citizens, rather than the commerce clause, in holding unconstitutional a Nevada statute imposing a tax upon each passenger leaving the state. And although the Court found that there were certain circumstances under which the transportation of passengers or freight admits of but one uniform rule,[10] it showed its reluctance to extend the application of this principle beyond the limits marked off by earlier decisions.[11] A decision of this kind which was to be of considerable economic importance in future years was that in which the power of the states to regulate foreign insurance companies was sustained.[12]

As against ten commerce cases in which state legislation was set aside, there were seven cases in which the principle that a state may not tax a federal instrumentality was applied, most of them concerning the recently established national banks. The other five cases in which the Court, acting as umpire of the federal system, ruled against state legislation are of less importance for the future growth of judicial review. Finally there are two cases in which the Court gave protection to civil liberties, both of them involving the *ex post facto* and bill of attainder provisions.[13]

Cummings v. Missouri and its companion case Ex parte Garland,[14] were cases in which state and federal statutes requiring a highly inclusive oath of nonsupport of the late wicked Rebellion as a prerequisite to the practice of certain

---

[10] Case of the State Freight Tax, 15 Wallace 232 (1873). See also Cox v. Lott, 12 Wallace 204 (1871), Morgan v. Parham, 16 Wallace 471 (1873).

[11] Gilman v. Philadelphia, 3 Wallace 713 (1866), Waring v. Mobile, 8 Wallace 110 (1869), Woodruff v. Parham, 8 Wallace 123 (1869), Ex parte McNeil, 13 Wallace 236 (1872), Osborne v. Mobile, 16 Wallace 479 (1873), Chicago and Northwestern R.R. v. Fuller, 17 Wallace 560 (1873).

[12] Paul v. Virginia, 8 Wallace 168 (1869). Also Ducat v. Chicago, 10 Wallace 410 (1871).

[13] Cummings v. Missouri, 4 Wallace 277 (1867), and Pierce v. Carskadon, 16 Wallace 234 (1873). [14] 4 Wallace 333 (1867).

professions were set aside.[15] A bare majority of the Court in each instance found that the *ex post facto* and bill of attainder provisions had been violated, but it seems reasonably clear now that those clauses were made to do service for the latter-day concept of due process. The majority needed a more flexible instrument. For the time being it had to rely upon a latitudinarian interpretation of ancient clauses, but it was heading for the channel which was not to become clearly marked on the navigation charts until a quarter of a century later.

Much the most striking steps in the expansion of judicial review under Chase are to be found in the Court's unfavorable vote against ten Congressional statutes. In this nine-year period there were five times as many such decisions as in the preceding seventy-five years. It would be unjustifiable to neglect the significance of that simple statistical datum. The Court is beginning to do for Congressional legislation what it had done for state legislation since 1810—act as a supervisor of legislative righteousness and as a guardian of the spirit of the Constitution. Probably not more than two of the decisions were of great popular interest,[16] the Garland case already mentioned, and Hepburn v. Griswold,[17] in which the Civil War legal tender legislation was set aside. That the latter decision was soon overruled under circumstances which led to the charge that Grant had packed the Court [18] is significant, but not more so than the tendency of the opinion

---

[15] In the state case the plaintiff was a Catholic priest, and in the second case, an attorney who desired to practice before the United States Supreme Court.

[16] I am not here dealing with the interesting case of Ex parte Milligan 4 Wallace 2 (1866), since the Court was then passing upon the validity of an action of the President. No statute was involved. [17] 8 Wallace 603 (1870).

[18] Cf. Allan Nevins, *Hamilton Fish* (1936), 305-307, for evidence that President Grant knew how his appointees would vote on the legal tender issue. See also Charles Fairman, "Mr. Justice Bradley's Appointment to the Supreme Court and the Legal Tender Cases," 54 *Harvard Law Review* 977, 1128 (April, May, 1941).

of Chief Justice Chase in the Hepburn case. Lacking a constitutional prohibition which was explicit on the issue Chase invoked the spirit of the Constitution with particular reference to the contract clause. Now that clause was not a limitation on Congress. Indeed, the Convention ignored a motion to include such a prohibition, the motion dying for lack of a second.[19] Chase also appealed to the due process clause of the Fifth Amendment, although he was obviously unwilling to place too much reliance upon it. But here, as in the Dred Scott case, the Court is unquestionably seeking to extend its censorial power over Congress. That it in some measure failed in these attempts does not, of course, mean that it was not laying a foundation for later expansion.[20]

One other decision of the series is well known. In Collector v. Day [21] the rule in Dobbins v. Erie County [22] was extended reciprocally to protect a state employee against taxation by the national government upon his salary. Heretofore that rule had served only to protect against state taxation of national instrumentalities.[23]

Even though the other rulings of unconstitutionality appear on first glance to be of lesser importance, some of them contain intimations of the future scope of judicial review. In the very interesting Klein [24] case the Court strengthened its claims to a position as referee among the three departments of the central government. Seven years earlier in Gordon v. U.S.[25] the distinction between constitutional and legislative courts, later to be productive of both confusion and litigation, was suggested although not clearly de-

---

[19] Farrand, *Records,* II, 619.

[20] Note also the use of the principle of "vested rights" in Reichert v. Felps, 6 Wallace 160 (1868). [21] 11 Wallace 113 (1871). [22] *Supra,* 68.

[23] In U.S. v. R.R. Co., 17 Wallace 322 (1873) the same doctrine was held to apply to an attempt under a Congressional act to tax the interest upon a mortgage paid to the city of Baltimore.

[24] U.S. v. Klein, 13 Wallace 128 (1872). [25] 2 Wallace 561 (1865).

fined.[26] Finally, in U.S. v. DeWitt [27] an act of Congress was, for the first time, declared invalid for lack of power under the commerce clause.

When Morrison R. Waite came to the bench as Chief Justice the full scope of judicial review as it has been exercised in this century had not been developed. In particular the possibilities of the commerce clause had only begun to be worked out, and the breadth of due process had, so far as the majority of the Court was concerned, been suggested only in the Dred Scott and Hepburn cases, neither of which was in good standing. The era of reconstruction had, nevertheless, materially extended the sphere within which the judicial veto operated, and by the very frequency of its use accustomed both the country and the Court itself to the existence of an agency of government, the function of which was to pass upon the validity of statutes, federal as well as state.

With this beginning the next quarter of a century witnessed the most extraordinary broadening of the judicial power since Marshall first began to indicate its potentiality as a force in American life. From 1874 through 1898 there were twelve decisions in which acts of Congress were declared unconstitutional and 125 involving state legislation. Those statistics prove only that the Court was becoming a more active agency of government, just as the statute books were becoming thicker and the population more numerous. The test is not how numerous were the decisions, but how important they were, both in their own time and in their bearing upon the future development of judicial review of legislation. The number of statutes providing in some way for the regulation of economic enterprise had been appear-

---

[26] The Alicia, 7 Wallace 571 (1869) was likewise decided on the basis of the jurisdictional clause of Article III. The Justices v. Murray, 9 Wallace 274 (1870) involved the removal of cases from state to federal courts and was decided on the basis of the Seventh Amendment.

[27] 9 Wallace 41 (1870). The act here held invalid attempted to regulate the sale of oil made from petroleum for illuminating purposes.

ing in the legislators' books at an ever-increasing rate since the closing years of the eighteenth century; the decades following the Civil War showed a new acceleration in the speed of this phenomenon. Having been earlier firmly established, the institution of judicial review was now ready to assume the role of censor of this changing order.

FEDERALISM IN THE AGE OF INVENTION

To a greater extent than during the first quarter of the twentieth century, review by the Supreme Court was concerned with issues of federalism. The rapid growth of interstate transportation and communication, together with the increase in the spread of business enterprise led to hundreds of state attempts at taxation and regulation and, a little later, to the beginnings of Congressional action. Furthermore the principles for the interpretation of state and national relationships had reached what may be termed a stage of maturity before the Civil War. On the other hand the doctrines which were so important after 1900 in controlling the relations of government and private or corporate persons were only being developed. That process will be considered later in this chapter.

Altogether there were over two hundred constitutional cases between 1874 and 1898 in which the Court acted as federal umpire. In sixty-five of them state laws were held unconstitutional. Only in the Trade Mark cases [28] was an act of Congress declared invalid exclusively on this ground, although several of the cases involving the reconstruction amendments had to do with federalism as well as with the rights of persons, but, for purposes of classification, they will be taken up later. Among the cases in which state legislation was set aside the great majority involved the commerce

---

[28] 100 U.S. 82 (1879).

clause.[29] From the large number of state laws and the absence of Congressional legislation held contrary to the commerce clause, one might easily jump to the conclusion that the Court had become antipathetic to the exercise of state powers. The answer is, of course, that it was the states which were the regulatory agencies during almost the whole of this period and that, although the Court was generally sympathetic with the exercise of state powers until Congress acted, it did find that the states had frequently exceeded their range of power. Before examining some of the run-of-the-mill decisions it may be best to consider a few of the landmarks.

In the great Granger cases of 1877 the major issue was the allowable sphere of governmental control, but the problem of state power in the absence of Congressional legislation was also involved. The Court upheld the states on the commerce as on the due process grounds. It is interesting to observe that Waite, in speaking of the position of the grain elevators in the Munn case when countering the due process argument, said that they stand "in the very 'gateway of commerce,' and take toll from all who pass." [30] In considering the relation of the state regulation to the commerce clause, however, he finds it to be "a thing of domestic concern." [31] It is indicated that if Congress should act with reference to this subject-matter the state regulation would stand on a different footing. The principle as applied in the Pensacola Telegraph case a few months later would come into play.[32] But in the silence of Congress and under the Cooley rule of selective exclusiveness, this was a type of regulation which did not require a single, uniform rule.

[29] Seven concerned the taxation of government instrumentalities, or of federal lands; three, taxes on tonnage; two, jurisdiction of the federal courts; one, power over the territories; and one, interstate privileges and immunities. [30] Munn v. Illinois, 94 U.S. 113, 132 (1877).

[31] *Ibid.*, 135.

[32] Pensacola Telegraph Co. v. Western Union Telegraph Co., 96 U.S. 1 (1877).

It is correct to say that the Waite Court, before 1886, ordinarily interpreted the Cooley rule so as to allow a generous breadth of power within which the states could operate, but it fails to indicate the number and variety of state statutes which were held contrary to the commerce clause. The Cooley rule was more liberal toward state regulation of commerce than a rule of Congressional exclusiveness, but, as I have earlier remarked, it was likewise one which required the Court to give a continuous supervision to the course of state legislation. Between 1877 and the Wabash case [33] of 1886 there were fourteen cases in which state commercial regulations were set aside. In the Pensacola case and in Spraigue v. Thompson [34] Congress had acted, but in a dozen others state legislation not in conflict with an act of Congress was held contrary to the commerce clause. Best known are the ones in which a Louisiana statute prohibiting discrimination against colored persons was held not to apply on boats engaged in interstate commerce,[35] that in which a Pennsylvania tax statute was sought to be applied to a ferry engaged in interstate commerce,[36] and that in which a Missouri license tax required of persons selling merchandise produced or manufactured outside the state was invalidated.[37] The others involved a variety of regulations and tax measures. They are cases in which the doctrinal developments are not of headline importance but they illustrate the frequency of the judicial veto on grounds of federalism even during a decade of comparative tolerance of state action.[38]

---

[33] Wabash, St. Louis, and Pacific Ry. Co. v. Illinois, 118 U.S. 557 (1886).
[34] 118 U.S. 90 (1886). [35] Hall v. DeCuir, 95 U.S. 485 (1878).
[36] Gloucester Ferry Co. v. Pa., 114 U.S. 196 (1885).
[37] Welton v. Missouri, 91 U.S. 275 (1876).
[38] See, e.g., Foster v. Wardens, 94 U.S. 246 (1877), R.R. Co. v. Husen, 95 U.S. 465 (1878), Cook v. Pa., 97 U.S. 566 (1878), Telegraph Co. v. Texas, 105 U.S. 460 (1882), Walling v. Michigan, 116 U.S. 446 (1886), Pickard v. Pullman Southern Car Co., 117 U.S. 34 (1886). On the interpretation of the commerce clause in this period see Frankfurter, *The Commerce Clause,* ch. III, and George G. Reynolds, *The Distribution of Power to Regulate Interstate Carriers* (1928), ch. II.

THE COMMERCE POWER OF CONGRESS

It is no coincidence that the Wabash decision of 1886 preceded the Interstate Commerce act by a single year. For in that case the majority of the Court made it impossible for the states to regulate the great bulk of freight transportation. An Illinois statute imposing a penalty for lower long haul rates was declared to be in conflict with the commerce clause even though Congress had not invaded this field. Doctrinally this is a modification, if not a reversal, of both language and conclusion in some of the Granger cases. In terms of governmental policy it was an invitation to the Congress to take action. It did so almost immediately. Judicial review at least helped to make clear the need for unified control of what had become a more than state-wide problem. But this decision did not bring an end to litigation over the constitutionality of state legislation under the commerce clause. Between this case and the end of 1898 there were twenty-nine cases in which statutes were declared unconstitutional on this ground. Some of the doctrines announced then are of case book importance [39] but in none is there a rule which marks any major extension of the scope of judicial review.

In reviewing acts of Congress, where the problem is the nature of the federal system, the Court passed upon a wide variety of issues. The legal tender legislation sustained in 1871, largely under the war powers, was, in 1884, justified as a normal, peace-time exercise of the national financial powers.[40] The language of the opinion is comparable to that of Marshall, so far as concerns its expression of the doctrine of loose construction of national powers, and of the authority vested in Congress as "the legislature of a sovereign nation."

---

[39] For example, Robbins v. Shelby County Taxing District, 120 U.S. 489 (1887), Bowman v. Chicago & Northwestern Ry. Co., 125 U.S. 465 (1888), Leisy v. Hardin, 135 U.S. 100 (1890), Minnesota v. Barber, 136 U.S. 313 (1890), Crutcher v. Kentucky, 141 U.S. 47 (1891).

[40] Juillard v. Greenman, 110 U.S. 421 (1884).

A similarly nationalistic opinion, written by Justice Gray, who had spoken for the Court in the 1884 legal tender case, is that in the Chinese deportation case in 1893.[41] In these opinions something very like a doctrine of inherent national power is accepted by the Court. But neither they nor the Wabash case, nor some others which could be cited,[42] can be taken as completely representative of the Court's attitude toward the federal structure. So long as the Congress was dealing with its traditional subject matter, and so long as its regulations did not threaten the foundations of *laissez faire* economics, the Court was generally well disposed toward a broad interpretation of its powers. When, however, the exercise of those powers seemed to the Court more likely to be harmful to the conduct of trade and industry, the interpretation of the commerce clause, or of the statutes themselves, became less uniformly liberal.

The Court made it clear early in the period that it saw no difficulty either in upholding federal power over telegraphic communication under the commerce clause or in denying to the states the power to interfere with the expansion of this means of communication.[43] So long as state regulations of the railroads were viewed as legitimate and as non-obstructive to the development of a national rail system the state statutes were approved. When, in the Wabash decision of 1886, the Court brought this era of exclusive state control to an end, it did not give its approval to any and all forms of federal regulation. The commerce as well as the due process cases of the next two decades show that the Court was highly critical of the kind of regulation as well as of the power to regulate. As

---

[41] Fong Yue Ting v. U.S., 149 U.S. 698 (1893). See also the Chinese Exclusion Case, 130 U.S. 581 (1889).

[42] See, e.g., Head Money Cases, 112 U.S. 580 (1884), Tennessee v. Davis, 100 U.S. 257 (1880), Ex parte Siebold, 100 U.S. 371 (1880), Ex parte Yarbrough, 110 U.S. 651 (1884).

[43] Pensacola Telegraph Co. v. Western Union Telegraph Co., 96 U.S. 1 (1877).

Professor Corwin has well said, "it tended to view Congress' power under the 'commerce' clause . . . as primarily a power to *foster, protect, and promote commerce.*" [44]

In its general principles the Interstate Commerce Act of 1887 was plainly acceptable. There was never any question of its constitutionality, but a general approval did not carry with it approval of specific ways and means of regulating the activities of interstate carriers. The first setback to the Commission was the Court's refusal to uphold its authority to require unwilling witnesses to testify.[45] After this difficulty had, with the aid of the Compulsory Testimony Act of 1893, been overcome,[46] the Court found that the Act of 1887 actually gave the Commission almost no substantial authority over the railroads. Powers to fix rates in place of those found unjust or unreasonable, and power to prevent long-and-short-haul discriminations were found not to be granted by the statute, although the Commission had been exercising those powers for nearly a decade.[47] The beginnings of business regulation through the use of commissions were viewed with a suspicious eye and the statute given a narrow interpretation. Not the purpose of the statute, but its letter, was invoked, and the Commission was left powerless "to carry out the primary purposes of the Act to Regulate Commerce—to protect the general public, irrespective of individual rights, against unreasonable and discriminatory charges." [48]

This attitude is even more clearly seen in the early interpretation of the Sherman Anti-Trust Act. In a case involving a combination which had, as the Court agreed, acquired "nearly complete control of the manufacture of refined sugar

[44] *The Twilight of the Supreme Court* (1934), 20.

[45] Counselman v. Hitchcock, 142 U.S. 547 (1892).

[46] Interstate Commerce Commission v. Brimson, 154 U.S. 447 (1894), Brown v. Walker, 161 U.S. 591 (1896).

[47] Texas & P. Ry. Co. v. I.C.C., 162 U.S. 197 (1896), Cin., N.O. & Texas P. Ry. v. I.C.C., 162 U.S. 184 (1896), I.C.C. v. Cin., N.O. & T.P. Ry., 167 U.S. 479 (1897), I.C.C. v. Alabama M. Ry. Co., 168 U.S. 144 (1897).

[48] I. L. Sharfman, *The Interstate Commerce Commission,* (1931) I, 27.

in the United States" it was held that the statute did not apply.[49] Here was surely a monopoly in the great sugar industry, and the Sherman Act was intended to prevent combinations in restraint of trade or commerce among the states. Yet, said the Court, manufacture is a purely local process. The object of the combination was "private gain in the manufacture of the commodity." This is not commerce, said Chief Justice Fuller, and it would be a violation of the principles of our dual system of government to permit the Congressional statute to be applied to such a transaction, even though the result of the combination was monopolistic control of the trading in sugar throughout the country. In this case, at any rate, "commerce" means little if anything more than physical movement across state lines. The attitude which the Court was subsequently to adopt toward the scope of the commerce clause[50] only serves to underline its early suspicion of national legislation which threatened to interfere with the "natural" course of economic development.

The beginnings of what was later to become an important and controversial problem of constitutional law is found in Field v. Clark,[51] probably the most important case of the time concerning the separation of powers. Here the Tariff Act of 1890 was upheld against the contention that it provided for an unconstitutional delegation of legislative power to the President. But in sustaining the act the Court made it plain that, although Congress could delegate authority to determine the conditions under which a statutory provision would come into effect, it could not "delegate its power to make a law." In short, it remained for the Court, as each case should arise, to determine whether the delegation was or was not within the allowable limits.

---

[49] U.S. v. E. C. Knight Co., 156 U.S. 1 (1895).

[50] Swift & Co. v. U.S., 196 U.S. 375 (1905). [51] 143 U.S. 649 (1892).

CONGRESS AND CIVIL RIGHTS

It is, however, neither in the realm of federalism nor in that of the separation of powers that the major extension of judicial review is to be found, but rather in the area where the courts serve to protect the rights of persons against the actions of governments. Here we find the greatest enlargement of judicial power since Marshall's day. This broadening process does not take place in protection of civil liberties. Cases involving such rights are somewhat more numerous than in preceding periods but neither in number nor scope do they begin to compare in importance with the cases involving economic rights. There are, for example, four cases [52] in which Congressional statutes are held invalid as infringements of civil liberties. That is a larger number than can be found in the entire previous history of the Court, but the interests given protection are limited and localized. Had the Court ruled otherwise in all four cases there would have been no serious loss of civil liberties on the part of any considerable number of persons.

In the Civil Rights cases,[53] on the other hand, a statute of very great importance was declared unconstitutional. By the Civil Rights Act of 1875 Congress had attempted to extend the protection of the national government to many of the civil liberties which had traditionally been under state protection. The object was, of course, to protect the negroes against discriminatory social and economic practices. Earlier legislation of the kind had been enacted before the adoption of the Fourteenth Amendment. It is clear that many of those in Congress who voted for the Fourteenth Amendment ex-

---

[52] U.S. v. Fox, 95 U.S. 670 (1878), Boyd v. U.S., 116 U.S. 616 (1886), Callan v. Wilson, 127 U.S. 540 (1888), Wong Wing v. U.S., 163 U.S. 228 (1896). It might be argued that the Fox and Boyd cases concern property rather than civil rights. Cf. Henry W. Edgerton, "The Incidence of Judicial Control over Congress," 22 *Cornell Law Quarterly,* 299 (1937). *Selected Essays on Constitutional Law,* I, 793. [53] 109 U.S. 3 (1883).

pected, or at least hoped, that it would afford a constitutional justification for legislation of this kind. The Court failed to agree. With but a single dissenter it held that the prohibitions of the amendments were effective only as against the states and that, therefore, the attempt to protect the negroes against discrimination on the part of persons or non-governmental groups was beyond the powers of Congress. The effect of this decision was virtually to erase Section 5 [54] of the amendment, for where the exercise of power by Congress has been sustained, the same result could ordinarily have been secured without benefit of statute.[55] This decision was, moreover, only one of a group in which the Court refused to allow Congress to extend its protection to the civil liberties of persons.[56] Taken together they constitute one of the two or three greatest setbacks to the extension of national power in our history. Had these decisions gone otherwise the federal system would probably have been permanently altered. Whatever the merits of the Court's interpretation of the Fourteenth Amendment, it is obvious that it prevented that amendment from becoming either a road to a new nationalism or an effective barrier against racial discrimination.

BEGINNINGS OF DUE PROCESS

The great extension of judicial power in this period came through the development of the due process of law concept and that development had, at this time, almost nothing to do with civil liberties. It is well to bear in mind, at the beginning of this discussion, that the importance of due process is not to be measured quantitatively until the twentieth century.

[54] "The Congress shall have power to enforce, by appropriate legislation, the provisions of this article."

[55] As in Strauder v. West Virginia, 100 U.S. 303 (1880), Ex parte Virginia 100 U.S. 339 (1880).

[56] U.S. v. Reese, 92 U.S. 214 (1876), U.S. v. Harris, 106 U.S. 629 (1883), Baldwin v. Franks, 120 U.S. 678 (1887).

Judged by number of cases and by the volume of decisions holding statutes unconstitutional the contract clause continues to be of foremost significance. Between 1874 and 1898 there were thirty-nine contract cases in which state laws were set aside.[57] In terms of the economic interests involved many of these were of more than local or private weight, but, from the point of view of this study, the important fact is that the period of expansion of the contract clause had come to an end. Partly because of the doctrine of strict construction of public grants, but mainly because of the general adoption of clauses in constitutions or statutes reserving to the states the right to alter or amend charters or franchises, that clause was of declining usefulness and the place that it so long held was about to be taken over by due process, a clause far more favorable to the proliferation of judicial power than had ever been true of the contract clause, at any rate after Marshall's defeat in Ogden v. Saunders.[58]

There had been a due process clause in the Fifth Amendment since 1791. Yet in only one case before 1868, the year when the Fourteenth Amendment went into effect, had due process been squarely before the Court. In Murray v. Hoboken Land & Improvement Co.[59] a Congressional statute was sustained which authorized certain administrative remedies, harsh in operation but of ancient lineage, against a defaulting customs collector. The Court held that the clause was a limitation upon Congress as well as upon the administrative and judicial agencies, but no issue of substantive right was considered, only procedural questions were discussed, and there is no intimation that due process might apply to substantive rights. The discussion seems to be based upon the premise that due process refers to those rights of

[57] Wright, *op. cit.,* 94-96.

[58] The only important innovation in the interpretation of the contract clause was the development of the doctrine of an inalienable police power. This doctrine was, however, applied in but few cases during these years. *Ibid.,* ch. VIII.

[59] 18 Howard 272 (1856).

procedure which guarantee a fair and open trial. In the very next year, however, Taney in his Dred Scott opinion does employ a substantive conception of due process.[60] Because of its uniqueness it is easy to exaggerate the importance of this portion of Taney's opinion. Some historians, led astray by the subsequent importance of due process, have written that the Missouri Compromise was held unconstitutional because it violated due process. Yet Taney gives but a few sentences in his fifty-six page opinion to this concept; he deals with it along with the other guarantees of the first eight amendments, which are similarly treated as if they were substantive protections to property; and only two other members of the majority, Grier and Wayne, gave even a perfunctory acceptance to this particular reasoning. Furthermore, not until Hepburn v. Griswold [61] in 1870 does substantive due process reappear in a Supreme Court opinion, and again the discussion is unclear. And when this decision was overruled fifteen months later this section of the Hepburn opinion was dismissed as being farfetched.[62]

If there was a dark conspiracy to write into the Fourteenth Amendment clauses which would serve to give protection to business corporations against governmental regulation, the conspirators could have found little support in the opinions of the Supreme Court for a hope that the due process clause would afford this protection. The Murray case concerned procedure only. Dred Scott was in very bad standing, especially with the authors of the Fourteenth Amendment, and the Hepburn case was yet to be decided. Decisions in the state courts may have given them more encouragement,[63] but it was not until the year that the amendment was finally ratified (1868) that Cooley's *Constitutional Limitations* ap-

[60] 19 Howard 393, 450 (1857). [61] 8 Wallace 603 (1870).

[62] Legal Tender Cases, 12 Wallace 457, 551-552 (1871).

[63] Edward S. Corwin, "The Doctrine of Due Process of Law before the Civil War," 24 *Harvard Law Review*, 366, 460 (1911). Reprinted in *Selected Essays on Constitutional Law*, I, 203.

peared, with its Chapter XI containing citations of scores of state cases demonstrative "Of the Protection of Property by the 'Law of the Land.'" The "conspirators"[64] may possibly have hoped to protect corporations against state legislation, but it seems likely that, if they entertained such hopes and made such plans, they counted more heavily upon the equal protection and privileges or immunities clauses. And the latter-day importance of due process as a defense for the rights of property should not cause us to forget that the discussion of all of these clauses, both in Congress and in the state legislatures which ratified the amendment, was in terms of giving protection to civil rights, particularly those of negroes.[65]

DUE PROCESS IN THE SEVENTIES

After all that has been written about the growth of substantive due process between 1868 and the end of the century the story remains, in some respects, curiously obscure. It is clear that the majority first repudiated the conception in the Slaughter House cases,[66] and that the explicit acceptance did not come for twenty years. But it is also true that during those two decades the Court, seemingly without quite realizing what was happening, was repeatedly accepting the two vital principles of modern due process: that it applies to substantive as well as to procedural matters, and that the word "person" in the Fifth and Fourteenth Amendments applies to corporate as well as to natural persons.

---

[64] The older accounts of the conspiracy have been superseded by Howard Jay Graham, "The Conspiracy Theory of the Fourteenth Amendment," 47 *Yale Law Journal,* 371, 48 *Yale Law Journal,* 171-94 (1938). The first section is reprinted in *Selected Essays on Constitutional Law,* I, 36. See also Louis B. Boudin, "Truth and Fiction about the Fourteenth Amendment," 16 *New York University Law Quarterly Review,* 19 (1938), and the review of the Graham and Boudin articles in 52 *Harvard Law Review,* 851 (1939).

[65] H. E. Flack, *The Adoption of the Fourteenth Amendment* (1908). Cf. also, B. B. Kendrick (ed.), *The Journal of the Joint Committee on Reconstruction* (1914), 305-311.

[66] 16 Wallace 36 (1873).

In the Slaughter House opinion Miller, after having drawn the teeth of the privileges or immunities clause, and having opined that the equal protection clause was intended to protect the freedmen, answered very briefly the argument from due process: "The argument has not been much pressed . . . it is sufficient to say that under no construction of that provision that we have ever seen, or any that we deem admissible, can the restraint imposed by the State of Louisiana . . . be held to be a deprivation of property within the meaning of that provision." [67] Thus the majority apparently assumed that due process meant due procedure, that it was a guarantee of a fair trial, not an inclusive guarantee of the substantive right to hold and enjoy property. It is impossible to determine how great was the effect upon the majority of the arguments of the three dissenters, two of whom were particularly insistent upon a broader conception of due process,[68] but in the very next year, in a case involving an Iowa liquor statute, the Court seemed to intimate that it would consider the possible conflict between this statute and the due process clause if the issue were properly presented.[69] Here, because the Iowa court had not considered the issue, it could not be discussed in the Supreme Court.

Far more significant is the fact that most of the discussion in Munn v. Illinois [70] proceeds upon the premise that the due process clause affords substantive as well as procedural

[67] 16 Wallace 36, 80-81.

[68] Mr. Justice Field was principally concerned with the privileges or immunities clause but Justices Swayne and Bradley emphasized the due process clause. The brief of ex-Justice Campbell, who appeared for the independent butchers, may also have exerted a considerable influence upon the Court. See Walton H. Hamilton, "The Path of Due Process of Law," in Conyers Read (ed.), *The Constitution Reconsidered* (1938), 167.

[69] Bartemeyer v. Iowa, 18 Wallace 129 (1874). The concurring opinions of Justices Bradley and Field reiterate the points of view of their former dissents and explain why they believe that this statute does not violate the Fourteenth Amendment. [70] 94 U.S. 113 (1877).

protection.[71] The procedural issue was not here involved, and the Chief Justice's opinion is addressed to a showing that the grain elevators are of such public concern that regulation is warranted. But, unless the due process clause is given a substantive meaning, there is no point to this part of the opinion. Why did not the Court dismiss the due process argument as it had done in the Slaughter House cases only four years earlier? The Munn case has many times been said to be a great victory for liberalism and the public interest. It is of course true that the Court here upheld the principle of government regulation. It did so, however, not as a universal right, but as one justifiable under circumstances to be determined by the Court. Because of this the case is another of the landmarks in the growth of the judicial power. Indeed, it might be said that the difference between the Slaughter House dismissal of the due process argument, and the elaborate justification of the statute as against the due process argument in the Munn case, is the measure of the gulf between an exclusively procedural and a broader conception of due process.

The Munn case involved an unincorporated partnership and neither the contract clause nor the question whether a corporation was a person under the Fourteenth Amendment was before the Court. In other Granger cases, however, corporations were concerned and in them the contract clause, at any rate, is considered.[72] And from the statement in the first paragraph of the first of the railroad cases, it seems apparent

---

[71] Notice Waite's curious statement on p. 125: "Down to the time of the adoption of the 14th Amendment, it was not supposed that statutes regulating the use, or even the price of the use, of private property necessarily deprived an owner of his property without due process of law. Under some circumstances they may, but not under all. The Amendment does not change the law in this particular: it simply prevents the States from doing that which will operate as such a deprivation."

[72] Chicago, B., & Q. R.R. Co. v. Iowa, 94 U.S. 155 (1877), Peik v. C. & N. Ry. Co., 94 U.S. 164 (1877), Winona and St. P. R.R. Co. v. Blake, 94 U.S. 180 (1877).

that the Court simply assumed that a corporate person was entitled to protection under the Fourteenth Amendment. There Waite says:

> Railroad companies are carriers for hire. They are incorporated as such, and given extraordinary powers, in order that they may the better serve the public in that capacity. They are, therefore, engaged in a public employment affecting the public interest, and, *under the decision in Munn v. Illinois, just announced, subject to legislative control* as to their rates of fare and freight, unless protected by their charters.[73]

Certainly there is neither here nor in any of the railroad regulation cases of this group any statement contradictory of the assumption that "person" is to be understood in this broad sense. Two years later, moreover, in the Sinking Fund cases, Waite, in discussing a Congressional statute requiring a railroad with a federal charter to establish a sinking fund, said of the United States that *"equally with the states* they are prohibited from depriving persons or corporations of property without due process of law." [74]

In 1883 Roscoe Conkling, who had been a member of the Joint Committee on Reconstruction which framed the Fourteenth Amendment, argued before the Court that the provisions of its first article were intended to give protection to corporate property as well as to civil rights.[75] Had it not been for the previous acceptance, implicit if not explicit, by the Court of the conclusion which Conkling was there con-

---

[73] Chicago, B. & Q. R.R. Co. v. Iowa, 94 U.S. 155 (1877). Italics not in the original. See also Richmond, F., & P. R.R. Co. v. Richmond, 96 U.S. 521 (1878) where the same assumption seems to have been made.

[74] 99 U.S. 700, 718-719 (1879). Italics not in the original.

[75] San Mateo County v. Southern R.R. Co., 116 U.S. 138 (1882). See also Kendrick, *op. cit.*, 28 *et seq.*, and Graham, *op. cit.* The most interesting discussion of this point is that of Mr. Justice Black, dissenting in Connecticut Gen. Life Ins. Co. v. Johnson, 303 U.S. 77, 83-90 (1938). Black denies flatly that the Amendment had any such purpose. On this issue see A. C. McLaughlin, "The Court, the Corporation, and Conkling," *American Historical Review,* XLVI, 45 (1940).

tending for, the Justices might have contented themselves with asking him why no hint of this conspiracy was given on the floor of Congress and whether so secretive a purpose, even assuming the accuracy of Conkling's statements,[76] deserved to be written into the law of the Constitution. Because Conkling's argument tended to fit in with their own drift his speech probably had an accelerating effect upon the growth of due process.

THE ACCEPTANCE OF SUBSTANTIVE DUE PROCESS

During the next decade there are a number of cases which show that the conception of due process as a substantive check was becoming familiar to the Court.[77] The only case, however, in which due process was the constitutional justification for holding an act of a state legislature invalid involved an exclusively procedural issue.[78] In two other cases [79] statutes discriminating against negroes and Chinese respectively, were thrown out as contrary to the equal protection clause.

The crucial case in this series is probably the Minnesota Commission case of 1890.[80] Here, over the dissent of Justices Bradley, Gray, and Lamar, the Court held that a statute giving final authority in rate-making to a commission was unconstitutional because it deprived the railroad of its right under the due process clause to have a judicial determination of the reasonableness of the rate. In the Munn case Waite

---

[76] The secret Journal of this committee, reprinted in 1914 by Professor Kendrick, gives little or no evidence to support Conkling's argument. See pp. 51, 54, 55, 61, 87, 98, 99, 106.

[77] See Missouri Pacific Ry. v. Humes, 115 U.S. 512 (1885), and Mugler v. Kansas, 123 U.S. 623 (1887). The latter case is a particularly good instance of the acceptance of due process as a limitation upon substantive legislation. Cf. Little Rock & Ft. Smith Ry. v. Worthen, 120 U.S. 97 (1887).

[78] Pennoyer v. Neff, 95 U.S. 714 (1878).

[79] Strauder v. West Virginia, 100 U.S. 303 (1880), Yick Wo v. Hopkins, 118 U.S. 356 (1886).

[80] Chicago, Milwaukee, & St. Paul Ry. v. Minnesota, 134 U.S. 418 (1890).

had said, *obiter,* that the reasonableness of the rate was not for the Court to determine, that that was a legislative question.[81] But what was a legislative question in 1877 had become a judicial question in 1890. It might be said that what the Court regarded as substantive in the earlier case was now regarded as procedural. Judicial procedure before a court had become an essential element in constitutional ratemaking. Because what the Court finds lacking here is procedure, this case is still one in the transition zone. Cases of the next few years show that the protection of property rights under the due process clause is becoming a more frequent constitutional issue.[82] And in 1896 two statutes are set aside which concern purely substantive issues. One, as interpreted by the state court, required a railroad to grant a right of way on which a private grain elevator was to be built,[83] the other required a lower rate schedule by a turnpike company.[84] In both of them the Court is dealing with the dueness or reasonableness of regulations affecting substantive rights of property.

Two years later came the decision in Smyth v. Ames.[85] Here the Court went even further than in its previous rulings on railroad rate cases, for it not only held that a final decision on the reasonableness of the rate must rest with the judiciary but also attempted to set forth the economic principles which the legislature and its agents must follow in determining rates.

> . . . the basis of all calculations as to the reasonableness of rates to be charged by a corporation maintaining a highway under legislative sanction must be the fair value of the

[81] 94 U.S. 113, 133-134 (1877).

[82] Budd v. New York, 143 U.S. 517 (1892), Brass v. Stoeser, 153 U.S. 391 (1894), Reagan v. Farmers' Loan & Trust Co., 154 U.S. 362 (1894).

[83] Missouri Pacific Ry. Co. v. Nebraska, 164 U.S. 403 (1896).

[84] Covington & Lexington Turnpike Co. v. Sandford, 164 U.S. 578 (1896).

[85] 169 U.S. 466 (1898). See also Gulf, Colorado, and Santa Fé Ry. Co. v. Ellis, 165 U.S. 150 (1897) for an application of the equal protection clause in a railroad case.

> property being used by it for the convenience of the public. And in order to ascertain that value, the original cost of construction, the amount expended in permanent improvements, the amount and market value of its bonds and stock, the present as compared with the original cost of construction, the probable earning capacity of the property under particular rates prescribed by statute, and the sum required to meet operating expenses, are all matters for consideration, and are to be given such weight as may be just and right in each case.[86]

It is apparent that the Court had finally taken unto itself the role of protector against undesired legislative activity which the corporations, and especially the railroads, had so long been urging it to assume. The rule in Smyth v. Ames has served to obscure and make more difficult rather than to assist in the determination of public utility rates, but it has undoubtedly been productive of litigation. It is one of a notable group of Supreme Court decisions in the 'nineties which increased the scope and the economic importance of judicial review.

There are three more cases of this period which deserve comment. Allgeyer v. Louisiana [87] involved a statute forbidding any person in Louisiana from making a contract for marine insurance with a firm which had not complied with the laws of that state. In holding this statute invalid, Justice Peckham, for a unanimous Court, simply wrote the dissenting opinions of Justices Swayne and Bradley in the Slaughter Houses cases into the Fourteenth Amendment.

> The liberty mentioned in that amendment means not only the right of the citizen to be free from the mere physical restraint of his person, as by incarceration, but the term is deemed to embrace the right of the citizen to be free in the enjoyment of all of his faculties; to be free to use them in all lawful ways; to live and work where he will; to earn his livelihood by any lawful calling; to pursue any livelihood

---

[86] 169 U.S., 466, 546-547. [87] 165 U.S. 578 (1897).

> or avocation, and for that purpose to enter into all contracts which may be proper, necessary and essential to his carrying out to a successful conclusion the purposes above mentioned.[88]

The importance of this principle for the future history of legislation dealing with the conditions of labor was not to be fully realized until some years later, but it is suggested in Holden v. Hardy [89] the next year. Here, over the dissent of Justices Peckham and Brewer, the Court sustained an eight-hour law applying to mines and smelters. In doing so, however, it made clear that not all such statutes, but only those which were reasonable in the eyes of the Court would be upheld. Much the same attitude is illustrated in Norwood v. Baker.[90] In the preceding decade a number of special assessment cases had been considered under the due process clause. Here one was declared unconstitutional, not for faulty procedure, the issue involved in the earlier cases, but because it provided for unreasonable assessments.

To the end of the year 1898 the significance of the due process and equal protection clauses is not to be measured by the number of statutory scalps hanging at their belts. The latter clause had been responsible for but three decisions of unconstitutionality, and of these one had involved the rights of negroes, one discrimination against Chinese, and only one a railroad. Due process had eight cases to its credit, but only the first involved an issue definitely procedural in character. It is not the number of decisions of unconstitutionality, or even the importance of the interests immediately concerned, but rather the possibilities for the future exercise of judicial review which makes of this period one of the most notable in American constitutional and economic history.

---

[88] *Ibid.*, 589. [89] 169 U.S. 366 (1898). [90] 172 U.S. 269 (1898).

THE INCOME TAX

Not until 1908 was due process the sole basis for declaring an act of Congress unconstitutional,[91] but in the income tax case of 1895 [92] the Court exhibited the attitude it was to express so many times in the years to come, only here it was in the guise of interpreting the direct tax clauses of the Constitution. These clauses had, as the records of the Federal Convention make perfectly clear,[93] been intended to apply only to the taxation of land and of persons. Their inclusion was part of a sectional compromise, they being a concession to the Southerners who feared a tax on their land by area and their slaves by numbers. In the carriage tax case of 1796,[94] the Court, which contained Wilson and Paterson who had participated in the writing of this clause, had stated clearly that this was the intent and scope of the clause. This interpretation had been reaffirmed more than once by the Court.[95] The clause had really ceased to have any meaning long before 1895. As recently as 1881 the Court had unanimously followed the doctrine of the Hylton case, holding that the income tax of 1864 did not violate the direct tax clauses since they applied only to taxes on land and on persons.[96]

Ordinarily when the Court reverses a long line of precedents it does so in interpreting a clause of uncertain meaning. Here there was no such excuse. A majority of the Court was persuaded that its duty required it to aid in stopping the "communist march." [97] Almost everyone agrees today that the decision was a very great error, a "self-inflicted

[91] Adair v. U.S., 208 U.S. 161 (1908).

[92] Pollock v. Farmers' Loan and Trust Co., 157 U.S. 429, 158 U.S. 601 (1895).

[93] Farrand, *Records,* I, 589-597. [94] Hylton v. U.S., 3 Dallas 171 (1796).

[95] E.g. in Veazie Bank v. Fenno, 8 Wallace 533 (1869). See also Scholey v. Rew, 23 Wallace 331 (1874). Cf. Story, *Commentaries on the Constitution,* I, § 950, Kent, *Commentaries,* I, 257. [96] Springer v. U.S., 102 U.S. 586 (1881).

[97] See the argument of Joseph H. Choate in pleading with the Court to give "protection now or never." 157 U.S. 532-533.

wound."[98] It is a perfect example of what judicial review should not be. As in Dred Scott the Court attempted to settle a great public issue, and again the result was not to take the controversy out of politics but to put the Court into politics. It is to be remembered, moreover, that at the same term the Court by interpretation virtually set aside the Sherman act,[99] and upheld the use of armed forces employed to put down the Pullman strike.[100] And in the next two years it so interpreted the Interstate Commerce Act as to leave the Commission almost powerless. The point of view that was being written into the due process clause of the Fourteenth Amendment is not confined to cases concerning state legislation.

By 1899 judicial review of the Hamilton, rather than the Madison type, was fully developed. The Court had become umpire-in-chief. It proceeded upon its interpretation of the spirit of the Constitution when that document's simple and general statements admitted of any latitude. When, as in interpreting the contract or due process or direct tax clauses, it preferred its interpretation to the meaning of the authors, it proceeded to give its views the force of law. In part, at least, it had taken over the functions thought of in 1787 as pertaining to a council of revision rather than to a court.

---

[98] Charles E. Hughes, *The Supreme Court of the United States* (1928), 50, 53. For a searching critique of the case, see Edward S. Corwin, *Court over Constitution* (1938), ch. IV. [99] U.S. v. E. C. Knight Co., 156 U.S. 1 (1895).
[100] In re Debs, 158 U.S. 564 (1895).

Chapter VI

UMPIRING THE FEDERAL SYSTEM

Between 1790 and the end of 1898 there were 23 cases in which Congressional statutes were held contrary to the Constitution. From 1899 to 1937 there were 55. In the same period there were 401 decisions invalidating state legislation, a figure considerably more than twice as large as that for the preceding thirty-eight years, and over six times as great as that for the first seventy-five years of the Court's history.

These raw statistics are, of themselves, sufficient to demonstrate just two things: the greatly increased use of the judicial veto, and the impossibility of discussing adequately either the scope or the incidence of judicial review within a brief compass. In this and the following chapters no such task can or will be attempted. An attempt will be made to consider some of the principal lines of development, to illustrate, rather than to describe, the incidence of the decisions of unconstitutionality, and to point out some of the rulings which indicate how broad was the area of discretion within which the Court functioned. For the most part those decisions and groups of decisions which culminate in the destructive rulings of 1935 and 1936 will be emphasized. This will be done not because they are always of greater intrinsic importance than many others which might well be taken up at length, but because of their contribution to the constitutional crisis of 1937.

Except for the group of cases dealing with the Roosevelt

recovery legislation, the constitutional decisions of the years of maturity will be considered under three functional headings. They will, that is to say, be discussed in terms of their relation to the nature of the federal system, to the separation of governmental powers, and to the rights of persons. Because of their peculiar unity and strategic importance, the cases involving the New Deal legislation of Congress will be taken up in a separate chapter.

PERSONNEL, POLITICS, AND ECONOMIC CHANGE

This scheme was not adopted upon the assumption that between 1899 and 1935, or, in the case of state legislation, 1899 and 1937, there were no events which strongly affected the course of judicial interpretation. Of such events there were many and they were of several kinds. Not the least interesting or important subject for study is the way in which the choice of successive Presidents affected the construction of the Constitution. It is difficult to generalize here, for, beyond the fact that the Democratic Presidents appointed Democrats, and that the Republican Presidents ordinarily appointed Republicans, the objective data does not always lead to what might seem to be the obvious conclusions. At least two of Cleveland's appointees, Fuller and Peckham, viewed the increase of governmental control with at least as jealous an eye as did the Republicans appointed by Harrison and McKinley. Theodore Roosevelt criticized the Court more vigorously than had any President since Lincoln, but some of the decisions of which he complained were written by Justices whom he had appointed. Taft's five appointees were, in general, of a conservative slant, although only Van-Devanter was on the Court during its period of greatest opposition to state economic legislation. This period was that in which the Chief Justice was former President Taft. The arch-conservative majority of that Court was made possible by the Harding appointments, particularly of Sutherland and Butler, but also of Taft and Sanford. But they were joined by Wilson's appointee, and former Attorney General, McReynolds, while Coolidge's appointee, and former Attorney General, Stone, frequently joined Roosevelt's Holmes and Wilson's Brandeis in dissent. Later Hoover was to appoint Cardozo, a Democrat but a fitting and worthy successor to the Republican Holmes, as well as Hughes, who had served on the Court from 1910 to 1916, when he resigned to become Republican candidate for the Presidency, and Roberts, a Republican whose participation in political activities had been relatively slight. A few years later Chief Justice Hughes and Associate Justice Roberts, particularly Roberts, were to hold the balance of power when the recovery legislation of the Democratic Roosevelt administration came before the Court.

Important as these changes were, the fundamental factor conditioning the course of judicial decision in these years was not the character of judicial personnel. It was the same force which was conditioning most of the legislation, state and national. Those who deal with case law are too prone to play their game of precedent matching as though nothing were involved save observance of the logical amenities. The central problem involved in the constitutional adjudication of the last half century was the accelerated movement toward an ever-increasing intervention of government in social and economic life. In this country, as earlier in the European countries where difficulties of an industrialized society were sooner apparent, the change from handicraft to machine production, from small to big business, from slow to fast transportation, from partnerships to corporations, from competition to monopoly, from merchant to finance capitalism, from unorganized to organized labor, resulted in legislative attempts to deal with some of the problems these changes produced. The Constitution had easily been accommodated to a doubling of territory and a multiplication of population, but it had required one of the bloodiest of Civil Wars to discover whether it could survive the sectional-slavery struggle. Toward the end of the century the vast increase in regulatory statutes coming before the Court raised a question quite as fundamental as that produced by the slavery struggle, whether the Constitution of 1787 could be interpreted to serve as an instrument of government for an industrialized population. The issue was not presented so clearly or directly as that. It came up in hundreds of cases involving the validity of statutory provisions, as well as in many cases concerning the actions of administrative agencies.

A comprehensive account of the history of American constitutional law would necessarily be concerned at some length with these statutes, and with their interpretation, as well as their constitutionality. President Wilson's Federal Trade Commission Act, for example, was not held invalid, but the Taft Court so interpreted its clauses as to make the Commission almost as impotent as the Court had made the Interstate Commerce Commission in 1896-1897. And although a federal income tax was made constitutionally possible by the Sixteenth Amendment, neither that Amendment nor the first income tax statute was interpreted by a group of Justices whose economic philosophy caused them to be enthusiastic about the taxation of incomes. The federal railroad statutes of this era were, on the other hand, interpreted with a relatively high degree of sympathy. The Court was not ready to accept the Interstate Commerce Commission in the 'nineties but it was prepared to do so after the first decade of the next century.

If the Justices did not, with one or two possible exceptions, dwell in the judicial equivalent of ivory towers before they came to the Court, and if the legislation upon which they passed did not come out of academic cloisters, it is nevertheless true that a detailed discussion of the relation of the one to the other would require an account far beyond the scope of this book. The statutes coming before the Court in this era were so numerous and the problems, both of constitutionality and of interpretation, so involved, that it must suffice here to discuss them as parts of a general movement. A very large proportion of the Court's decisions of unconstitutionality in these decades was concerned with statutes resulting from the unrest of which the Granger, Greenback, Populist, and Progressive movements were but symptoms. The decisions of 1935-1936, like those of the preceding decades, were very largely the product of the Court's reluctance to accept the consequences of the technological revolution which had begun to affect American society during the closing years of the eighteenth century. The social and economic problems produced by this revolution led almost immediately to legislative attempts to solve them, although there are relatively few constitutional cases involving such legislation until the last quarter of the nineteenth century.

That the Court delayed somewhat the final acceptance of many forms of governmental control of economic life in this country is apparent. Few legislative categories were, however, denied all possibility of acceptance, and, until 1935, the Court fought a rear-guard action rather than an engagement on a broad front. But in that long-drawn-out delaying campaign it developed a number of tactical devices. Almost all of these it employed when it gave open battle with the Roosevelt recovery legislation in 1935 and 1936. The scale of that engagement was unprecedented, but the Court's weapons were those devised and employed in the restricted warfare that had been going on for over a generation.

FEDERALISM AND COMMERCE

It has earlier been pointed out that under Marshall most of the cases involving the relative powers of central government and states grew out of the disputes over the jurisdiction of the federal courts. With the power of those courts once firmly established cases involving the commerce clause soon became the most numerous group, those involving the taxation of government instrumentalities being second. In the first two decades of the period now under consideration the commerce clause was the most frequent basis for decisions against the validity of state laws. After that the due process clause came to the fore. Between 1899 and the end of Chief Justice White's term in 1921 there were 194 cases in which state laws were invalidated, and of them 102 were decided in terms of federalism. Under Chief Justice Taft (1921-1930) of 141 decisions against state laws, only 54 primarily involved federalism, and this ratio continued during the next seven years.

When we look at the cases in which Congressional statutes were set aside the picture is, until 1935, a little different. For one thing there are few cases involving the commerce clause, indeed probably not more than four are to be so classified,[1] and two of these were of narrow application. This small number is, however, no measure of the importance of the litigation involving the national commerce power, and although there were fifteen cases having to do with the federal system in which acts of Congress were held invalid without reference to the commerce clause, the problems dealt with in some varieties of commerce cases are clearly of prior interest and importance.

---

[1] Matter of Heff, 197 U.S. 488 (1905), Employers' Liability Cases, 207 U.S. 463 (1908), Keller v. U.S., 213 U.S. 138 (1909), Hammer v. Dagenhart, 247 U.S. 251 (1918). The Employers' Liability and Hammer cases will be considered below. The Heff case set aside a Congressional act here interpreted to forbid sale of liquor to Indians who had, by an earlier statute, been given citizenship and were therefore under state jurisdiction. This decision was overruled by U.S. v. Nice, 241 U.S. 591 (1916). The Keller case held invalid a statute punishing those persons harboring alien women who had earlier been brought into the country for immoral purposes. Three members of the Court dissented.

The commerce clause is a grant of power to Congress. For almost a century the statutes for which it was the constitutional basis were confined largely to the promotion and regulation of water-borne commerce. Since 1887 there has been a great body of legislation dealing with the railroads, corporations, labor conditions and relations, health, morals, agriculture, marketing, and the conservation of natural resources, which has, in whole or in part, been justified constitutionally by the same brief grant of power. Obviously, if the Court refused its approval in but four commerce cases before 1935, the term commerce was given a broad interpretation. But just how broad was the federal power cannot be so easily indicated, nor can we by use of that simple statistic determine where, and in what variety of cases, the Court drew the line. Sometimes statutes have been so interpreted as greatly to restrict their applicability even though their constitutionality was sustained.

FEDERAL RAILROAD LEGISLATION

It has been indicated that in 1896 and 1897 the Court found that under the act of 1887 the Interstate Commerce Commission had powers of such limited scope as to render it incapable of performing the functions for which it was presumably established. In the acts of 1903, 1906, and 1910 Congress added materially to the powers of the Commission, particularly its powers over the rate structure.[2] These powers the Court was not reluctant to sustain. Indeed it upheld the Commission's application of these acts to intrastate railroad rates where those rates were closely tied in with interstate traffic. In 1913 it announced the principle in these words:

> The authority of Congress extends to every part of interstate commerce, and to every instrumentality or agency by which it is carried on; and the full control by Congress of

[2] Sharfman, *op. cit.*, I, ch. I.

> the subjects committed to its regulation is not to be denied or thwarted by the commingling of interstate and intrastate operations.[3]

In the Shreveport Case of the following year Justice Hughes stated the doctrine even more strongly:

> Wherever the interstate and intrastate transactions of carriers are so related that the government of the one involves the control of the other, it is Congress, and not the State, that is entitled to prescribe the final and dominant rule, for otherwise Congress would be denied the exercise of its constitutional authority and the State, and not the Nation, would be supreme within the national field.[4]

Following the period of government operation during the World War the roads were returned to private control, but under the even stricter supervision by the Commission prescribed in the Transportation Act of 1920. This act was sustained, as was its application to what, a few years before, would have been considered purely intrastate commerce, in the Wisconsin Commission Case.[5] Said Chief Justice Taft:

> Commerce is a unit and does not regard state lines, and while, under the Constitution, interstate and intrastate commerce are ordinarily subject to regulation by different sovereignties, yet when they are so mingled together that the supreme authority, the Nation, cannot exercise complete effective control over interstate commerce without incidental regulation of intrastate commerce, such incidental regulation is not an invasion of state authority. . . .[6]

The nationalistic inclusiveness of this doctrine, particularly when supported by the other rulings of the same period,[7] made it clear that the Court was willing to uphold the constitutionality of a Congressional statute which applied to many aspects of intrastate transportation. This does not

[3] The Minnesota Rate Cases, 230 U.S. 352, 399 (1913).

[4] Houston, E. & W.T. Ry. v. U.S., 234 U.S. 342, 351-352 (1914).

[5] Railroad Commission of Wisconsin v. Chicago, Burlington & Quincy R.R., 257 U.S. 563 (1922). [6] *Ibid.*, 588. [7] Reynolds, *op. cit.*, ch. IV.

mean that the Court was no longer concerned with litigation involving the regulation of the railroads. It means only that thereafter the issues concerning the constitutionality of acts of Congress were rare. There were scores of cases involving the interpretation and application of the national legislation, and although the attitude of the Court after 1920, or, for that matter after 1906, was in marked contrast to that of 1896-1897, the orders of the Commission were not invariably sustained.[8] Nor did the Court's approval of the Act of 1920 mean that the states were deprived of all control over intrastate railroad transportation. Indeed it is surprising how far the Court went in sustaining state regulations interfering with interstate railroads.[9] Even though under the Cooley rule and the Court's recent decisions the rail system had apparently been held to be a field in which a single, uniform system of regulation was required, dozens of state acts affecting, in varying degrees, that system of regulations were sustained. Many of them had to do with health, as quarantine laws and laws requiring the cleanliness and ventilation of cars, others concerned safety, and some of these specified details of equipment or man-power on interstate as well as intrastate trains, or the elimination of grade crossings. The Court, in brief, though upholding the broad powers of Congress and of the Interstate Commerce Commission, did not thereby pronounce the death of its own power as umpire over the play-by-play aspect of the game. It continued to rule upon the reasonableness of particular state regulations. Jurisdiction over nearly all rates and fares was taken from the states, but they continued, under the Court's presiding watchfulness, to determine many of the other, and not always trivial, rules under which the carriers operated.

Between 1899 and 1935 there were only two cases in which the Court held Congressional attempts at regulation of the

[8] Sharfman, *op. cit.*, II, 384-452.

[9] See Reynolds, *op. cit.*, 157ff. for a survey of these cases.

railroads to be invalid. Both involved the relation of the roads to their employees. In the Employers' Liability Cases [10] a bare majority of the Court rejected a statute amending the common law rules as to the liability of the railroads to their employees who were injured or killed while engaged in their occupations. The majority held that the provisions of the act were unconstitutionally made applicable not only to employees actually engaged in interstate commerce, but to all employees, even if at the time of their injury or death their employment had no direct relation to interstate commerce. An act complying with the principles set forth by the Court was later sustained,[11] but it is significant that the Court saw fit to draw so fine a distinction between the interstate and intrastate activities of the carriers in a case involving the interests of labor. In the same year the Court passed unfavorably upon a statute prohibiting interstate carriers from discharging employees solely because of their membership in a labor union; [12] but here the constitutional basis was due process. It will be pointed out later that these are not the only instances in which the line was drawn just short of statutes beneficial to labor.

TRUSTS AND BOYCOTTS

The commerce clause was the sole constitutional basis for the Sherman Anti-Trust Act of 1890, for there is nothing in the Constitution about trusts or conspiracies in restraint of trade. It was pointed out in the last chapter that although the act was accepted as constitutional the Court virtually stripped it of meaning in the Knight case in 1895. Four years later, however, the act was successfully applied against an industrial combination,[13] one involving a division of terri-

[10] 207 U.S. 463 (1908).
[11] Second Employers' Liability Cases, 223 U.S. 1 (1912).
[12] Adair v. U.S., 208 U.S. 161 (1908).
[13] Addyston Pipe and Steel Co. v. U.S., 175 U.S. 211 (1899).

tory among several concerns, and consequently one which to the visual imagination of the Court had a more "direct" bearing upon commerce among the states than the comprehensive monopoly of the sugar refiners in 1895. The application of the act was carried a step further when, in Northern Securities Co. v. U.S.,[14] the Court held that the acquisition by a holding company of stock control of competing carriers was a violation of its provisions. And in the Swift case of 1905 the Knight variety of myopia disappeared and a combination of meat packers was viewed not as a group exercising control of the stockyards in a given city located in a given state, but as a controlling factor in the extremely interstate process of meat production and distribution.

> Commerce among the States [said Justice Holmes for a unanimous Court] is not a technical legal conception, but a practical one, drawn from the course of business. When cattle are sent for sale from a place in one State, with the expectation that they will end their transit, after purchase, in another, and when in effect they do so, with only the interruption necessary to find a purchaser at the stock yards, and when this is a typical, constantly recurring course, the current thus existing is a current of commerce among the States, and the purchase of the cattle is a part and incident of such commerce.[15]

This comprehensive acceptance by the Court of the spirit of the Sherman Act was not to be the final stage in the judicial supervision of the legislation. Six years later, in the well-known Standard Oil and American Tobacco[16] cases, the Court abandoned both the literal wording of the Sherman Act and its own earlier interpretation of those words. Where the act stipulated that "Every contract, combination, . . . or conspiracy, in restraint of trade or commerce among the several states is . . . illegal," the Court decided that this meant every agreement in "unreasonable" restraint of trade. Again,

[14] 193 U.S. 197 (1904). [15] Swift & Co. v. U.S., 196 U.S. 375, 398-399 (1905).
[16] 221 U.S. 1, 106 (1911).

as so often before, the Court established itself in the strategic position as interpreter of the just and reasonable. In many cases since that time in which the meaning and applicability of the Sherman Act, as well as the later Clayton and Federal Trade Commission Acts, was involved, the Court has acted almost in the manner of a jury trying to get at the facts in order to determine whether a given combination reasonably restrained competition, or whether it unreasonably and therefore illegally blocked competition and tended to establish a monopoly.

One other aspect of the judicial application of this act should be given brief mention, even though the cases do not involve the problem of constitutionality. But in its finding that the anti-trust legislation served to restrict the activities of labor unions the Court was adding an important item to its record as referee. It has been indicated that in the Adair case in 1908 the Court held invalid the attempt of Congress to prohibit the discharge of railroad employees because of membership in a labor union. Justice Harlan wrote:

> There is no such connection between interstate commerce and membership in a labor organization as to authorize Congress to make it a crime against the United States for an agent of an interstate carrier to discharge an employé because of such membership on his part.[17]

Just one week later the Court held that the Sherman Act was applicable to a combination of labor union members who by boycotting an employer's business had acted "in restraint of trade or commerce" among the states.[18] This is not the place to attempt to deal with the much disputed question whether the Sherman Act was intended to apply to labor unions,[19] nor can we here trace the interesting history of

[17] Adair v. U.S., 208 U.S. 161, 179 (1908).

[18] Loewe v. Lawlor, 208 U.S. 274 (1908).

[19] A. T. Mason, *Organized Labor and the Law* (1925), Edward Berman, *Labor and the Sherman Act* (1930), E. E. Witte, *The Government in Labor Disputes* (1932).

the effective application of the anti-trust acts against labor boycotts. But it may at least be indicated that there was some basis for the strongly expressed opinion of the unions that the Court viewed the scope of the commerce clause with a more liberal eye when the act of Congress served to hamper the powers of labor organizations than it did when the act in question helped to strengthen the unions.

THE FEDERAL POLICE POWER

That the Court in its capacity as federal umpire has occasionally exhibited sympathies with one of the contestants is again illustrated in the series of cases dealing with the growth of the federal police power under the commerce clause. According to the principle of the Tenth Amendment what is called the police power, that is the general power to legislate for the health, morals, and general welfare, is reserved to the states. The federal government has only delegated powers. But under certain of those powers, particularly the commerce, tax, and postal powers, that government has built up a considerable body of police legislation and almost all of these acts have been sustained by the Court. The measures vary greatly in the closeness of their connection with commerce, or with what is ordinarily visualized as commerce. Those prescribing safety devices on interstate carriers, for example, present no constitutional difficulties, but when Congress prohibited the transporting of lottery tickets in interstate commerce the scope of the federal commerce power was sharply presented. The statute was upheld on the ground that lottery tickets are subjects of traffic and of commerce.[20] The power to regulate includes the power to prohibit, for if Congress has power to prescribe the rule according to which commerce is carried on, it may require the exclusion of articles deemed harmful. There is, the Court

[20] Champion v. Ames, 188 U.S. 321 (1903).

held, no violation of the states' reserved powers, since they have no reserved authority over interstate commerce.

In all Congress has enacted at least twelve statutes prohibiting one or another kind of commerce. With a single exception they have been sustained by the Supreme Court.[21] Of principal constitutional interest were the cases sustaining the Pure Food and Drug Act of 1906,[22] the acts restricting the shipment of intoxicating liquor into dry states,[23] and the Mann Act forbidding the transportation of women for immoral purposes.[24] It is apparent that these statutes were concerned with health and morals, not with the means or conditions of transportation. Nevertheless, since interstate transportation was essential to the accomplishment of the end which the act sought to deal with, the Court had little difficulty in finding that the coverage of the commerce clause was broad enough to include the prohibition. There is the one exception to be accounted for and that is the Child Labor Case of 1918.[25] Once more the Court draws the line of its tolerance just short of a labor statute. By a five-to-four decision the Court held that the commerce clause did not authorize Congress to exclude from interstate commerce the products of mines and manufacturing establishments in which, during the preceding month, children under certain specified ages had been employed.

There is little difficulty in agreeing with the statements in the majority opinion concerning the intent behind the act. Obviously it sought to prevent the existence of child labor in certain industries. But it is also just as obvious that the lottery, pure food, and Mann acts were not enacted out

---

[21] Edward S. Corwin, "Congress' Power to Prohibit Commerce," 18 *Cornell Law Quarterly* 477 (1933). Reprinted in *Selected Essays on Constitutional Law*, III, 103. Cf. U.S. v. DeWitt, 9 Wallace 41 (1870).

[22] Hipolite Egg Co. v. U.S., 220 U.S. 45 (1911).

[23] Clark Distilling Co. v. Western Maryland Ry. Co., 242 U.S. 311 (1917).

[24] Hoke v. U.S., 227 U.S. 308 (1913).

[25] Hammer v. Dagenhart, 247 U.S. 251 (1918).

of an interest in the means and conditions of transportation. They were aimed at lotteries, adulterated or harmful foods and drugs, and prostitution, yet the Court had sustained those statutes, on the ground that since Congress had the power to regulate commerce among the states, it was constitutionally permissible for it to affect intrastate activities so long as it was employing its delegated power. In justifying the distinction which he draws between these earlier cases, Mr. Justice Day apparently sees commerce as primarily, if not exclusively, transportation. This narrow conception is, of itself, inadequate, for the Congress had provided only for the regulation of transportation. He then inserts "expressly" in the Tenth Amendment, finding thereby that the states have the expressly reserved power to regulate production and manufacturing, one of the central doctrines, by the way, of the old E. C. Knight case. Under this statute, he continues, Congress is seeking to control intrastate activities (production) which take place before the transportation began. The transportation was not necessary to the achievement of some harmful use of materials sent from state to state.

But in any realistic sense the earlier prohibitions of transportation did affect conditions preceding transportation. The business interests involved in lottery, liquor, and white slave enterprises suffered and the methods of the packers and patent medicine manufacturers had to be changed a little. Indeed the distinctions which the majority drew between the child labor and the valid statutes made very little sense, and Mr. Justice Holmes' caustic dissenting opinion does not hesitate to indicate just that.[26] The majority seems, however, to have believed that a line had to be drawn, or else there would be no limit to Congress' power to prohibit commerce. So child labor was held to be a local problem.

[26] The literature on the case is extensive and for the most part critical. Several of the articles are reprinted in *Selected Essays on Constitutional Law,* III, ch. 2.

In 1925 the Court sustained the National Motor Theft Act which made it a crime to transport or conceal a stolen automobile.[27] Now a stolen automobile is in itself no more harmful than furniture made in a factory employing children. The evil sought to be prevented, moreover, took place before the transportation occurred. Nevertheless the Court voted unanimously in favor of this act. That inarticulate major premise which is found in judges as in all men, and in commerce as well as in due process problems, made it easy for the Justices to see the "traffic" in stolen cars as a more legitimately national problem than the "production" of goods in factories or mines where children were employed.

The two decisions dealing with the prison-made goods statutes also served to weaken the Hammer ruling, although they did not overrule it. In the Hawes-Cooper Act of 1929 Congress, following the example of the old Wilson Act of 1890, provided that convict-made goods should, upon transportation into any state, be subject to the laws of such state. This act was upheld,[28] as was the Ashurst-Summers Act prohibiting the transportation of convict-made goods into any state wherein they are to be sold or used in violation of that state's laws.[29]

The tax clauses of the Constitution have, like the commerce clause, been the basis for legislation in which the purpose behind the act was obviously not the same as that appearing on its face. Tax laws, in other words, have not always been exclusively or even primarily revenue statutes.[30] A completely protective tariff, for example, is not a revenue measure. Protective tariffs are not new in our history, but

[27] Brooks v. U.S., 267 U.S. 432 (1925).

[28] Whitfield v. Ohio, 297 U.S. 431 (1936).

[29] Kentucky Whip & Collar Co. v. Illinois Central R.R., 299 U.S. 334 (1937).

[30] Robert E. Cushman, "Social and Economic Control Through Federal Taxation," 18 *Minnesota Law Review,* 759 (1934), *Selected Essays on Constitutional Law,* III, 543.

it was not until 1928[31] that the Supreme Court passed upon, and upheld, the principle embodied in such acts. It did so partly on the basis of long-established practice, and partly on the ground that so long as the tariff was ostensibly a revenue measure, any other motive was an irrelevant consideration.

With but two exceptions the Court has sustained the "tax" measures coming before it which also provided for economic or social control. The destructive tax imposed on state bank notes in 1866 was sustained on the principle that Congress and not the Courts must determine the rate and incidence of the tax.[32] Even where the tax measures also included regulatory provisions they were sustained. Thus the Dingley Tariff Act of 1897, in addition to levying a tax on tobacco and cigarettes, prohibited the inclusion in such packages of premiums or prize certificates. Congress, said the Court, is entitled to regulate the thing taxed in order to prohibit inclusion therein of anything except that which is taxed.[33] A similar method of control has been employed in the acts dealing with narcotic drugs. Persons importing, selling, or even giving away such drugs were required to register with the commissioner of internal revenue, pay a tax of one dollar per year, and abide by a detailed set of regulations. Violations of these rules were punishable by fine and imprisonment. The tax feature was obviously slight, but it was the constitutional basis of the act, and the measure was sustained, although by a five-to-four vote.[34] Four of the Justices believed that the relation to the tax power was too slight to justify this encroachment upon the reserved police power of the states. One of them, Mr. Justice McReynolds, was, for reasons which are a secret

[31] Hampton v. U.S., 276 U.S. 394 (1928).
[32] Veazie Bank v. Fenno, 8 Wallace 533 (1869).
[33] Felsenheld v. U.S., 186 U.S. 126 (1902).
[34] Doremus v. U.S., 249 U.S. 86 (1919).

of the judicial chamber, permitted to include two sentences in a case decided seven years later which virtually invited someone to bring up another case on the subject in order that the Court might overrule the error of 1919.[35] Two years later the issue was reconsidered, but the Court sustained its earlier ruling, partly on the theory that since Congress had raised the rates from the dollar-a-year levy earlier imposed, the narcotic act was now an important revenue measure.[36] But this conception of constitutionality measured by amount of revenue was evidently a secondary argument, as it should have been. Indeed, little excuse for introducing it can be found, and the Court continued to hold that the regulatory provisions were incidental to those imposing the taxes.

Perhaps the most striking instance in which the Court sustained a tax measure which was patently not a tax measure was the oleomargarine case.[37] Here a divided Court upheld an act imposing a tax of ten cents per pound on oleomargarine colored to look like butter. The profession that this tax was intended to protect the health of users of oleomargarine was easily shown to be a pretext. The tax upon uncolored oleomargarine, or probably upon oleo given any color of the spectrum excepting only yellow, was one-fourth of one cent per pound. It is also well known that nearly all butter is artificially colored to resemble the stereotyped conception of butter. It was, indeed, claimed in this case that the oleomargarine was colored with the same substance commonly employed to lend the desired shade to butter. The act was passed to protect the creamery interests, not the public health. If it had, for that matter, been enacted for the

[35] "The constitutionality of the Anti-Narcotic Act, touching which this Court so sharply divided in United States v. Doremus, was not raised below and has not been again considered. The doctrine approved in Hammer v. Dagenhart . . . Child Labor Tax Case . . . Hill v. Wallace . . . and Linder v. U.S. . . . may necessitate a review of that question if hereafter properly presented." U.S. v. Daugherty, 269 U.S. 360, 362-363 (1926).

[36] Nigro v. U.S., 276 U.S. 332 (1928). Justices McReynolds, Sutherland, and Butler dissented. [37] McCray v. U.S., 195 U.S. 27 (1904).

purpose of benefiting the public health, it would, under the Tenth Amendment, have been in the domain reserved to the states. Yet the Court upheld the measure as an excise tax. To the argument that the tax power was being employed "for an unlawful purpose . . . to accomplish a result not intended by the Constitution," Mr. Justice White answered: "The decisions of this court from the beginning lend no support whatever to the assumption that the judiciary may restrain the exercise of lawful power on the assumption that a wrongful purpose or motive has caused the power to be exerted." [38]

Shortly after the first child labor case Congress passed a statute imposing a tax of ten per cent of the net income upon various forms of industry in which children had knowingly been employed during the preceding year. This act was held to be unconstitutional in the Child Labor Tax Case.[39] The Court found that "the analogy of the Dagenhart case is clear." There Congress sought to stop interstate commerce in various necessary commodities, "and to deny the same to the people of a state, in order to coerce them into compliance with Congress' regulation of state concerns." Here "the so-called tax is a penalty to coerce people of a state to act as Congress wishes them to act in respect of a matter completely the business of the state government under the Federal Constitution." [40]

It is difficult to disagree with either of Taft's propositions. The tax was not a tax in any usual sense; it was a penalty. Congress obviously sought to get at the problem of child labor through the tax power. So much is clear. But what of the precedents? The Chief Justice finds that the Veazie, Doremus, and McCray cases offer no difficulties. The measures sustained in those cases were all tax measures. That the "taxes" were not for revenue, that they were enacted for

[38] *Ibid.*, 54, 56. [39] 259 U.S. 20 (1922). [40] *Ibid.*, 39.

regulatory or prohibitory purposes was evident, but Taft professes to find that the ends were incidental to the means. One is tempted to remark that the Court was willing to shut its eyes to the purpose of these police power acts, whether passed under the commerce or the tax powers, so long as labor legislation was not involved and so long as reputable business was not interfered with. For this, after all has been said about the distinction between taxes which are clearly penalties, and regulatory or prohibitory measures which are constitutionally taxes, is another instance of the Court's habit of drawing the line between the allowable and the invalid just at the point where a labor law is involved.

In this instance, however, the verdict of invalidity was not confined to the Child Labor Tax Act. The case following immediately had to do with the Future Trading Act of 1921, an act imposing a tax of 20 cents per bushel on all contracts for the sale of grain for future delivery, except sales on boards of trade designated as contract markets by the Secretary of Agriculture, and by him regulated. This act was held invalid on the authority of the Child Labor Tax Case.[41] The Court went on to hold that the act could not be justified under the commerce clause. That part of the ruling, however, was not long to have the effect that might have been expected, for the Court also pointed out the Constitutional defects of the act and almost invited Congress to reenact it in improved form. This Congress did and the next year the Court sustained the Grain Futures Act of 1922 under the commerce clause.[42] In this act, said the Chief Justice, Congress has observed the principles stated in Hill v. Wallace and the regulation of trading in grain futures is allowable under the doctrine first announced in the Swift case of 1905. The Chicago Board of Trade is located in Chicago, but, like

[41] Hill v. Wallace, 259 U.S. 44 (1922).
[42] Board of Trade v. Olsen, 262 U.S. 1 (1923).

the stockyards,[43] it is also a part of that stream or current of commerce which is as much subject to Congressional regulation as are the arteries of transportation. But the first Child Labor Case had shut off that possibility so far as the regulation of child labor was concerned. At that time it appeared that only through an amendment to the Constitution could Congress acquire the power necessary to the enactment of a valid statute on that subject. The liberality of construction which enabled Congress to establish and to regulate banks, to tax banknotes issued by state banks out of existence, to charter and to regulate corporations, including those engaged in production or manufacturing, to restrict the traffic in lotteries, in white slaves, in foods and drugs, to regulate the activities of brokers on the Chicago Board of Trade and of commission men in the Chicago stockyards, to tax prohibitively yellow oleomargarine while taxing that of less delectable colors at a nominal rate, did not extend to the regulation of child labor, for that was a subject left to the states.

INTER-GOVERNMENTAL TAXATION

Among the most curious chapters in the history of the Court as federal umpire is that concerned with the doctrine of the taxation of governmental instrumentalities. The basic principles originating in McCulloch v. Maryland and given application in the Weston and Dobbins cases and applied reciprocally in Collector v. Day remained virtually intact

[43] See Stafford v. Wallace, 258 U.S. 495 (1922) in which the Packers and Stockyards Act of 1921 was upheld. In sustaining the extensive regulations there imposed the Court said, "The application of the commerce clause of the Constitution in the Swift case was the result of the natural development of interstate commerce under modern conditions. It was the inevitable recognition of the great central fact that such streams of commerce from one part of the country to another which are ever flowing are in their very essence the commerce among the States and with foreign nations which historically it was one of the chief purposes of the Constitution to bring under national protection and control." *Ibid.*, 518-519.

until 1939, but the course of those principles during the first third of the present century has left a network of paths which can be followed only with an elaborate paraphernalia of maps and guidebooks. It will be remembered that Marshall here laid down not the rule of reasonableness, but the rule of absoluteness. No tax upon a governmental instrumentality was allowable; none, in other words, could be reasonable and constitutional. It may be that a doctrine of reasonableness would, in this field of constitutional law, have led to even more litigation than Marshall's rule of absolutes, although the evidence does not appear to indicate that. Certain it is that the absolute doctrine has not shut off litigation, nor did it produce simple and logical end-results in the way of judicial formulae. Consider some of the problems and the answers given by the Court.

When the state of South Carolina established liquor dispensaries the problem of the validity of the national excise tax upon liquor dealers when applied to these state-owned establishments was presented. There was no doubt that the state was the lawful and constitutional owner, and the sole owner, whereas the national government had been but a minority owner of the Bank of the United States. Yet the Court held that the liquor dispensaries were subject to fed eral tax, since the exemption is limited to those which are of a strictly governmental character.[44] Just what this latter category includes has never been entirely certain, but it is certain that the Court here decided to take upon itself the function of determining as it went along.[45] The rule of reason had crept back into one part of the field. So far as the liquor business is concerned it is both interesting and significant of a

[44] South Carolina v. U.S., 199 U.S. 437 (1905). Justices White, Peckham, and McKenna dissented.

[45] Although no perfectly clear line of demarcation was worked out by the Court, it roughly approximated the principles observed by the courts in determining the liabilities of municipalities for torts committed by their officers. Alden L. Powell, *National Taxation of State Instrumentalities* (1936), 85.

peculiar variety of intransigence in the Court that, after many state and two national constitutional amendments dealing with that traffic, the Court continued to hold it to be a private rather than a strictly governmental function for purposes of exemption from taxation.[46] The entire story is a perfect illustration of the *laissez faire* conception of government.

Some of the oddest results in the sphere were developed in cases where the national or state government was trustee or lessor. An Oklahoma income tax was held unconstitutional as applied to the income of one of its citizens derived from certain oil and gas lands because the lands were owned by an Indian ward of the federal government and the lease had been negotiated by the government.[47] The tax was non-discriminatory but Mr. Justice Holmes, for a divided Court, said that "a tax upon such profits is a direct hamper upon the efforts of the United States to make the best terms that it can for its wards." Subsequently another Oklahoma tax levied upon ore taken from Indian-owned lands under a lease arranged by the Department of the Interior was held to be a tax upon a national instrumentality.[48] The result is a curiosity of American federalism. Not only were the taxes non-discriminatory, they were not upon a federal instrumentality. The national government came into the picture only as agent of the Indians, who were presumably, but only in a very long-run sense, the beneficiaries of this application of Marshall's principle. It is not clear why these Indians should be favored over other persons, including those Indians who were legally competent to manage their own affairs.

The same rule was applied to a federal tax upon the gross production of oil and gas lands, where the lands were state-owned public school lands but leased to a private corpora-

---

[46] Ohio v. Helvering, 292 U.S. 360 (1934).

[47] Gillespie v. Oklahoma, 257 U.S. 501 (1922).

[48] Jaybird Mining Co. v. Weir, 271 U.S. 609 (1926).

tion.[49] A slight modification of the absurdities of these rulings is found in two decisions of the next year.[50] The Court does not abandon its peculiar principles but it reaches a different conclusion on similar facts, by considering the remoteness of the government's interest from the tax as levied. It is highly probable that if the Court had always gone upon the theory that "the subject of the tax is so remote from any governmental function as to render the effect of the exaction inconsiderable as respects the activities of the city," [51] it would not have reached the conclusions it did in some of the earlier decisions.

Another kind of situation that perplexed the Court was the taxation of sales to governmental agencies. An excise tax upon the sale of gasoline was held not to be applicable where the sale was to the Coast Guard Fleet,[52] but it is to be remarked that the Court divided five-to-four and that Justice Holmes, who wrote the Gillespie opinion, here wrote one of the dissenting opinions, arguing that the question of interference with the government is one of reasonableness and degree, and here the interference is too remote. But eight years later, and with only two dissenters, the Court disallowed a tax upon the storage of gasoline when brought from outside the state, stored therein, and later sold to the United States.[53] Earlier the Court had, as if to show that it was not attemping to favor the national government, held that where a motorcycle is sold by its manufacturer to a municipal government, for use in a strictly governmental function, the transaction cannot be taxed by the United States.[54] A tax, on the other hand, levied upon gasoline sold to a private contractor who is carrying on work for the federal government is valid, for

[49] Burnet v. Coronado Oil & Gas Co., 285 U.S. 393 (1932).

[50] Indian Territory Oil Co. v. Board of Equalization, 288 U.S. 325 (1933), Burnet v. Jergins Trust, 288 U.S. 508 (1933).

[51] 288 U.S. 508, 516 (1933).

[52] Panhandle Oil Co. v. Mississippi, 277 U.S. 218 (1928).

[53] Graves v. Texas Co., 298 U.S. 393 (1936).

[54] Indian Motorcycle Co. v. U.S., 283 U.S. 570 (1931).

here there is no burden upon the government.[55] And a license tax assessed against a warehouse operating under a federal license was not invalid,[56] nor was a tax imposed upon the production and sale of electric power when the company taxed had a federal license.[57] These corporations were not federal agencies and the taxes were not on the licenses.

There are a good many strained doctrines expressed in this series but surely the most far-fetched conclusion was reached in Long v. Rockwood [58] where it was held that a state income tax might not be imposed upon royalties received from patent rights, a doctrine which had earlier been expressed by several state courts. Aside from the evident fact that patents are not government instrumentalities, it is to be remarked that the majority conceded that the states would continue "to exercise control over articles manufactured by patentees, to regulate the assignment of patent rights, and to prevent fraud in connection therewith." The line-up of the Court is also interesting. Holmes, who wrote the opinion in the Gillespie case and concurred in the Jaybird case, here wrote the dissenting opinion, while McReynolds, who dissented in Jaybird, here wrote the majority opinion. Sutherland, who had been with the majority in virtually every case sustaining exemption, was with the minority, as were Brandeis and Stone, who had more frequently sought to lessen the rigors of the doctrine of tax immunity. Four years later a unanimous Court sustained a state tax upon gross receipts arising from the licensing of copyrighted moving pictures,[59] and expressly overruled Long v. Rockwood. But this reversion to a rational basis of decision applied only in the restricted area of patents and copyrights.

It was not carried into the taxation of officers and/or employees of governments. Here the old fine-spun distinctions persisted. The Court, to be sure, sustained taxes on the in-

[55] Trinity-farm Construction Co. v. Grosjean, 291 U.S. 466 (1934).
[56] Federal Compress & Warehouse Co. v. McLean, 291 U.S. 17 (1934).
[57] Broad River Power Co. v. Query, 288 U.S. 178 (1933).
[58] 277 U.S. 142 (1928). [59] Fox Film Corp. v. Doyal, 286 U.S. 123 (1932).

come of consulting engineers employed to advise states or their sub-divisions about water supplies,[60] and on the salaries of Trustees of the Boston Elevated Railway.[61] But the first was upheld on the ground that the consulting engineer was not an employee of the government, his only relation being one of contract, and the second on the theory that although the Elevated trustees were appointed by the governor, performed duties prescribed by statute, and received a regular salary, they must pay the tax since the street railway was, from the point of view of tax-immunity, like the liquor business. Here the business was operated by a private corporation under strict governmental supervision and by state-chosen officers, but even if the state owned and operated the business, it would be the same. On the other hand the immunity denied to the rulers of a street railway system was allowed to a resident of New York who was general counsel for the Panama Railroad, a federal government enterprise.[62] This railroad, the Court held, was auxiliary to the Canal and was consequently an instrumentality of the United States which the states could not tax. And the water system of New York City is similarly a strictly governmental function so that the salary of its chief engineer may not be taxed by the federal government.[63] In a dissenting opinion Mr. Justice Roberts recognized the need for rationalization and restatement in the field of tax immunity and suggested two general limitations upon the powers of taxation of the branches of the federal system: that the taxes be non-discriminatory and that they not directly burden the operations of the other government.[64] Two years later the Court was to go even further than

[60] Metcalf & Eddy v. Mitchell, 269 U.S. 514 (1926).
[61] Helvering v. Powers, 293 U.S. 214 (1934).
[62] New York *ex rel.* Rogers v. Graves, 299 U.S. 401 (1937).
[63] Brush v. Commissioner of Internal Revenue, 300 U.S. 352 (1937).
[64] *Ibid.*, 375. Mr. Justice Brandeis concurred in the dissent. Justices Stone and Cardozo concurred with the majority on grounds which made it unnecessary to pass on the constitutional issue.

Roberts suggested, but that case belongs to another chapter.

In Weston v. Charleston [65] Marshall had held that the income from federal securities could not be taxed by the states or their subdivisions, even though the securities were owned by private persons. This doctrine has not yet been altered, but it, like other portions of the rule of tax immunity, has led to some interesting drawing of lines between the allowable and the unconstitutional. Perhaps the most striking exception to the general rule is in the case of inheritance taxes. Where neither Congress nor a state may levy an income tax against the securities issued by the other, the capital value of such securities may be included in the estate subject to state or federal inheritance taxes. In 1899 the Court in sustaining a state tax upon an estate consisting of United States government bonds not only held that the power to take property by will or descent is derived from and regulated by municipal law and that the tax upon "such right or privilege" might be measured by the value of the property passing, but also dismissed the argument that taxation here would impair the borrowing power of the federal government as being far-fetched.[66] "The injury ought to be obvious and appreciable." [67] That has hardly been the criterion when applied in other phases of the law of intergovernmental taxation, but it has persisted here.[68] Indeed the Court has gone beyond this rule-of-reason criterion, and has allowed bequests to the federal government to be taxed by the states [69] and bequests to state and municipal governments to be taxed by the federal government, even though those bequests were to be used for public and governmental purposes.[70]

A somewhat similar attitude is found in the willingness to uphold an income tax upon the profit derived from the sale

---

[65] *Supra,* p. 50. [66] Plummer v. Coler, 178 U.S. 115 (1900).
[67] *Ibid.,* 138. [68] Cf. Greiner v. Lewellyn, 258 U.S. 384 (1922).
[69] U.S. v. Perkins, 163 U.S. 625 (1896).
[70] Snyder v. Bettman, 190 U.S. 249 (1903).

of state and local bonds.[71] The profits on the sales of bonds are in a different category from the interest on the bonds. And before the power of the government to lay a tax on the profits can be denied it must appear that the burden is real, not imaginary, substantial, not negligible. A reasonable rule of reason, which, if applied generally throughout the field of intergovernmental taxation would have produced an overhauling of the precedents long before 1939.

THE SCOPE OF THE TREATY POWER

Before leaving the subject of the Court as federal umpire one final illustration may be given in the treaty power. Presumably the Tenth Amendment applied to that section as to all parts of the Constitution adopted in 1788. That is not to say that the powers reserved to the state limit the powers which were delegated to the central government, but only that the reserved powers were reserved as against the treaty as well as the commerce or tax powers. So far, however, the Court has never held a treaty to be unconstitutional. What the limits to the treaty power are we do not know, but we do know that the power is indeed an extensive one, and, more definitely, that it extends to certain important subjects upon which Congress could not enact legislation.[72] If this were not so the national government would be denied authority to deal with many subjects of international concern. As far back as 1817 the Court applied the provisions of a treaty with France to the inheritance of land in Maryland,[73] a question which is normally within the exclusive domain of the states. Two generations later much the same issue produced the same ruling, and in this case there was a conflict between the treaty and the state law.[74]

---

[71] Willcuts v. Bunn, 282 U.S. 216 (1931).

[72] Edward S. Corwin, *National Supremacy* (1913).

[73] Chirac v. Chirac, 2 Wheaton 259 (1817).

[74] Hauenstein v. Lynham, 100 U.S. 483 (1880).

Doubtless a treaty would be held invalid if, in the Court's opinion, it dealt with a matter which was not an appropriate subject of international agreement and which invaded the domain of powers reserved to the states. That a broad scope will be allowed to the subject matter properly coming within the area of international agreement was well illustrated in the migratory bird case.[75] The regulation of hunting is ordinarily assumed to be within the range of the states' police powers. Nevertheless when a treaty was made between the United States and Great Britain providing for the protection of wild birds which annually toured across the Canadian border, the Court sustained not only the treaty but also the Congressional statute which was passed for its enforcement. The statute, without the treaty, would probably have been unconstitutional, for Mr. Justice Holmes, after pointing out that the supreme law clause did not specify that treaties, like statutes, must be made in pursuance of the Constitution, goes on to say:

> We do not mean to imply that there are no qualifications to the treaty-making power, but they must be ascertained in a different way. It is obvious that there may be matters of the sharpest exigency for the national well being that an act of Congress could not deal with but that a treaty followed by such an act could, and it is not lightly to be assumed that, in matters requiring national action, "a power which must belong to and somewhere reside in every civilized government" is not to be found.[76]

[75] Missouri v. Holland, 252 U.S. 416 (1920). [76] *Ibid.*, 433.

Chapter VII

JUDICIAL REVIEW AND THE SEPARATION OF POWERS

FOR over a century it has been generally assumed that the Supreme Court has final authority to decide any jurisdictional dispute between the three branches of the national government. There is no Constitutional provision explicitly authorizing the Court to exercise this power. And in the 49th and 51st numbers of the *Federalist,* of which Madison was probably the author, we find perfectly clear evidence that not all of the framers anticipated the later assumption. In the 49th paper it is asserted that "The several departments being perfectly co-ordinate by the terms of their common commission, none of them, it is evident, can pretend to an exclusive or superior right of settling the boundaries between their respective powers. . . ." [1] In the 51st it is not so much asserted as assumed that "In republican government, the legislative authority necessarily predominates." [2] It appears that "The remedy for this inconveniency" is not judicial review, but bicameralism. The discussion of checks and balances in the *Federalist* does not proceed upon the assumption that the judicial will have any more powerful check, or any superior authority as an arbiter, than the legislative or executive branches. And this was ever the doctrine to which Madison and Jefferson adhered.

[1] Ford ed., 335. [2] *Ibid.,* 345.

In the years before Marshall transformed the Court into the most powerful judicial body known to history there was evidently some uncertainty in the Court itself concerning its proper relation to the separation of powers. The inconclusive Hayburn case in Jay's term is evidence of this uncertainty.[3] Although the Justices were apparently agreed that "neither the Legislative nor the Executive branches can constitutionally assign to the Judicial any duties, but such as are properly judicial," [4] they hesitated to go beyond this assertion of separateness. But Marshall had no doubts concerning the final authority of the Court to interpret and apply the fundamental law. The sections of the Constitution allotting the legislative, the executive, and the judicial powers to the three branches of government were no exception to the general rule. The assertion of judicial supremacy in Marbury v. Madison was general, not specific. The judicial power, contrary to the view expressed in the 49th *Federalist,* included the authority to rule upon the proper workings of the tripartite separation of powers.

During the first half of the Court's history the principal judicial issues growing out of the system of a tripartite separation of governmental powers into legislative, executive, and judicial departments had to do with the position and powers of the courts. Until quite recently there were few controversies involving the relative powers of the executive and legislative branches of the national government, but, particularly during the last few decades, those issues have begun to furnish an increasing number of constitutional problems. Even though the number and importance of such cases has grown it is evident that judicial review was probably less frequently employed in this area than might have been anticipated. The separation of powers may not have worked automatically, or always smoothly, but the safeguarding of this device, which John Adams was not alone

[3] *Supra,* 30. [4] 2 Dallas, 411.

in believing essential to a government of laws, has not been a primary concern of the courts. At least until 1935 there were surprisingly few constitutional cases of the first magnitude in which the principle so much discussed in the Convention of 1787 and so carefully analyzed in the *Federalist* was involved.

JUDICIAL REVIEW OF PRESIDENTIAL POWERS

It is especially notable how rare were the cases in which were reviewed the exercise of powers by the President, when those powers were not based upon acts of Congress. At the beginning of the Civil War President Lincoln proclaimed a blockade, suspended the privilege of the writ of *habeas corpus,* provided for the enlistment of three-year volunteers and for the enlargement of the regular army and navy, all before Congress met. A closely divided Court upheld his blockade proclamation, apparently because Congress subsequently authorized the action.[5] Chief Justice Taney held that the suspension of the writ of *habeas corpus* was invalid unless made by Congress, since the Constitutional provision on the subject was placed in Article I, dealing with the legislative department.[6] This opinion was disregarded by Lincoln but it is significant that Congress in 1863 declared that the President is authorized to suspend the writ. By its choice of words it dodged the issue whether he is authorized by the law or by the Constitution, but the inclusion of the provision in a statute lends some support to Taney's interpretation.

The Emancipation Proclamation was issued without Congressional authorization. Lincoln believed that Congress had no power to deal with the subject, but that he, as Comman-

---

[5] The Prize Cases, 2 Black 635 (1863). *Supra,* 81.

[6] Ex parte Merryman, Fed. case 9, 487 (1861). This was not a decision of the Supreme Court. The writ of *habeas corpus* was issued by Taney and the opinion is, therefore, that of only one member of the Court.

der in Chief, did have power to deal with this war-time problem. The adoption of the Thirteenth Amendment two years later prevented the constitutionality of his Proclamation from being passed upon by the Supreme Court.

Only in the Milligan case,[7] decided more than a year and a half after Lincoln's death, did the Court rule against one of his acts. It held unanimously that a trial by military commission of a civilian in an area remote from the theater of military operations could not be constitutionally authorized by the executive. Four members of the Court believed that the war powers of Congress would justify a legislative provision for such trial, but they agreed with the majority that executive authorization was invalid.

During the latter part of the nineteenth century the most notable case in which the authority of the President was questioned before the Court was In re Neagle.[8] Justice Field had been threatened by one Terry, who was bitter about a decision rendered by Field.[9] The President ordered Neagle, a United States deputy marshal, to protect Field from Terry. While Field was on circuit duty in California Terry attempted to attack the Justice, whereupon Neagle shot and killed Terry. Neagle was arrested by California authorities and indicted for murder, but secured his release upon a writ issued by the federal circuit court. The Supreme Court affirmed the judgment of the circuit court. It sustained, that is, the power of the President to order a federal marshal to protect a federal judge even though there was no statute specifically providing for this duty. Upon the President is devolved the duty of seeing that the laws of the United States, including the Constitution, "be faithfully executed." His power and duty are not limited to enforcing the express terms of the statutes or treaties. The breadth and impor-

---

[7] Ex parte Milligan, 4 Wallace 2 (1866).

[8] 135 U.S. 1 (1890). Cf. Tennessee v. Davis, 100 U.S. 257 (1880).

[9] Carl B. Swisher, *Stephen J. Field, Craftsman of the Law* (1930) ch. XIII.

tance of his obligation requires that he be given a considerable range of discretion.[10]

A number of less spectacular problems dealing with the exercise of the veto power and with the signing of Congressional bills have been decided by the Court. These have, for the most part, had to do with the time at which the President may exercise the silent veto or at which he may affix his signature to a bill. Thus, in the Pocket Veto case [11] the Court held that the words of Article I section 7 which stipulate that an unsigned bill does not become a law if "the Congress by their adjournment prevent its return," refer to the adjournment of any session of a Congress and not to its final adjournment only. In making this decision, it is worth noting, the Court was only following a presidential interpretation which went back to the term of Madison.

In 1899 the Court held that the President might sign bills during the recess of Congress, such as that taken over the Christmas holidays.[12] A generation later it sustained the right of the President to sign a bill after the final adjournment of a Congress, provided it be done within the ten-day period explicitly stipulated.[13]

THE REMOVAL POWER

A very important issue, which was never clearly ruled upon until 1926, is the extent to which the removal power of the President depends upon the provisions of the statute creating the office. It had often been assumed, but not definitely decided, that the Congress could not limit the President in this regard, not, that is, if the appointment was made by the President, either with or without Senatorial confirma-

[10] This ruling was reinforced by In re Debs, 158 U.S. 564 (1895). On the entire problem see Edward S. Corwin, *The President: Office and Powers* (1940) ch. IV. [11] Okanogan Indians v. U.S., 279 U.S. 655 (1929).

[12] La Abra Silver Mining Co. v. U.S., 175 U.S. 423 (1899).

[13] Edwards v. U.S., 286 U.S. 482 (1932).

tion. In the important Myers decision the Court held that an Act of 1876 requiring the Senate's approval for the removal as well as the appointment of postmasters was invalid to the extent that it limited the executive power of removal. The majority opinion, written by Chief Justice Taft, is a very long one and deals at length with a variety of historical evidence and with previous decisions of the Court touching on this issue. But, as the three dissenters were able to show, the evidence drawn from history and precedents is, at best, equivocal.[14] The majority case appears to rest essentially upon an interpretation of the "executive power" as described in Article II of the Constitution. Taft, who had not been entirely happy in his relationships with Congress while chief executive, argues that the clause instructing the President to "take care that the laws be faithfully executed" assumed that he must be in control of his subordinates. It is the "reasonable implication" that

> he should select those who were to act for him under his direction in the execution of the laws. The further implication must be, in the absence of any express limitation respecting removals, that as his selection of administrative officers is essential to the execution of the laws by him, so must be his power of removing those for whom he cannot continue to be responsible.[15]

The obvious answer to this argument would be that the Constitution has limited the President's power of appointment. Certain officers can be appointed only with Senatorial consent, and the method of appointment for the inferior officers is to be determined by Congress to the extent that their appointment may be vested in "the President alone, in the courts of law, or in the heads of departments." [16] To this Taft's reply was that "The power of removal is incident

---

[14] Myers v. U.S. 272 U.S. 52 (1926). In addition to the dissenting opinions of Justices McReynolds and Brandeis see E. S. Corwin, "The President's Removal Power under the Constitution" (1927), reprinted in *Selected Essays on Constitutional Law,* IV, 1467. [15] 272 U.S. at 117. [16] Article II, 2, cl. 2.

to the power of appointment, not to the power of advising and consenting to appointment, and when the grant of the executive power is enforced by the express mandate to take care that the laws be faithfully executed, it emphasizes the necessity for including within the executive power as conferred the exclusive power of removal." It appears that Congress may, when it vests the appointment of an inferior officer in the head of a department, "prescribe incidental regulations controlling and restricting the latter in the exercise of the power of removal." But it could not require that Congress participate in the removal process. "To do this would be to . . . infringe the constitutional principle of the separation of powers." [17]

The dissenting opinions of Justices McReynolds and Brandeis contain long and detailed examinations of the historical evidence and the judicial precedents. That of Justice Holmes was very brief but unequivocal in its doctrine.[18] The office involved is one "that owes its existence to Congress and that Congress may abolish tomorrow." Congress defined the duties of the office and provided that it should be filled by appointment by the President and Senate. Congress fixed the term of the office, and by virtue of the same power, could alter that term. "The duty of the President to see that the laws be executed is a duty that does not go beyond the laws or require him to achieve more than Congress sees fit to leave within his power." To this may be added Justice Brandeis' conclusions concerning the nature and purpose of the separation of powers:

> The doctrine of the separation of powers was adopted by the convention of 1787 not to promote efficiency but to preclude the exercise of arbitrary power. The purpose was not to avoid friction, but, by means of the inevitable friction incident to the distribution of the governmental powers among three departments, to save the people from autocracy.

---

[17] 272 U.S. at 161. [18] *Ibid.*, 177.

> In order to prevent arbitrary executive action, the constitution provided in terms that presidential appointments be made with the consent of the Senate, unless Congress should otherwise provide; and this clause was construed by Alexander Hamilton in the Federalist, No. 77, as requiring consent to removals.[19]

The majority doctrine is clear in its rejection of this interpretation, so far as the particular office here involved was concerned, but the decision left unsettled a number of important governmental problems, including the status of members of the administrative commissions and of federal employees under the classified civil service. Some of these questions were to be considered in the Humphrey case which will be discussed in Chapter IX.

THE DELEGATION OF LEGISLATIVE POWERS

An issue of even greater potential importance was that discussed in the cases involving the delegation of discretionary authority to executive and administrative officers. There is no constitutional injunction prohibiting delegation as delegation, but the first section of the Constitution specifies that "All legislative powers herein granted shall be vested in a Congress of the United States. . . ." The constitutional issue arises, therefore, only if it is alleged that Congress has attempted to bestow its legislative power upon some other agency or officer. Although there is a very long legislative history of delegated authority[20] judicial discussion of the problem hardly begins before 1892. Early in the century in a case involving the authority conferred upon the President by the Non-intercourse Act of 1809, Joseph Ingersoll, as counsel, argued that Congress could not and had not granted to the President the "legislative power" to determine when the

---

[19] 272 U.S. at 293.

[20] James Hart, *Ordinance Making Powers of the President* (1925), Ch. IV.

act should be in operation. But the Court barely referred to this feature of the act, and was content to "see no sufficient reason" why Congress should not exercise its discretion in determining how the act should be revived.[21]

The first real discussion by the Supreme Court of this issue, the importance of which was only beginning to be realized, came in 1892. The case of Field v. Clark [22] involved, among other questions, the reciprocal trade provision of the Tariff Act of 1890. This section of the act authorized the President, when he believed that discriminatory duties were imposed upon any one of a number of American commodities named in the act, to suspend the provisions for the free importation of certain articles into this country. Justice Harlan for the majority found no unconstitutional delegation. He pointed to a long array of statutes conferring discretion upon executive officers but, except for the brief mention in the Aurora case, he could instance no decision under Article I, section 1, which was clearly in point. But from the state decisions he could and did get useful precedents. For the Ohio Supreme Court Judge Ranney had said: "The true distinction is between the delegation of power to make a law, which necessarily involves a discretion as to what it shall be, and conferring authority or discretion as to its execution, to be exercised under and in pursuance of the law." [23] And from a Pennsylvania opinion he quoted with approval a statement of the theory of constitutional delegation, one which the Supreme Court was frequently to reaffirm:

> To assert that a law is less than a law, because it is made to depend on a future event or act, is to rob the legislature of the power to act wisely for the public welfare whenever a law is passed relating to a state of affairs not yet developed, or to things future and impossible to fully know. . . . The

[21] The Brig Aurora v. U.S., 7 Cranch 382 (1813). [22] 143 U.S. 649 (1892).
[23] Cincinnati, W. & Z. R. Co. v. Clinton County Comrs., 1 Ohio St. 88.

> legislature cannot delegate its power to make a law; but it can make a law to delegate a power to determine some fact or state of things upon which the law makes, or intends to make, its own action depend. To deny this would be to stop the wheels of government. There are many things upon which wise and useful legislation must depend which cannot be known to the law-making power, and must, therefore, be a subject of inquiry and determination outside of the halls of legislation.[24]

The Court seems never to have been seriously concerned about the delegated authority in the statutes establishing the regulatory commissions.[25] They apparently came well within the allowable scope described in Field v. Clark. But surely it is one of the really significant facts about the expansion of American constitutional law that these latter-day creations which combined elements of executive and judicial power and which exercised authority frequently bearing a close family resemblance to legislative power were accommodated within the old separation of powers theory without even a struggle. Without, indeed, a thorough examination of their constitutional character.

In the cases decided before 1935 where the Court did go into the delegation issue there is little more than a reiteration of the doctrine expressed in 1892. Thus in a case concerning the authority vested in the Secretary of War to prohibit the construction of bridges over navigable waters which would constitute obstructions to navigation the Court said that Congress had not abdicated its constitutional power.[26] It had itself determined the policy and had committed to the Secretary of War no power save that "of ascertaining all the facts essential" to determining upon the application of the policy in particular instances. Upon the same principle it was constitutional for Congress to delegate

[24] Locke's Appeal, 72 Penn. St. 491 (1873).

[25] Cf. Interstate Commerce Commission v. Illinois Central R.R., 215 U.S. 452 (1910). [26] Union Bridge Co. v. U.S., 204 U.S. 364 (1907).

to a board selected by the Secretary of the Treasury the determination of standards for tea to be imported into the United States.[27]

Other opinions reinforced the principle that "it was impracticable for Congress to provide general regulations for these various and varying details of management," [28] as well as the need for leaving to an executive agency the problem of deciding "exactly when its exercise of the legislative power should become effective." [29] There was, in short, an ungrudging recognition by the Court of the impossibility of legislation which would remove the necessity for discretion in the administration of the laws. But there was also, in nearly every opinion dealing with the problem, a reminder that Article I, section 1, prohibited Congress from delegating its legislative power. It was this reminder which the Court invoked when it passed upon the validity of the National Industrial Recovery Act in 1935.

[27] Buttfield v. Stranahan, 192 U.S. 470 (1904).

[28] U.S. v. Grimand, 220 U.S. 506, 516 (1911).

[29] J. W. Hampton, Jr. & Co. v. U.S., 276 U.S. 394, 407 (1928) and cases there cited.

Chapter VIII

THE RIGHTS OF PERSONS

IN SHARP contrast to the very small number of cases concerned with the relation of the three powers is the great mass of those involving the relation of governments and persons. Unfortunately it is impossible to convey an adequate conception of the character of the cases of this kind by citing statistics, but this procedure does at least suggest the size of the problem. Between 1899 and 1937 there were 212 cases in which state legislation was held to be unconstitutional for failure to preserve the guarantees of the Constitution regarding the rights of persons.[1] There were 18 such cases involving Congressional acts.

CIVIL RIGHTS

It has been pointed out that throughout the nineteenth century the cases involving civil liberties formed but a tiny proportion of the total number in which statutes were set aside. This continues to be true up to 1937, although after about 1930 the number of decisions giving protection to the civil rights of persons begins to show an appreciable increase. The increase is to be found entirely in the cases involving state laws, for in this entire period there were at

[1] This figure does not include 17 cases in which the Court relied upon the commerce and either the due process or the equal protection clause.

most four cases[2] in which Congressional statutes were set aside on this ground and the last came in 1922. All have to do with the protection of persons accused of crimes. None is of unusual interest or importance. There are two possible conclusions: either the Court was not giving adequate protection under the bill of rights, or Congress was not enacting legislation threatening the exercise of the rights there guaranteed. It may be pointed out in passing that the Espionage and Sedition Acts, as well as the Selective Service Act of the World War period, were sustained,[3] and that the only Congressional statute of these years held unconstitutional was one attempting to prevent profiteering in the necessities of life.[4]

The increased importance of the civil liberties cases where state legislation was held invalid results from the Court's changed attitude toward the scope of due process in the Fourteenth Amendment. To be sure there are a few cases where this revision is not the basis of decision. The "peonage" cases,[5] in which laws enforcing labor contracts were set aside, rested upon the Thirteenth Amendment, and the "grandfather" clauses were found to violate the Fifteenth Amendment.[6] That both sets of cases carried out the intentions of those amendments there can be no doubt. It is also not open to doubt that the combined effect of the reconstruction amendments did not serve to produce an equality of civil or

---

[2] Kirby v. U.S., 174 U.S. 47 (1899), Rassmussen v. U.S., 197 U.S. 516 (1905), U.S. v. Evans, 213 U.S. 297 (1909), U.S. v. Moreland, 258 U.S. 433 (1922). It is doubtful whether a statute was set aside in the Evans case but most lists of such decisions include it. Perhaps it should be listed as an instance of strained statutory construction.

[3] Schenck v. U.S., 249 U.S. 47 (1919), Debs v. U.S., 249 U.S. 211 (1919), Abrams v. U.S., 250 U.S. 616 (1919), U.S. v. Burleson, 255 U.S. 407 (1921), Selective Draft Law Cases, 245 U.S. 366 (1918). Cf. Carl B. Swisher, "Civil Liberties in War Time," *Political Science Quarterly,* LV, 321 (1940), Zechariah Chafee, Jr., *Free Speech in the United States* (1941), Part I.

[4] U.S. v. Cohen Grocery Co., 255 U.S. 81 (1921).

[5] Bailey v. Alabama, 219 U.S. 219 (1911), U.S. v. Reynolds, 235 U.S. 133 (1914). [6] Guinn v. U.S., 238 U.S. 347 (1915).

social standing for the negroes. After the Civil Rights cases it seemed that Congress had gained no effective authority from the sections in each of the amendments granting to that body power to enforce their prohibitions. There are a few cases in which the Supreme Court reversed convictions of negroes in the state courts,[7] but, between 1899 and 1937, the cases in which state laws discriminating against negroes were held contrary to the Fourteenth Amendment number but three, and two of those were later rendered of no effect by another Supreme Court ruling.

An ordinance of Louisville providing that negroes might not move into residential blocks where the occupants were primarily whites, and *vice versa,* was held contrary to due process as being an undue interference with property rights.[8] The equal protection clause was the basis for a ruling that Texas could not by statute exclude negroes from the Democratic primary.[9] The same ruling greeted a statute allowing the executive committee to prescribe the membership of the party.[10] In both instances it was found that the state was depriving citizens of their rights under the Amendment. But a rule of the party itself, even though the rule excluded negroes from participation in primary elections, was not an act of the state and consequently was constitutional.[11] The Court continued to see parties as private agencies even though they had become a closely integrated part of the machinery of election, one regulated by scores, if not hundreds, of statutes.

That a great many of those who voted for the Fourteenth

[7] Moore v. Dempsy, 261 U.S. 86 (1923), Brown v. Mississippi, 297 U.S. 278 (1936).

[8] Buchanan v. Warley, 245 U.S. 60 (1917). The effect of this decision was somewhat weakened by Corrigan v. Buckley, 271 U.S. 323 (1926) in which the Court held that a restrictive covenant in a deed or conveyance of real estate providing that the property shall never be leased or sold to a negro did not violate the due process clause.

[9] Nixon v. Herndon, 273 U.S. 536 (1927).

[10] Nixon v. Condon, 286 U.S. 73 (1932).

[11] Grovey v. Townsend, 295 U.S. 45 (1935).

Amendment thought that it would, somehow, make the first eight amendments binding upon the states is demonstrable. After the Court had laid the privileges and immunities clause to rest in the Slaughter House Case, only the due process clause remained as a constitutional basis for such a result. This prop was knocked out in 1884 and not explicitly restored until 1931. When California provided for indictment by information rather than by the traditional grand jury, it was argued by one so indicted that this violated due process of law. The Court held, however, that due process did not require indictment by grand jury.[12] The Fifth Amendment contains both the due process and the grand jury guarantees. Following the canon of interpretation according to which nothing is superfluous, it is evident that due process does not include the other guarantees set forth in the Fifth Amendment, or in the other amendments of the "bill of rights." This interpretation did not hinder the application of the due process clause to economic legislation, but it meant that its importance in the civil liberties field would be slight indeed.

In the first quarter of this century there is probably only one case in which due process in its traditional meaning was the basis for a holding of unconstitutionality as against a state statute. An Ohio statute providing that the mayor of rural villages might try offenses against the state prohibition law without jury, the mayor retaining the amount of costs in case of conviction, was found to lack due process because of the pecuniary interest of the judge in the outcome of the trial.[13] Such a ruling is in clear relation to precedent. But when the Court held invalid a Nebraska statute prohibiting teaching in any language other than English or teaching foreign languages before the eighth grade it was breaking new ground.[14]

[12] Hurtado v. California, 110 U.S. 516 (1884).

[13] Tumey v. Ohio, 273 U.S. 510 (1927).

[14] Meyer v. Nebraska, 262 U.S. 390 (1923). Variations on this ruling are found in Bartels v. Iowa, 262 U.S. 404 (1923), and Farrington v. Tokushige, 273 U.S. 284 (1927).

And Mr. Justice McReynolds wrote the opinion in this case, and also in the one invalidating the Oregon statute abolishing private schools for children between the ages of eight and sixteen,[15] as if only property rights were involved.

The Court was heading toward a broader protection of civil rights but it was hesitant in recognizing it. Or perhaps it may be more accurate to say that the Court saw the rights of education as property rather than as civil rights, for only a week after the Oregon public school case came the decision in which the Court both upheld a conviction under the New York criminal anarchy law and assumed that due process in the Fourteenth Amendment served to protect freedom of speech and of the press guaranteed in the First Amendment.[16] That the immediate effect of this assumption was not vast may be illustrated by the Whitney case sustaining a conviction under the California criminal syndicalism act.[17] Its scope was, however, narrowed slightly by the case immediately following, in which a conviction under a similar Kansas statute was set aside because it was not shown that the organization in which the defendant secured members advocated crime or violence.[18] Here the Court was overturning one application of a statute on the basis of a theory of the due process clause which had been ruled out in the Hurtado case forty years earlier, for in the Fiske case it was not a fair trial, in the traditional sense, but rather the right of free speech which was presumably involved. This is only a presumption, however, for the Court avoids explicitness on the point.

In 1931 two cases were decided in which, for the first time, state statutes were held to deny due process because of infringement of rights of freedom of speech and freedom of the

[15] Pierce v. Society of Sisters, 268 U.S. 510 (1925).
[16] Gitlow v. New York, 268 U.S. 652, 666 (1925).
[17] Whitney v. California, 274 U.S. 374 (1927).
[18] Fiske v. Kansas, 274 U.S. 380 (1927).

press.[19] This meant that the canon of interpretation followed in the Hurtado decision had been abandoned. To an as yet unsettled extent the guarantees of the first eight amendments had become limitations upon the states as well as upon the national government. There were several decisions of the next six years in which state judicial decisions were set aside for lack of due process in this broader sense,[20] but in only two cases were statutes found to violate the Bill of Rights. Both were ruled contrary to the First Amendment, a section of the Constitution which has not yet been the basis of a ruling against a congressional statute. In the first of them a "license tax" upon advertising revenues of all newspapers in Louisiana having a circulation of more than 2,000 per week was held to be a deliberate attempt to stifle the freedom of the press.[21] One of the facts brought to the attention of the Court was that twelve of the thirteen newspapers so taxed were in active opposition to the Huey Long regime. In the DeJonge case not an entire statute but one application of a criminal syndicalism act was held to deprive the defendant of the right to assemble and to discuss the public issues of the day.[22] It was not alleged that criminal syndicalism or communism was advocated at the meeting in question and the Court did not pass upon the validity of the statute if and when such doctrines were being advocated.

THE RIGHTS OF PROPERTY

As contrasted with the handful of civil liberties cases in this period there was a flood of decisions involving protection to the rights of property. It has been previously pointed out that up to the closing years of the nineteenth century the great majority of such cases were decided under the contract

[19] Stromberg v. California, 283 U.S. 359 (1931), Near v. Minnesota, 283 U.S. 697 (1931). [20] See especially Powell v. Alabama, 287 U.S. 45 (1932).

[21] Grosjean v. American Press Co., 297 U.S. 233 (1936).

[22] DeJonge v. Oregon, 299 U.S. 353 (1937).

clause. But because of the spread of the practice according to which the states reserved the right to alter or rescind charters or grants of tax immunity, and, to a lesser extent, because of the growth of the principle that there are certain powers which the states may not contract away, the usefulness of the contract clause as a bulwark of vested rights declined.[23] After the Court, during the nineties, finally and explicitly accepted the substantive interpretation of due process, that concept was of much greater usefulness to a Court which had taken upon itself a role which appeared to be similar to that discussed in the Convention of 1787 as belonging to a council of revision. To an unprecedented degree the Court became a censor of legislative reasonableness and rationality. States could not reserve powers as against the expanding concept of due process.

Excluding the civil liberties cases, there were 159 decisions under the due process and equal protection clauses in which state statutes were held to be unconstitutional, plus 16 in which both the due process and commerce clauses were involved, plus 9 more involving due process and some other clause or clauses. Had the Court adhered to the interpretation of the due process and equal protection clauses stated in the Slaughter House opinion less than a score of these decisions would have been possible. Indeed, not more than five of them are concerned with procedure.

As a result of Marshall's interpretation of the contract clause the Court gave an amount of protection to corporations which had not been anticipated, save possibly by Hamilton. As a consequence of the expansion of the due process and equal protection clauses the corporations were again the beneficiaries, a result anticipated by those who advocated that

---

[23] Wright, *op. cit.,* 95-100. By the time of Chief Justice Taft the proportion of contract clause cases to all others in which state laws were held unconstitutional was rather less than one-fourth as high as it had been before 1890.

expansion. A good many of the decisions are difficult to classify in these terms, but approximately three-fourths of them are concerned with the rights of corporations. Nearly a third involve public utilities. Obviously no simple generalization or set of generalizations can give an accurate picture of the results to be found in this body of decisions. Anything like accuracy would require a careful examination not only of all cases in which statutes, state and national, were held to violate the Fourteenth and the Fifth Amendments, but also a simultaneous consideration of the much larger number in which they were sustained. All that can be attempted in a brief compass is to indicate the character of the statutes held to be unconstitutional. Such a summary view may convey an impression of the scope and character of the Supreme Court's work in protecting the rights of property against the state and national legislation. After first indicating the principal groups of cases in which statutes were invalidated a few cases which appear to be of particular interest and to have had an appreciable impact upon recent events will be considered in more detail.

DUE PROCESS AND THE UTILITIES

After the Granger cases there was never any doubt that the states had the power to regulate the rates of public utilities. But after the series of decisions culminating in Smyth v. Ames [24] it was quite as certain that the legislative decision concerning rates was not final, that the courts must be allowed to pass upon its reasonableness. The courts, that is to say, would intervene to prevent the imposition of rates deemed to be so low as to deprive the owner of his right to a fair return on his property. The majority of the rate regulation cases involve the validity of the actions of administrative commissions rather than the validity of legislation, but there are many cases in which state laws were held to violate the

[24] *Supra,* 103-104.

maxims of a fair return. The largest group of these involves the railroads,[25] but the gas and electric companies figure in almost as many decisions,[26] and there are similar cases involving statutes or city ordinances regulating the rates of street railways,[27] water companies,[28] and telephone companies.[29] Still another concerned stockyards.[30]

There is considerable variety in the statutory devices held invalid in these decisions, but in all of them the Court is attempting to apply the principle that the investor is entitled to a fair return on his investment. That confidence in the finality of legislative decisions regarding rate-making which was expressed by Waite in the Granger cases gave way, during the reactionary eighties and nineties, to a Marshallian distrust of legislative competence. The reaction did not carry far enough explicitly to deny to the legislatures or their agents the power to fix rates for the utilities, although, as will be pointed out later, this power was sharply restricted outside of the utility field, but it did result in imposing upon the courts the duty of overseeing and reviewing this work of rate fixing. And it is to be understood that the Court was not concerned alone with procedure or method, nor even with the character of the factors to be taken into account. It went

[25] Lake Shore & Mich. S. Ry. Co. v. Smith, 173 U.S. 684 (1899), N. Pacific Ry. Co. v. N. Dakota, 216 U.S. 579 (1910), Mo. Pacific Ry. Co. v. Tucker, 230 U.S. 340 (1913), Minnesota Rate Cases, 230 U.S. 352 (1913), Missouri Rate Cases, 230 U.S. 474 (1913), Northern Pacific Ry. v. N. Dakota, 236 U.S. 585 (1915), Norfolk & Western Ry. Co. v. W. Va., 236 U.S. 605 (1915), Groesbeck v. Duluth Ry. Co., 250 U.S. 607 (1919).

[26] Wilcox v. Consolidated Gas Co., 212 U.S. 19 (1909), S. Iowa Elec. Co. v. Chariton, 255 U.S. 539 (1921), Newton v. Consol. Gas Co., 258 U.S. 165 (1922), Pacific Gas & Electric Co. v. San Francisco, 265 U.S. 403 (1924), Ottinger v. Consol. Gas Co., 272 U.S. 576 (1926), Columbus Gas Co. v. Ohio P.U. Comm., 292 U.S. 398 (1934).

[27] San Antonio v. San Antonio Public Service Co., 255 U.S. 547 (1921), Paducah v. Paducah Ry. Co., 261 U.S. 267 (1923).

[28] Denver v. Denver Union Water Co., 246 U.S. 178 (1918), San Joaquin Co. v. County, 233 U.S. 454 (1914).

[29] Home Tel. & Tel. Co. v. Los Angeles, 227 U.S. 278 (1913), Board v. New York Tel. Co., 271 U.S. 23 (1926).

[30] Cotting v. Kansas City Stockyards, 183 U.S. 79 (1901).

beyond those and examined into the adequacy of particular rates under the conditions of the given situation. Systems of accounting, fluctuations in values, interest rates, business conditions, obsolescence, standards of efficiency and of safety, these and many other factors were considered by the Court in the attempt to see that a fair return was being secured upon a fair valuation of the property devoted to the public service.

It may be added that although no similar act of Congress was held unconstitutional there are a number of cases dealing with the rate-fixing powers of the Interstate Commerce Commission in which the same elaborate technique is applied to the problem of attempting to balance the conflicting interests of the public in lower rates and of the railroads in higher rates.

So much attention has been given to the rate-making cases that the extent to which judicial review has been concerned with protecting the utilities against impositions of other kinds has not always been realized. Several decisions invalidated attempts to require the railroads to pay damages for livestock killed or fires set by trains promptly and in full, on penalty of double damages.[31] Others found that under particular circumstances, or without adequate notice and hearing, grade crossings could not be ordered abolished.[32] Requirements regarding compensation for street grading,[33] regarding the giving of a location for an elevator and maintaining a spur track,[34] regarding the interchange of cars and terminal facilities between railroads,[35] and imposing drastic penalties

---

[31] St. Louis, I.M. & Southern Ry. Co. v. Wynne, 224 U.S. 354 (1912), Chicago, M. & St. P. Ry. Co. v. Polt, 232 U.S. 165 (1914), Chicago M. & St. P. Ry. Co. v. Kennedy, 232 U.S. 626 (1914)

[32] Chicago, St.P., M., & O. Ry. Co. v. Holmberg, 282 U.S. 162 (1930), Southern Ry. Co. v. Va., 290 U.S. 190 (1933).

[33] Ettor v. Tacoma, 228 U.S. 148 (1913).

[34] Mo. Pacific Ry. Co. v. Nebraska, 217 U.S. 196 (1910).

[35] L. & N. R.R. Co. v. Central Stockyards Co., 212 U.S. 132 (1909).

for violation of the law [36] were all held to violate the due process or equal protection clauses. Municipal ordinances prohibiting gas works in certain localities,[37] taking over the rails and poles of a street railway whose franchise had expired,[38] and attempting to remove the property of a private utility in order to make way for a municipal system [39] are among the varied subjects to which the Supreme Court directed its attention in carrying out its self-imposed burden of acting as the defender of the rights of private property, even though that property had been devoted to a public use.

REASONABLE TAXES

A closely related group of cases are those in which taxes imposed upon public utilities were found to be discriminatory, or unreasonable because not related to the benefits derived by the property taxed.[40] But in the field of taxation the equal protection and due process clauses were by no means confined to the cases involving the railroads and other utilities. Indeed a body of case law of formidable proportions and astonishing complexity developed out of the expanded version of the Fourteenth Amendment. This was not foreshadowed in the earliest cases decided under that amendment, for when the Court in 1875 held a tax to be invalid because not levied for a "public" purpose it could find no more definite basis for its decision than the principles of free government and the general nature of the constitutional system.[41] Before the turn of the century the due

[36] Ex parte Young, 209 U.S. 123 (1908).
[37] Dobbins v. Los Angeles, 195 U.S. 223 (1904).
[38] Cleveland Electric Ry. Co. v. Cleveland Ry. Co., 204 U.S. 116 (1907).
[39] Los Angeles v. Los Angeles Gas & Electric Corp., 251 U.S. 32 (1919).
[40] Duluth & Iron Range R.R. Co. v. St. Louis, 179 U.S. 302 (1900), Kansas City S. Ry. Co. v. Road Dist., 256 U.S. 658 (1921), Thomas v. K.C.S. Ry. Co., 261 U.S. 481 (1923), Road Improvement District v. Missouri Pacific Ry. Co., 274 U.S. 188 (1927), Hopkins v. Southern Cal. Tel. Co., 275 U.S. 393 (1928).
[41] Loan Assn. v. Topeka, 20 Wallace 655 (1875).

process clause had become the justification for decisions of this kind. The Court has not been inclined to narrow the meaning of "public" so as to exclude taxes levied for the support of enterprises ordinarily or previously engaged in by private business,[42] but it has exercised a supervisory control over other features of tax policy. Not only must the procedure followed in assessing property be due procedure, but it must allow taxpayers the right to object in the courts.[43] And even if the procedure be fair, the tax, and usually such decisions apply to special assessments, will be invalidated if the Court believes that it does not bear a reasonable relation to the benefits or purposes for which it is levied.[44]

A recent variation of the tax problem has been the result of attempts to tax chain stores in relation not to the size or value of the stores considered individually, but in relation to the size of the entire chain. The Court, by a majority of one, upheld an Indiana occupation tax graduated according to the number of stores in the chain,[45] but later invalidated the feature in the Florida chain store tax which increased the tax when the stores were located in more than one county.[46] Three Justices dissented from this decision as they did from a subsequent finding that a tax upon gross sales denied equal protection when laid upon a graduated basis.[47]

By far the greater proportion of the cases in which tax statutes fell afoul of the due process and equal protection clauses was not concerned with public purpose or proce-

[42] Green v. Frazier, 253 U.S. 233 (1920).

[43] Londoner v. Denver, 210 U.S. 373 (1908), Turner v. Wade, 254 U.S. 64 (1920), Browning v. Hooper, 269 U.S. 396 (1926).

[44] Myles Salt Co. v. Board, 239 U.S. 478 (1916), Gas & Realty & Investment Co. v. Schneider Granite Co., 240 U.S. 55 (1916), Standard Pipe Line Co. v. Miller County District, 277 U.S. 160 (1928).

[45] State Board v. Jackson, 283 U.S. 527 (1931).

[46] Liggett Co. v. Lee, 288 U.S. 517 (1933).

[47] Stewart Dry Goods Co. v. Lewis, 294 U.S. 550 (1935).

dure, or, in the ordinary sense, benefits derived, or chain stores. They involved the question of jurisdiction to tax. It is one of the surprising characteristics of modern American constitutional law that an elaborate set of rules and precedents concerning what is essentially one phase of federalism should have been built up under protection of the clauses of the Fourteenth Amendment which were expected to give protection to certain civil liberties. The problem is not federalism in the traditional sense, the relative rights of states and national government not being involved. It is rather the relationship between state and state, or, perhaps it would be more accurate to say, between state and property located in other states.

The Court early held that attempts to tax property located outside the jurisdiction of the state were invalid because they would deprive the owners of their property without due process of law. This principle held for both tangible[48] and intangible[49] property. But it would be more difficult than profitable to attempt to follow the decisions of the Court through the maze of distinctions in which the subject abounds. In 29 cases between 1899 and 1937 the Court held state legislation to be in violation of the due process and equal protection clauses[50] which in some way discriminated against out-of-state enterprises or attempted to tax property which was found not to be within the tax jurisdiction of the state. A good number of these cases grew out of the proliferation of business beyond state lines, and the issue of foreign corporations was dealt with, in part at least, not as a question involving the commerce clause, but as one coming under the due process rubric.[51] When a cor-

---

[48] Delaware, L. & W. R.R. Co. v. Pa., 198 U.S. 341 (1905), Union Refrigerator Transit Co. v. Ky., 199 U.S. 194 (1905).

[49] Buck v. Beach, 206 U.S. 392 (1907).

[50] Four of the decisions were also based upon the commerce clause.

[51] Some issues other than taxation but involving foreign corporations are discussed in Ky. Finance Corp. v. Paramount Auto Exchange Corp., 262

poration operates in several states it may, under the so-called unit rule, be taxed in the relation which the business done in the state bears to the value of the entire system. But the acceptance of this general rule was not an end of the problem.[52] Similarly the problem of taxing intangibles was not settled by acceptance of the general principle of *mobilia sequuntur personam*. The Court found exceptional circumstances in which this seemed to be an unjust basis of decision.[53] The taxation of inheritances has been particularly productive of difficult problems, of fine distinctions, and of changes of doctrine.[54]

Income and gift taxes, both state and national, produced a further crop of decisions in which legislation was held to deny due process. It is particularly significant of the character of the task performed by the Court in these cases that the division of the Justices so frequently found in cases involving legislation concerning social policy and government regulation of labor or industry is usually repeated here. The differences of opinion on the Court resulted not from varying logical devices but from divergent premises, and the premises were the product of different attitudes toward governmental policy and toward the role of judicial review. This is made clear again and again in the dissenting opinions of Justices Holmes, Brandeis, and Stone.[55]

U.S. 544 (1923), Fidelity & Deposit Co. of Maryland v. Tafoya, 270 U.S. 426 (1926), Power Mfg. Co. v. Saunders, 274 U.S. 490 (1927), Louis K. Liggett Co. v. Baldridge, 278 U.S. 105 (1928).

[52] See, e.g., Hans Rees' Sons Inc. v. North Carolina, 283 U.S. 123 (1931), as well as cases there cited.

[53] Safe Deposit & Trust Co. v. Va., 280 U.S. 83 (1929).

[54] See especially Farmers Loan & Trust Co. v. Minnesota, 280 U.S. 204 (1930), Baldwin v. Missouri, 281 U.S. 586 (1930), Frick v. Pennsylvania, 268 U.S. 473 (1925), Blodgett v. Silverman, 277 U.S. 1 (1928), First National Bank of Boston v. Maine, 284 U.S. 312 (1932).

[55] See Schlesinger v. Wisconsin, 270 U.S. 230 (1926), Untermyer v. Anderson, 276 U.S. 440 (1928), Hoeper v. Tax Comm., 284 U.S. 206 (1931), Heiner v. Donnan, 285 U.S. 312 (1932), Senior v. Braden, 295 U.S. 422 (1935), Binney v. Long, 299 U.S. 280 (1936).

To leave the due process field for a moment, it is significant that the Court did not follow the scheme of interpretation when viewing the words of the Sixteenth Amendment that it had employed for the Fourteenth. It will be remembered that the literal application of "no state shall" in the earlier amendment had served to render ineffective the positive power of Congress which many thought had been granted by Section V of that provision. In the Sixteenth Amendment it is stipulated that "The Congress shall have power to lay and collect taxes on incomes, from whatever source derived, without apportionment. . . ." If given a literal interpretation, and certainly there were those who believed that it should be so read, the phrase "from whatever source derived," would very considerably increase the breadth of Congress' tax power. But, said the Court, in a very involved opinion, the effect of the amendment was not to broaden the scope of the taxing power; only the method of taxation had been changed by altering the rule laid down in the Pollock case so as to relieve income taxes [56] from the necessity of apportionment. The income from state securities and salaries paid by the state could no more be taxed now than before the adoption of the amendment. Nor could Congress subject the salaries of the federal judges to an income tax.[57] In short the Court here followed not the words of the amendment, as it had done when considering the power of Congress under the Fourteenth Amendment, but the purpose behind the new provision—as the Court interpreted it. In one important sense the result was the same in both sets of decisions, to narrow the scope of Congressional power. The spirit of the majority decision in the Pollock case lived on long after the adoption of the income tax amendment.

---

[56] Brushaber v. Union Pacific R.R. Co., 240 U.S. 1 (1916).

[57] Evans v. Gore, 253 U.S. 245 (1920).

PRIVILEGES AND IMMUNITIES

A decision which, as much as any other, represents the culmination of the point of view expressed so frequently in the tax cases of this period is Colgate v. Harvey.[58] A Vermont income tax law exempted income from money loaned inside the state while taxing income from loans outside the state. This was held to deny the equal protection of the laws. The majority, as if not content with the breadth of the Court's discretion in tax cases when applying the equal protection and due process clauses, then went on to hold that this statute also violated the privileges and immunities provision of the Fourteenth Amendment. A citizen of the United States has the right to engage in business, to make loans in any state other than that in which he resides, and for a state to restrict or discriminate against this right is a denial of the privileges or immunities clause. There was no precedent for this decision, at least none nearer than the Allgeyer case, and there this clause was not invoked. The novelty of the Court's ruling, as well as the possibilities that it held for the future scope of judicial review, were well described in Mr. Justice Stone's dissenting opinion, one in which Justices Brandeis and Cardozo concurred:

> Feeble indeed is an attack on a statute as denying equal protection which can gain any support from the almost forgotten privileges and immunities clause of the Fourteenth Amendment. The notion that that clause could have any application to any but the privileges and immunities peculiar to citizenship of the United States, as distinguished from those of citizens of states, has long since been rejected. . . . Since the adoption of the Fourteenth Amendment at least forty-four cases have been brought to this Court in which state statutes have been assailed as infringements of the privileges and immunities clause. Until today none has held that state legislation infringed that clause. If its sweep were

[58] 296 U.S. 404 (1935).

> now to be broadened to include protection of every transaction across state lines, regardless of its connection with any relationship between the citizen and the national government, a step would be taken, the gravity of which might well give us concern. . . .[59]

STATE POLICE POWERS

Important and numerous as are the cases involving taxation they are, after all, but one group in which the Court was concerned with the relationship between state or national power and the rights of property. There are many others. The legal doctrines set forth in these cases amount to a great number of variations upon the theme that statutes must be reasonable and not arbitrary. It is not sufficient that the general principle and purpose of the statute be valid; particular applications of a generally valid statute may deny due process. Thus the example of zoning ordinances. In 1926 a divided Court sustained the principle that municipalities might regulate the character and use of buildings in the interest of the health, safety, and property of their citizens.[60] Two years later another zoning ordinance was found invalid to the extent that one particular piece of property had been incorrectly placed in a residential zone rather than in a business zone.[61] Somewhat similar situations are found where the Court, though upholding the power of the states to enact anti-trust legislation, refused to sustain all acts of this kind. Classification is allowable, but not all classification, and an anti-trust act exempting agricultural products while in the hands of the producer denied equal protection.[62]

---

[59] *Ibid.*, 443, 445-446.

[60] Euclid v. Ambler Realty Co., 272 U.S. 365 (1926).

[61] Nectow v. Cambridge, 277 U.S. 183 (1928). Cf. Washington v. Roberge, 278 U.S. 116 (1928).

[62] Connolly v. Union Sewer Pipe Co., 184 U.S. 540 (1902). Cf. International Harvester Co. v. Kentucky, 234 U.S. 216 (1914), Collins v. Kentucky, 234 U.S. 634 (1914), Cline v. Frink Dairy Co., 274 U.S. 445 (1927).

Only a comprehensive survey of the cases can give an accurate picture of the extent to which the state police power was, before 1937, limited by the doctrines developed by the Court in its interpretation of the Fourteenth Amendment.[63] The recitation of a few such decisions may at least give a rough indication of some of the kinds of statutes held invalid.

An act prohibiting the mining of coal under a city to such an extent as to cause the subsidence of buildings was found to deny due process when applied to a mine where this right was reserved in a grant.[64] The requirement that loaves of bread must weigh one-half pound or one pound or multiples thereof denied due process wherever applied.[65] A law forbidding the use of shoddy in comfortables also denied vested rights of property under the Fourteenth Amendment.[66] A statute requiring private carriers using the public highways to be subject to the duties and burdens of common carriers,[67] and an ordinance making the road from the railroad station available to all taxicabs when the railroad had previously contracted with a single cab company to allow it exclusive use of the road, which was stipulated to be not a public road, were both held to be unconstitutional.[68] In none of these cases were all of the members of the Court in complete agreement. There was no dissent, however, from the holding that a pipe line company would not be required to

[63] Such a survey for the period of Chief Justice Taft, an era in which the Court viewed state legislation with an exceptionally suspicious eye, is found in the series of articles by Thomas Reed Powell, "The Supreme Court and State Police Power, 1922-1930," in 17 and 18 *Virginia Law Review* (1931, 1932). In the appendix to Felix Frankfurter, *Mr. Justice Holmes and the Supreme Court* (1938) will be found a comprehensive list of cases in which state action was held contrary to the Fourteenth Amendment through 1938. As the one-sentence summaries indicate, this list includes decisions invalidating the action of state courts and administrative agencies as well as those ruling against state statutes.

[64] Pennsylvania Coal Co. v. Mahon, 260 U.S. 393 (1922).

[65] Jay Burns Baking Co. v. Bryan, 264 U.S. 504 (1924).

[66] Weaver v. Palmer Brothers Co., 270 U.S. 402 (1926).

[67] Frost v. R.R. Commission, 271 U.S. 583 (1926).

[68] Delaware, L. & W. R.R. Co. v. Morristown, 276 U.S. 182 (1928).

remove or lower its pipes when new highways were laid across its right of way.[69] And a statute was unanimously held to deprive oil-well owners of their property without due process which so limited the daily production of the oil wells owned by companies owning pipe lines as to furnish a market for those wells having no pipe-line connections.[70] This decision was, by the way, handed down just before the President introduced his judiciary proposal on February 5, 1937, and it stands today as one of the last of the old-style due process rulings.

"A PUBLIC INTEREST"

Among the most interesting episodes in the history of due process is that associated with the concept of business affected with a public interest.[71] The origin of the concept is found in a short essay on the ports of the sea written by Lord Chief Justice Hale about 1670, but not published until 1787. Two centuries after it was written the attorneys appearing for the plaintiff in Munn v. Illinois cited this treatise in support of the proposition that the grain elevators subjected to price regulation were not among the kinds of business which had traditionally been considered subject to government control of this kind, and that therefore the owners of the elevators were being deprived of their property without due process of law. In the Munn opinion Chief Justice Waite borrowed the phrase, but held that the elevators were a business affected with a public interest.[72] He engaged in the practice observed by generations of common law judges of pouring a new content into an old concept. The underlying assumption of

---

[69] Panhandle Eastern Pipe Line Co. v. Highway Comm., 294 U.S. 613 (1935). [70] Thompson v. Consolidated Gas Co., 300 U.S. 55 (1937).

[71] Walton H. Hamilton, "Affectation with a Public Interest," 39 *Yale Law Journal,* 1089 (1930), Breck P. McAllister, "Lord Hale and Business Affected with a Public Interest," 43 *Harvard Law Review,* 759 (1930). Both articles are reprinted in *Selected Essays on Constitutional Law,* II.

[72] Munn v. Illinois, 94 U.S. 113 (1877).

Waite's ruling, that changing economic conditions may enlarge the sphere of business enterprises which might be regulated by statute, was, so far as concerns this particular concept, adhered to by the Court until the twenties of the next century. Thus in two later cases statutes regulating the prices charged by grain elevators were sustained, and, whether Waite had believed that monopolistic conditions existed in this field in Illinois, they did not exist in at least one of the areas where similar legislation was upheld.[73] And in German Alliance Insurance Co. v. Kansas [74] the Court sustained the regulation of fire insurance rates on the ground of the importance of the business in the particular circumstances existing in Kansas. There was no monopoly and no franchise. The business was not comparable to any discussed by Lord Hale. Only a realistic view of the position of fire insurance in the Kansas rural economy justified the holding of the Court.

Five decisions handed down between 1923 and 1932 indicated that the concept borrowed by Waite from counsel arguing against price control could be employed as well by a majority suspicious of legislative regulation. The statutes dealt with a variety of subjects and of regulative devices, but all were held invalid as violating the injunctions of the Fourteenth Amendment. A Kansas compulsory arbitration act as applied to the packing industry,[75] a New York statute forbidding the resale of theatre tickets at an increase of more than fifty cents per ticket,[76] a New Jersey law requiring persons operating employment agencies to secure licenses from a state commission and subjecting them to price regulation,[77] a Tennessee act regulating the price of gasoline,[78] and an Oklahoma statute prohibiting anyone from entering the ice

---

[73] Budd v. New York, 143 U.S. 517 (1892), Brass v. Stoeser, 153 U.S. 391 (1894). [74] 233 U.S. 389 (1914).

[75] Wolff Packing Co. v. Court of Industrial Relations, 262 U.S. 522 (1923).

[76] Tyson v. Banton, 273 U.S. 418 (1927).

[77] Ribnik v. McBride, 277 U.S. 350 (1928).

[78] Williams v. Standard Oil Co., 278 U.S. 235 (1929).

business without a certificate of necessity and convenience from a state agency [79] were all found to be regulations which were not justified in businesses which were not affected with a public interest.

Only in the first of these cases was the Court unanimous and only there is an attempt made to supply general criteria according to which a business affected with a public interest may be recognized as such. Chief Justice Taft says that such enterprises are of three kinds: those carried on under a public grant or franchise (in general, public utilities), those traditionally subject to regulation, and those "which though not public at their inception may be said to have risen to be such and have become subject in consequence to some government regulation." [80] But this set of criteria does not go far toward solving the constitutional issues involved in government regulation. The first two categories had long been recognized as such; the entire debate was over the inclusiveness of the third. In the theatre ticket, employment agency, gasoline, and ice cases it is obvious that a Court which had unanimously believed that the business of meat packing was not so affected with a public interest as to justify compulsory arbitration was sharply, even bitterly, divided over the further applications of the doctrine. Finally, in 1934 the unsatisfactory character of the concept was recognized by a bare majority of the Court when it decided to reverse the trend of the twenties and return to the attitude of Waite.

In the course of his opinion in the Oklahoma Ice case Mr. Justice Sutherland (who wrote the opinions in all of this group excepting the Wolff case) said that the ice business was "as essentially private in its nature as the business of the

---

[79] New State Ice Co. v. Liebmann, 285 U.S. 262 (1932).

[80] 262 U.S. at 535. It may be remarked that this concept was never employed to sustain a decision of unconstitutionality as against an act of Congress. It was, however, referred to in opinions upholding certain statutes. Cf. Stafford v. Wallace, 258 U.S. 495 (1922), Tagg Brothers and Morehead v. U.S., 280 U.S. 420 (1930).

grocer, the dairyman, the butcher, the baker, the shoemaker, or the tailor. . . ." [81] Evidently there could be no doubt about the immunity of such business from government regulation, save that justified as necessary for the protection of public health, safety, or morals. Yet just two years later the Court voted five-to-four to sustain price regulation involving both dairymen and grocers. Two of the five, Chief Justice Hughes and Mr. Justice Roberts, had voted with Sutherland in the Ice case. Here they voted with Justices Brandeis, Stone, and Cardozo to sustain an elaborate New York milk-control statute, one under which a small grocer was held subject to a penalty for selling milk at less than the prescribed price.[82] This could not possibly be justified on the basis of the criteria and points of view expressed in the cases just considered. What Mr. Justice Roberts, who wrote the majority opinion, does is to accept the point of view of the former dissenters, the doctrine strongly urged by Holmes and Stone, and expressed by Brandeis in the Oklahoma Ice Co. dissent in these words: "In my opinion, the true principle is that the State's power extends to every regulation of any business reasonably required and appropriate for the public protection." [83] But Roberts was not content to bury the test of affectation with a public interest, and to substitute the less faulty principle that regulation is to be exercised subject to the general requirements of due process. Having done this he goes on to say:

> "The due process clause makes no mention of sales or of prices any more than it speaks of business or contracts or buildings or other incidents of property. The thought seems nevertheless to have persisted that there is something peculiarly sacrosanct about the price one may charge for what he makes or sells, and that, however able to regulate other elements of manufacture or trade, with incidental effect upon price, the state is incapable of directly controlling the price

[81] 285 U.S. at 277. [82] Nebbia v. New York, 291 U.S. 502 (1934).
[83] 285 U.S. at 302-303.

itself. This view was negatived many years ago. Munn v. Illinois."[84]

Both in holding and in doctrinal justification the Nebbia decision cuts squarely across the line pursued by the Court for at least a dozen years. The majority opinion ignores rather than overrules the conflicting cases of the past, but in the dissenting opinion of Mr. Justice McReynolds there is no such restraint.

It might reasonably be assumed that the Nebbia decision would mean a virtual end of substantive due process employed for the protection of property rights. This it did not mean any more than it had the effect of restoring equal protection to the meaning expressed by the Court in the Slaughter House Cases. Between Nebbia and the Court battle there were ten cases in which the due process and equal protection clauses were employed in the fashion so generously used during the twenties.

Of these decisions the one most closely related to the Nebbia case is that in which a section of the New York Milk Control Act was held invalid for denial of equal protection.[85] This section permitted those small milk distributors who were in business before 1933 to sell at a slightly lower price than those dealers having a well-advertised trade name. Mr. Justice Roberts again wrote the majority opinion, but three of the four who had been with him in the Nebbia case dissented. The crucial proof that the Nebbia opinion did not mean all that might be found in it is the minimum wage decision of 1936. But before considering the series of labor cases, of which it is the culmination, it may be well to take a brief glance at the contract clause decisions which offer a parallel instance to the 1934 interpretation of due process.

---

[84] 291 U.S. at 532.

[85] Mayflower Farms Inc. v. Ten Eyck, 297 U.S. 266 (1936). Cf. the earlier case of Fairmont Creamery Co. v. Minnesota, 274 U.S. 1 (1927).

DEPRESSION LEGISLATION AND CONTRACTS

It has been pointed out that the founding fathers were apparently seeking to prevent legislative interference with existing private contracts when they accepted the provision in Article I, section 10, prohibiting impairment of the obligation of contracts. Until 1934 the Court, while applying the clause principally to protecting charter rights and other contracts to which states were parties, did interpret it so as to render invalid all statutes coming before it which retrospectively affected such contracts.[86] The Great Depression, like the lesser depression of the Confederation era, produced a variety of statutes attempting to ease the plight of mortgage debtors. One such statute was sustained in the surprising Blaisdell decision.[87]

The statute here sustained by a five-to-four vote authorized the courts to extend the existing one-year period of redemption from foreclosure sales. It was to be in effect only during the emergency, but not beyond May 1, 1935. While the statute was more carefully drafted than most of those previously held unconstitutional, and while it attempted to protect the interest of the creditor, it did alter the debtor-creditor relationship retrospectively, and it applied to more than the remedial elements of the contract. Chief Justice Hughes, in sustaining the act, relied heavily upon the theory that in a time of economic distress the state may act to prevent "the immediate and literal enforcement of contractual obligations by a temporary and conditional restraint." But, as Mr. Justice Sutherland argues in dissent, the clause was written at the end of a period of depression and was intended to prevent just such "stay" laws in just such circumstances. Nor is there difficulty in showing that the decision is out of line with the precedents.

---

[86] Wright, *The Contract Clause,* 104ff.

[87] Home Building & Loan Assn. v. Blaisdell, 290 U.S. 398 (1934).

Here, in brief, is a holding which taken with the Nebbia ruling appeared to show that the Court was prepared to take a much more tolerant attitude toward the statutes which represented the almost frantic attempt to deal with the acute situations produced in the economic life of the nation by depression. During the next two years, however, the decisions under the contract clause indicated that the Blaisdell ruling, for all its implications, was to be confined within narrow bounds and that statutes altering contract relationships would be viewed with almost, if not quite, as suspicious an eye as before.[88]

DUE PROCESS AND LABOR LEGISLATION

While the number of cases in which the Court has held unconstitutional statutes seeking to ameliorate the conditions of labor has not been large, these decisions have a significance out of all proportion to their quantity. They dramatized, as did no other decisions between 1895 and 1935, the breadth of the discretionary power within which the Court operated. And to students of constitutional history they helped to make clear the gap between the intentions and the accomplishment of those who voted for the adoption of the Fourteenth Amendment.

The transformation of due process from its earlier meaning of due procedure to a primary concern with the reasonableness of legislation involving not procedure but the substantive rights of property was sketched in the preceding chapter. Of the many decisions between 1899 and 1937 in which statutes fell afoul of the Fourteenth Amendment, it is doubtful whether more than seven [89] of them can be classi-

[88] In Wright, *op. cit.*, 111-119, these cases are reviewed and their tendency analyzed.

[89] Roller v. Holly, 176 U.S. 398 (1900), Central of Georgia Ry. v. Wright, 207 U.S. 127 (1907), Ex parte Young, 209 U.S. 123 (1908), Coe v. Armour, 237 U.S. 413 (1915), McDonald v. Mabee, 243 U.S. 90 (1917), Flexner v. Farson,

fied as dealing with exclusively, or even primarily, procedural matters, although there is a somewhat larger group of cases in which the Court employed that amendment as the basis for invalidating the rulings of state judicial or administrative agencies on grounds of faulty procedure. But with the maturity of the liberty of contract concept the way was prepared for a group of decisions against labor laws which did much to bring about the controversy of 1937.

In 1898 the Court sustained a Utah statute limiting the working day for men employed in mines and smelters to eight hours.[90] The Court accepted, however, the liberty of contract theory as expressed the previous year in the Allgeyer case, and justified this statute as a legitimate exercise of the police power under the circumstances of the particular occupations here involved. In short the act was a health law and as such was valid.[91] When, however, the Court was asked, seven years later, to rule upon the constitutionality of a New York statute limiting the number of hours which an employee could be required to work in bakeries to sixty in one week, or not over ten per day, except for the purpose of making a shorter workday on Saturdays, the majority ruled that the statute was not a health law, but was a "mere meddlesome interference with the rights of the individual." [92] Mr. Justice Peckham, who had dissented in Holden v. Hardy, wrote the Lochner opinion. It is a classic example of that brand of *laissez faire* ideology which the judiciary grafted on to the due process stem after 1890. One would hardly get the impression from reading his opinion that liberty of contract, as he envisages it, had been discovered less than fifteen years

---

248 U.S. 289 (1919), Turner v. Wade, 254 U.S. 64 (1920), Wuchter v. Pizzutti, 276 U.S. 13 (1928). Most of these deal with the service of legal process on nonresidents. [90] Holden v. Hardy, 169 U.S. 366 (1898).

[91] The Court has traditionally been inclined to sustain statutes seeking to protect the public health and morals. See Ray A. Brown, "Police Power-Legislation for Health and Personal Safety," 42 *Harvard Law Review,* 866 (1929). [92] Lochner v. New York, 198 U.S. 45 (1905).

earlier.[93] To him it is one of the eternal verities that this liberty was guaranteed by the Constitution and that it preserves the inalienable right of employer and employee alike to make contracts for their mutual advantage. That being so, "the limit of the police power has been reached and passed in this case."

This was the first case in which a labor statute was held contrary to the Fourteenth Amendment. That alone would have made it of exceptional interest. The further fact that four members of the Court dissented added to the case's notoriety. The dissenting opinion of Justice Harlan, concurred in by Justices White and Day, was a vigorous, lawyer-like disputation. But the separate dissent of Justice Holmes was something new under the sun. After expressing regret that he is unable to agree with the majority he bluntly remarks, "This case is decided upon an economic theory which a large part of the country does not entertain."[94] Now Holmes, appointed to the Court three years before, was easily the member of the Court most learned in the history and system of the common law, as his edition of Kent, his *The Common Law* (1882), and his opinions during his twenty years on the Supreme Judicial Court of Massachusetts all demonstrated. He was not a partisan, certainly not a reformer. His conception of the scope of judicial review, rather than his legal learning or his economic conservatism, furnishes the key to this extraordinarily influential dissenting opinion. "If it were a question whether I agreed with that theory," he continues, "I should desire to study it further and long before making up my mind. But I do not conceive that to be my duty, because I strongly believe that my agreement or disagreement has nothing to do with the right of a majority to embody their opinions in law." After pointing to some of the instances of laws sustained by the Court which

---

[93] Roscoe Pound, "Liberty of Contract," 18 *Yale Law Journal* 454 (1909), *Selected Essays on Constitutional Law,* II, 208. [94] 198 U.S. at 75.

interfere with the liberty of contract, he remarks that the "Fourteenth Amendment does not enact Mr. Herbert Spencer's Social Statics," and the agreement or disagreement of the judges with the purpose of the laws is an irrelevant consideration. The Constitution is not intended to embody a particular economic theory, either of *laissez faire* or paternalism. "It is made for people of fundamentally differing views, and the accident of our finding certain opinions natural and familiar or novel and even shocking, ought not to conclude our judgment upon the question whether statutes embodying them conflict with the Constitution of the United States."

Holmes did not retire from the Court for twenty-seven years after the Lochner case, but nevertheless it was not until five years after his retirement that the point of view expressed in 1905 really began to represent the attitude of the majority of the Court. But, in the meantime, his dissenting opinions continue to reiterate the gospel of judicial tolerance. Thus, when the Court, dividing five-to-four, held invalid an Arizona act prohibiting injunctions against terminating any relation of employment, Holmes concludes a brief dissent in much the words used in 1905:

> There is nothing that I more deprecate than the use of the 14th Amendment beyond the absolute compulsion of its words to prevent the making of social experiments that an important part of the community desires, in the insulated chambers afforded by the several states, even though the experiments may seem futile or even noxious to me and to those whose judgment I most respect.[95]

It has earlier been remarked that the first case in which an act of Congress was held invalid for violation of due process

[95] Truax v. Corrigan, 257 U.S. 312, 344 (1921). It should not be assumed that Holmes was opposed to all use of substantive due process for the protection of property rights. He concurred in approximately three-fourths of the cases in which state action was held contrary to the Fourteenth Amendment. Cf. Frankfurter, *op. cit.*, appendix.

in the Fifth Amendment was the section of the Erdman Act imposing a penalty upon interstate carriers who discharged employees solely because of membership in labor unions.[96] Holmes and McKenna dissented. A few weeks later, however, a unanimous Court sustained the Oregon law limiting the working day for women to ten hours.[97] The opinion was written by Mr. Justice Brewer who had dissented in Holden v. Hardy, as well as in the case sustaining the Massachusetts compulsory vaccination statute.[98] The having and dissemination of smallpox was apparently a right under the Fourteenth Amendment, according to Brewer and Peckham. It was Brewer who had ended his dissent in Budd v. New York [99] by a diatribe against "the paternal theory of government." He was willing to make an exception of a labor statute protecting women, but he is careful to add that this does not question "in any respect the decision in Lochner v. New York."

It is highly probable that the brief submitted by Mr., subsequently Mr. Justice, Brandeis, in the Muller case helped to account for the decision. He devoted two pages to legal citations and a hundred to evidence drawn from reports of public health authorities, bureaus of statistics, and inspectors of factories, all with the intent of indicating the relation between the Oregon statute and the health of women.[100] The same kind of brief was presented a few years later when the Court passed in the Bunting case upon the Oregon statute providing for the ten-hour day for men employed in factories

[96] Adair v. U.S., 208 U.S. 161 (1908). There are twelve cases after this in which Congressional statutes were held to violate due process. All involve property rights, none civil liberties. In only two is there even a remote relation to a procedural issue. See the lists in Haines, *op. cit.*, 541ff., and the Library of Congress pamphlet, *Provisions of Federal Law held Unconstitutional* (Government Printing Office, 1936).

[97] Muller v. Oregon, 208 U.S. 412 (1908).

[98] Jacobson v. Massachusetts, 197 U.S. 11 (1905). [99] 143 U.S. 517 (1892).

[100] Alpheus T. Mason, *Brandeis: Lawyer and Judge in the Modern State*, 108 (1933).

in that state.[101] Doubtless the criticism leveled at the Lochner decision was not without its effect, and the opinion of Mr. Justice McKenna for the majority almost assumes the validity of an hours law, and considers whether the statute is in reality a wages law, because of the time-and-a-half for overtime provision. This too is sustained, the Court deferring, as it certainly had not in the Lochner opinion, to the legislative judgment. Apparently Lochner was disregarded but it was not explicitly overruled.

The Bunting decision is hardly proof that the Court was in an era of tolerance so far as labor legislation was concerned, for in 1915 a Kansas act, which was similar in character to the Congressional act held invalid in the Adair case, was held to be in denial of due process,[102] and in 1917 a Washington statute forbidding employment agents from receiving fees from workers for whom they found places was set aside.[103]

A more serious setback to the hopes raised by the Bunting decision, as well as those sustaining workmen's compensation legislation,[104] was the minimum wage decisions. The Court had upheld statutes requiring redemption in cash of store orders issued in payment of wages,[105] and prohibiting mining operators from screening coal in order to reduce the wages paid the miners.[106] But the regulation of the rate of wages proved to be a different question. In 1919 (Justice Brandeis who had been of counsel not taking part), the Court divided evenly on the validity of an Oregon minimum wage law.[107] Six years later, in Adkins v. Children's Hospital, it voted five-to-three, Brandeis again not participating, against an act

[101] Bunting v. Oregon, 243 U.S. 426 (1917).

[102] Coppage v. Kansas, 236 U.S. 1 (1915). Justices Holmes, Day, and Hughes dissented. [103] Adams v. Tanner, 244 U.S. 590 (1917).

[104] New York Central R.R. Co. v. White, 243 U.S. 188 (1917), Mountain Timber Co. v. Washington, 243 U.S. 219 (1917).

[105] Knoxville Iron Co. v. Harbison, 183 U.S. 13 (1901).

[106] McLean v. Arkansas, 211 U.S. 539 (1909).

[107] Stettler v. O'Hara, 243 U.S. 629 (1917).

of Congress providing a minimum wage law for women in the District of Columbia.[108]

The point of view is essentially that of the Lochner opinion, of which Mr. Justice Sutherland notes that "Subsequent cases in this Court have been distinguished from that decision, but the principles therein stated have never been disapproved." A brief of the Brandeis type, submitted by Mr., later Mr. Justice, Frankfurter, drew the comment that materials have been presented to show the great benefits of such laws in the states, "all of which we have found interesting but only mildly persuasive." The standards set forth in the statute according to which the wage board was to fix a minimum wage were found to be vague and indefinite, demonstrating the "fatal uncertainty of the act." The act takes into account the needs of only one party to the contract, and the wage as fixed "need have no relation to the capacity or earning power of the employee." It is therefore arbitrary and a taking of property without due process. "To sustain the individual freedom of action contemplated by the Constitution, is not to strike down the common good but to exalt it; for surely the good of society as a whole cannot be better served than by the preservation against arbitrary restraint of the liberties of its constituent members."[109]

A few years later two *per curiam* decisions disposed of state minimum wage laws on the authority of the Adkins decision.[110] In 1926 an Oklahoma statute punishing contractors on public works for paying workmen less than the current *per diem* rate in the locality was held to deny due process because of its uncertainty and indefiniteness.[111] The sharp distinction drawn by Justice Sutherland between the regulation of wages, on the one hand, and the regulation of hours or other features of the wage contract, on the other, is paral-

[108] 261 U.S. 525 (1923). Justices Taft, Holmes, and Sanford dissented.

[109] *Ibid.*, 561.

[110] Murphy v. Sardell, 269 U.S. 530 (1925), Donham v. West-Nelson Mfg. Co., 273 U.S. 657 (1927).

[111] Connally v. General Construction Co., 269 U.S. 385 (1926).

leled in a number of the cases discussed in connection with the affectation with a public interest concept. That distinction should have perished with Mr. Justice Roberts' declaration in the Nebbia opinion that the Fourteenth Amendment said nothing of prices, that they were not particularly sacrosanct. That it did not was made dramatically evident in Morehead v. New York *ex rel.* Tipaldo.[112] Here the Court held a New York minimum wage for women statute invalid on the basis of precisely the same theory employed thirteen years earlier in the Adkins case. The Court divided five-to-four, Mr. Justice Roberts, author of the Nebbia opinion, being of the majority which spoke through Mr. Justice Butler. Chief Justice Hughes dissented, arguing that a distinction should be drawn between this act and those earlier held unconstitutional, in that the New York law provided that the minimum wage should correspond to the fair value of the service performed. Mr. Justice Stone, with whom Mr. Justice Brandeis and Mr. Justice Cardozo concurred, dissented on broader grounds. He argued, in terms reminiscent of Holmes, that the entire principle of the Adkins case should be repudiated by the Court.

Had this case been decided two years earlier it would probably have attracted relatively little comment, but it came on June 1, 1936. It came, that is to say, at the end of a seventeen-month period in which an unprecedented number of Congressional acts had been invalidated, at a time when most of the judicial vetoes of national legislation were justified on the principle of states' rights. But with this ruling it appeared that the rights of the states, as well as the powers of the national government, were to be strictly construed. It supported the charge that the Court had built up a twilight zone in which business management could operate free from any control. Because of this particular set of circumstances the decision was to have a prominent place in the spectacular series of reversals which began ten months later.

[112] 298 U.S. 587 (1936).

Chapter IX

THE NEW DEAL AND THE OLD SUPREME COURT

BETWEEN January 7, 1935, and May 25, 1936, the Supreme Court handed down twelve decisions in which Congressional statutes were held to be unconstitutional. The number is a very large one for so short a period. Even between 1925 and 1935, a period in which the Court was at least normally vigilant in the employment of its powers of review, there had been only twelve such cases. But it is not the number of decisions which makes these seventeen months a critical period in the history of judicial review. It is rather that all except one of these statutes [1] were of more than local importance and that together they stood for a very large, probably the major, part of the attempt being made by the President and Congress to meet and deal with the consequences of the Great Depression.

In the entire preceding history of the Supreme Court there had been relatively few decisions in which statutes of broad general interest had been invalidated. Most of this number checked attempts by Congress to extend national protection of civil liberties, to stop the spread of slavery in the northern

[1] In Stewart v. Keyes, 295 U.S. 403 (1935) an act of 1926 of very limited application and having no relation to the depression legislation was held invalid in one application. This case is not included in *Provisions of Federal Law Held Unconstitutional by the Supreme Court of the United States* (1936). The opinion of Mr. Justice VanDevanter, especially at page 417, would seem to indicate that one application of the act in question was, however, held invalid.

territories, to impose higher taxes upon the wealthy, or to improve the conditions of laborers. After one has named the Dred Scott and Civil Rights cases, the Income Tax case and some later cases involving income and gift taxes, the Child Labor, Adair, and Minimum Wage cases, there are surprisingly few decisions left which set aside even part of a Congressional statute having any very general application. Furthermore, as has been remarked, the statutes held unconstitutional in this period were part of a comprehensive, although not necessarily a well coordinated attempt to deal with the consequences of an economic downswing which had been in effect for nearly four years when the first of these statutes was enacted. The Court took upon itself the great responsibility of saying that this attempt, under the Constitution, could not be made.

The statutes held unconstitutional in whole or in part [2] were the National Industrial Recovery Act,[3] the abrogation of the gold clause in Liberty Bonds,[4] the Railroad Pension Act,[5] the Frazier-Lemke Act for the relief of farmer-mortgagors,[6] the federal tax on liquor businesses conducted contrary to state laws,[7] the section of the Home Owners' Loan Act allowing conversion of state associations into federal ones,[8] the Agricultural Adjustment Act,[9] and the amend-

[2] It has been indicated at various points that the Court does not always hold an entire act invalid. Frequently it deals only with a particular application of a general statute, the act remaining valid, at least presumptively, for other applications. The editor of the Library of Congress publication, *Provisions of Federal Law Held Unconstitutional,* concludes that, in a technical sense, in only eight cases have entire acts of Congress been invalidated (p. 92). It is not irrelevant to note that five of the eight were New Deal statutes. As the editor goes on to point out, the same effect was secured in at least six other cases, including the Schechter case involving the National Industrial Recovery Act.

[3] Panama Refining Co. v. Ryan, 293 U.S. 388 (1935), Schechter Poultry Corp. v. U.S., 295 U.S. 495 (1935). [4] Perry v. U.S., 294 U.S. 330 (1935).

[5] Railroad Retirement Board v. Alton R.R. Co., 295 U.S. 330 (1935).

[6] Louisville Joint Stock Bank v. Radford, 295 U.S. 555 (1935).

[7] U.S. v. Constantine, 296 U.S. 287 (1935).

[8] Hopkins Federal Savings & Loan Assn. v. Cleary, 296 U.S. 315 (1935).

[9] U.S. v. Butler, 297 U.S. 1 (1936).

ments to this act providing for the collection of processing taxes,[10] the Bituminous Coal Act,[11] and the Municipal Bankruptcy Act.[12] To this formidable list should be added the case in which President Roosevelt's removal of a member of the Federal Trade Commission not for malfeasance in office, or other cause stipulated in the statute, but because of his desire to secure a more vigorous application of the Federal Trade Commission Act.[13] The power of removal sustained in the Myers decision is here very considerably qualified.

ACTS SUSTAINED

Not quite all of the New Deal measures which came before the Court were rejected. In the other Gold Clause cases [14] the power of the government to abrogate the gold clause in private contracts and to refuse to redeem gold certificates in gold or its equivalent was sustained under the grant of power to Congress to "coin money" and "regulate the value thereof." But it is to be remarked that four dissenters thought that these measures involved the "confiscation of property rights," and the "repudiation and spoliation of citizens by their sovereign," all of which was as unconstitutional as it was abhorrent. "The impending legal and moral chaos is appalling." [15]

Something of the reluctance with which certain members of the majority voted to sustain the government came out in the extraordinary decision in the Liberty Loan Bond case.[16] There the Court held that the government could not

---

[10] Rickert Rice Mills v. Fontenot, 297 U.S. 110 (1936).

[11] Carter v. Carter Coal Co., 298 U.S. 238 (1936).

[12] Ashton v. Cameron Cty. Water District, 298 U.S. 513 (1936).

[13] Humphrey's Executor [Rathbun] v. U.S., 295 U.S. 602 (1935).

[14] Norman v. Baltimore & Ohio R. Co., 294 U.S. 240 (1935), Nortz v. U.S., 294 U.S. 317 (1935). For later decisions carrying the doctrine of these cases somewhat further see Smyth v. U.S., 302 U.S. 329 (1937), Guaranty Trust Co. v. Henwood, 307 U.S. 247 (1939). [15] 294 U.S. at 361, 362, 381.

[16] Perry v. U.S., 294 U.S. 330 (1935).

constitutionally modify the obligations of its own gold bonds, even though the government's power "to borrow money" is a grant with no restraints attached. But having held that the act of Congress was to this extent invalid the Court went on to hold that the creditor could not prove actual damage by being required to accept $10,000 in "depreciated" money. The government had acted unconstitutionally but the wrong was without a remedy. Perry may have won a moral victory but the financial policy of the New Deal was not disturbed.

In a case decided a few weeks later Section 77 of the 1933 Bankruptcy Act, which provided that insolvent railroads might reorganize with the consent of two-thirds of the creditors and stockholders and of the Interstate Commerce Commission, was upheld.[17] And in the Ashwander case [18] the water-power program of the Tennessee Valley Authority was sustained so far as the construction of the Wilson Dam and sale of its surplus power was concerned. The decision was carefully limited to apply only to this dam, which was built under the National Defense Act and thus could be justified in part under the war power. The validity of the remainder of the T.V.A. was left in doubt.

But the principal way in which the Court sustained the New Deal measures was by refusing to pass upon the validity of the spending power. It had long been a paradox of American constitutional law that while states and their subdivisions were jealously watched as to their regulatory powers, their powers of public ownership were, under the national Constitution, virtually unlimited, provided that they paid for any property taken for public use. Their power to regulate the rates and services of the utilities was recognized but limited. Their power to own and operate was accepted with-

---

[17] Continental Illinois Nat. Bank & Trust Co. v. Chicago, R.I. & Pac. Ry. Co., 294 U.S. 648 (1935).

[18] Ashwander v. T.V.A., 297 U.S. 288 (1936). Justice McReynolds dissented. Justices Brandeis, Stone, Roberts, and Cardozo thought that the constitutional issue should not be discussed.

out dispute. And where they could not, at least before the Nebbia case, regulate rates or even services, they could own and operate enterprises which by no stretch of the pre-1934 judicial vision could be found within the magic circle of businesses affected with a public interest. This state socialism could extend even to fuel yards, gasoline stations, flour mills, and the building and selling of homes to private citizens.[19] It could be done at cost; no attention need be paid to the rule of Smyth v. Ames.

The same paradox was to be found in the powers of the national government. "So long," wrote Professor Corwin, just before the New Deal decisions, "as Congress has the prudence to lay and collect taxes without specifying the purposes to which the proceeds from any particular tax are to be devoted, it may continue to appropriate the national funds without judicial let or hindrance."[20] In the Maternity Act cases[21] the Court had refused to review the constitutionality of national expenditures for a purpose that was clearly within the domain of the powers reserved to the states. Neither a state nor an individual taxpayer could challenge the validity of such a use of moneys in the courts. Thus the spending of billions of dollars in civilian relief, and in the building of public works was beyond the range of constitutional litigation.

TAXATION AND AGRICULTURE

No case better illustrates the strangeness of the resulting situation than United States v. Butler,[22] in which the first Agricultural Adjustment Act was held invalid. Under this act a tax was laid upon the processors of certain basic agricultural commodities. The proceeds from this tax were used to com-

---

[19] Jones v. Portland, 245 U.S. 217 (1917), Green v. Frazier, 253 U.S. 233 (1920). [20] *The Twilight of the Supreme Court* (1934), 176.

[21] Massachusetts v. Mellon, Frothingham v. Mellon, 262 U.S. 447 (1923).

[22] 297 U.S. 1 (1936).

pensate farmers who agreed to produce less or none of those commodities. Some means had to be found to get money into the sorely distressed farm areas. It is a wry commentary upon contemporary economic life that the method chosen was that of paying the farmers to produce less at a time when millions in this country, and hundreds of millions in other countries, were habitually undernourished. But the Roosevelt administration was not the first to face a situation in which hunger at home and abroad existed simultaneously with a great unsaleable surplus of farm products. Other devices had been tried and had failed. The A.A.A. would increase the cost to the consumer, and in this respect it would be the agricultural equivalent of the protective tariff. It would also send money into the distressed rural communities where foreclosures of farm mortgages were becoming more common than painted buildings. And it would at least have the merit of being self-financing.[23]

An imposition which produces millions of dollars for government purposes is ordinarily considered to be a tax. But to Justice Roberts, who spoke for the majority, it was not a tax, for a tax has "never been thought to connote the expropriation of money from one group for the benefit of another." A very large proportion of taxation consists of doing just that, although the transfer may be more carefully disguised, and the majority was not content to rule that this measure was not a tax law. Roberts went on to discuss the provision in Article I, section 8, granting Congress the power to lay and collect taxes "to pay the debts and provide for the common defense and general welfare of the United States." For over a century there had been doubt whether the general welfare phrase added to the powers of Congress. The issue had been debated by, among others, Hamilton and Madison. Roberts finds that this is a distinct power, that the phrase is not a bit

[23] Cf. Robert H. Jackson, *The Struggle for Judicial Supremacy* (1941), 125-130.

of supererogation. But his own conclusions on the subject quickly turn out to be unnecessary, if not sheer *obiter dicta,* because he goes on to hold that the "tax" is invalid because it is "a mere incident" of a plan for the regulation of agriculture. The regulation of agriculture was, by the Tenth Amendment, reserved to the states, for the powers not "expressly [24] granted, or reasonably to be implied from such as are conferred," are reserved to the states. "It is an established principle that the attainment of a prohibited end may not be accomplished under the pretext of powers which are granted."

It is clear that the national government was granted no power to regulate agricultural production. It is equally clear that it was given power to lay and collect taxes to provide for the general welfare. "To say that the national government has not a specifically delegated power to regulate agriculture is one thing; to say that it may never so exercise any of its delegated powers as to regulate agriculture whether indirectly, as in the A.A.A., or directly, as in war, is quite another thing." [25] As though conscious of the weakness of his argument based upon the intent of the act Justice Roberts distinguishes between plans for "purely voluntary cooperation" and a scheme which, like the A.A.A., provides for enforced control. Even neglecting the patent fact that many farmers, including about one-fourth of the cotton producers, had exercised their privilege under the statute and had refused to reduce their acreage, the distinction is of doubtful constitutional importance. The question was whether Congress had power under the taxing-spending clauses to establish the system of taxes and payments.

The resulting contradictions are striking and important.

---

[24] The word "expressly" is contributed by Justice Roberts. It was deliberately omitted from the Tenth Amendment, for it was contained in the amendments proposed by Massachusetts, New Hampshire and South Carolina in 1788.

[25] Edward S. Corwin, *Constitutional Revolution, Ltd.* (1941), 60-61.

A tax, called a tariff, may constitutionally be levied though it be solely for protective, i.e., promotional purposes, and bring in no revenue at all. Such a "tax" has a very direct bearing upon industrial production. A tax upon processors levied for the purpose of promoting agricultural prosperity is invalid. And grants to farmers, or to agricultural colleges, were presumably as constitutional after the Butler decision as before, provided that no tax was levied for the express purpose of raising the money thus to be expended. It is no wonder that Justice Stone, dissenting for himself and Justices Brandeis and Cardozo, called this a "tortured construction of the Constitution," and said that "courts are not the only agency of government that must be assumed to have capacity to govern."

CODES, PENSIONS, AND COAL

Some of the interpretations of the commerce clause were only a little less serious in their restrictive implications. The National Industrial Recovery Act was made unworkable because of the ruling on delegation of powers and that issue will be considered presently. In the Schechter case, however, the Court "went beyond the necessities of the litigation in announcing limitations upon the commerce power of Congress." [26] The Court here went out of its way to expound a narrow conception of the commerce power, to emphasize the limits of that power rather than, as it so often had done, to find a justification for the national regulation of local activities whether the effect upon commerce was "direct" or "indirect." And the emergency doctrine successfully invoked in Wilson v. New [27] was here bluntly dismissed.

Clearer evidence of the majority attitude in 1935 and 1936 toward the scope of the commerce power is found in the

[26] Thomas Reed Powell, "Commerce, Pensions, and Codes," 49 *Harvard Law Review,* 1, 193 at 197 (1935). [27] 243 U.S. 332 (1917).

Railroad Pension [28] and Bituminous Coal [29] cases. In both of these cases the majority saw the commerce power through the lenses of due process. It was not so much the range of power as the propriety with which the power is exercised which seems to animate the opinions, particularly the first of them. Justice Roberts could hardly deny to the national government the power to regulate railroads, not without overruling almost every case on the subject. But his result amounts to declaring that a statute imposing the requirement of pensions cannot be constitutional. For, after finding defects in the particular statute here before the Court, he goes on to say that plans of this kind "are really and essentially related solely to the social welfare of the worker, and therefore remote from any regulation of commerce as such. . . . We feel bound to hold that a pension plan thus imposed is in no proper sense a regulation of the activity of interstate transportation." [30]

This was from a Court which had, only eleven years before, in upholding the radical recapture clause of the Transportation Act of 1920, spoken unanimously of the power to regulate as the power "to foster, protect and control the commerce with appropriate regard to the welfare of those who are immediately concerned." [31] It is not difficult to understand why Chief Justice Hughes, in his dissenting opinion with which three other Justices concurred, went beyond the restraint which marked his rare dissenting opinions, in expressing his astonishment that the Court would "raise a barrier against all legislative action of this nature," and his regret at this "departure from sound principles [which] places an unwarranted limitation upon the commerce clause of the Constitution." [32]

The majority opinion is not, however, a departure from

---

[28] Railroad Retirement Board v. Alton R.R. Co., 295 U.S. 330 (1935).

[29] Carter v. Carter Coal Co., 298 U.S. 238 (1936).

[30] 295 U.S. 330, 368, 374.

[31] Dayton-Goose Creek Ry. Co. v. U.S., 263 U.S. 456 (1924).

[32] 295 U.S. 330, 374-375.

the principles of the Adair and the First Employers Liability Cases.[33] It is the third case in which a Congressional act regulating the railroads was held unconstitutional and, like its predecessors, it is an act seeking to promote the interests of railroad labor.

In holding unconstitutional the Bituminous Coal Conservation Act of 1935 the majority relies somewhat less upon due process than in the Pension case, but both due process and the due process point of view are there, as well as the delegation of powers principle. The signal feature of the case, however, is the close relation which a good part of the argument bears to the commerce clause interpretations of the Knight and Child Labor cases.[34] The emphasis is upon the distinction between production and commerce, the latter being subject to national regulation, the former not. As in the Schechter case, so here the effect upon interstate commerce of coal mining is held to be indirect. The act contained general price provisions and also provisions for the protection of laboring conditions, labor unions, and wages. It was these latter that the majority found to be so obnoxious that it struck down the entire act, even though the statute specifically provides that if any sections of the act were held invalid the remainder should not thereby be affected.

The Chief Justice agreed that the labor provisions were invalid but dissented from the more sweeping holding that the entire act was unconstitutional. Justices Cardozo, Brandeis, and Stone dissented from the entire opinion. The former found many precedents to justify his statement that

> "Congress was not condemned to inaction in the face of price wars and wage wars so pregnant with disaster. Commerce had been choked and burdened; its normal flow had been diverted from one state to another; there had been bankruptcy and waste and ruin alike for capital and for

[33] *Supra,* 117. [34] *Supra,* 92, 121.

labor. The liberty protected by the Fifth Amendment does not include the right to persist in this anarchic riot." [35]

BANKRUPTCY, MUNICIPAL AND AGRICULTURAL

The same five-to-four division (although here as in the Pensions case the minority dissented on all counts) is found in the Municipal Bankruptcy case.[36] When hearings were held in 1934, before enacting the law held invalid in this case, some 2,000 communities were found to be in default of their obligations. The act provided that, if the states consented and two-thirds of the creditors of these communities agreed, the federal courts might approve plans for scaling down or compromising the debts. Although the consent of the states was an essential part of the proceedings, and although the State of Texas had here passed a law to render the Congressional act applicable in that state, Mr. Justice McReynolds found that "If obligations of states or their political subdivisions may be subjected to the interferences here attempted, they are no longer free to manage their own affairs; the will of Congress prevails over them. . . ." He continues: "Neither consent nor submission by the states can enlarge the powers of Congress; none can exist except those which are granted." In support of this doctrine he cites United States v. Butler. The parallel between the two cases is a fairly close one. In both instances Congress was exercising a delegated power; in both instances the Court found that that power could not be exercised because its employment represented an attempt to control subjects left to the states. The consent of the states in the bankruptcy case, like the consent of the farmers in the A.A.A. case, made no more difference than did the desperate plight of the agricultural population or the appalling prevalence of bankruptcy among local governmental units.

---

[35] 288 U.S. 238, 331.

[36] Ashton v. Cameron County District, 298 U.S. 513 (1936).

In some respects the most interesting contrast to the Municipal Bankruptcy case is the Blaisdell decision [37] of 1934. That case did not involve the problem of federalism, but it was concerned with the relief of mortgagors in a depression. In the Ashton case McReynolds said little about the contract clause, but he was emphatic in his rejection of the notion that the prohibition against impairment of the obligation of contracts could be set aside by any such means as here employed. There is none of the willingness to consider either the exigencies of the situation or the fairness of the methods to be employed which is to be found in the earlier opinion, written by Chief Justice Hughes. And it is evident that eight members of the Court saw the two statutes from much the same point of view. Four of them, that is, thought both unconstitutional; four thought both constitutional. Only Justice Roberts was a variable quantity; only he was in the majority in both cases.

The bankruptcy power was involved again in the decision holding invalid the act for relief of farm mortgagors.[38] The act was based upon the explicit grant to Congress of the power to legislate on the subject of bankruptcy and this act was clearly a bankruptcy statute. It is invalid, said the Court, because it contravenes the due process clause of the Fifth Amendment. Now the statute here invalidated is of the kind which the fathers evidently had in mind when they forbade the states to impair the obligation of contracts, and it is very similar to a number of acts held contrary to that clause. But the fathers also, and deliberately, refused to impose that restriction upon the central government. Nor is there the slightest evidence that the due process clause, until recently, had the remotest relation to such matters. If the act was unconstitutional it was so only because the due process concept

[37] Home Building & Loan Assn. v. Blaisdell, 290 U.S. 398 (1934). *Supra,* 171.
[38] Louisville Joint Stock Bank v. Radford, 295 U.S. 555 (1935).

had been so expanded as to render the obligation of contract clause supererogatory.

DELEGATION AND CODES

One final example of the doctrinal developments of the period must be considered. In the final section of Chapter VII it was indicated that the Court had said that Congress could not, consistently with Article I, section 1, delegate its power to make a law. But it had always found that the statutes brought before it did not make that attempt. In the Panama Refining and Schechter cases,[39] for the first time, an act was found to violate the principle that Congress must do its own legislating. Of course the Court could not hold that Congress had not enacted a statute, for it was a statute that was being held to violate the provision that "all legislative powers herein granted shall be vested in Congress." What the Court did was to find that the statute attempted to delegate an excessive amount of rule-making authority to the President and to industrial groups. Just how much discretion there must be in order to be excessive is not made clear. The rules of the game are the products of the umpire's decisions. That there was extremely little awareness of the possibility of a decision going on this basis is attested by the government's brief in the Schechter case. A brief of 227 pages plus 200 more of appendix contained just 13 pages devoted to this subject.[40]

In Field v. Clark the Court had said that the true distinction is between delegating the power to make a law, which necessarily involves determining an issue of public policy, and conferring discretionary authority as to its execution, to be exercised under and in pursuance of the law.[41] But in

[39] Panama Refining Co. v. Ryan, 293 U.S. 388 (1935), Schechter Poultry Corp. v. U.S., 295 U.S. 495 (1935). [40] Jackson, *op. cit.*, 92.
[41] 143 U.S. 649, 693-694 (1892).

the Panama Refining, or "Hot Oil" Case as it was usually called, the Court found that section 9 (c) of the N.I.R.A. was invalid, because Congress did not sufficiently define in advance the terms and conditions under which the President must operate in prohibiting the shipment in interstate commerce of oil produced in violation of state laws which fixed production quotas. The entire N.I.R.A. went down in the Schechter case when the Court found that the Live Poultry Code involved undue delegation of legislative authority. This code was one of the more than 700 codes of fair competition prepared, under authority of the National Industrial Recovery Act, by representatives of the respective industries and approved by the President. By the statute the President was charged with the duty of seeing that certain standards with respect to working conditions, wages and freedom from monopoly were observed. If the trade representatives were unable to agree, the President was authorized to impose a code. He might, furthermore, impose code changes when "in his discretion" he finds such changes necessary "to effectuate the policy of the act."

The Court found that Title I of the act did not establish adequate standards "for any trade, industry, or activity. . . . Instead of prescribing rules of conduct, it authorizes the making of codes to prescribe them." In conferring this power upon the representatives of various enterprises and upon the President the Congress had unconstitutionally attempted to delegate to them the legislative power which it alone could exercise.[42]

This principle applied to all of the N.I.R.A. codes. If the

---

[42] In U.S. v. Curtiss-Wright Export Corp., 299 U.S. 304 (1936), the Court sustained the delegation to the President by a joint resolution of Congress, of the authority to declare an embargo on the shipment of arms to South America. The Court was careful to point out that such a delegation might not be valid if confined to internal affairs, but in the field of foreign relations, the President as spokesman for the nation might constitutionally exercise a range of discretion which could not be conferred upon him in other fields.

Live Poultry Code had been unconstitutionally prepared, so had the other 700. Had the decision ended here the Congress could, however, have rescued the act, had it wished to do so. More specific Congressional definitions of code policy, together with a withdrawal from the code authorities of much of their power, would have remedied this defect in the statute. But, as has been pointed out, even though the act had been held to violate Article I, section 1, of the Constitution, the Court gratuitously went on to set forth so narrow a definition of the national commerce power that it appeared that the entire industrial life of the nation, except transportation, was beyond the regulatory power of Congress. This point of view was reinforced in the Coal decision a few months later.

AS GOES JUSTICE ROBERTS—

At the beginning of this chapter emphasis was placed upon the number and importance of the Congressional statutes held unconstitutional in 1935 and 1936. The scale of statutory mortality was as unprecedented as was the breadth and intensity of the effort made by the Roosevelt administration to alleviate the economic and social hardships of the depression. According to the orthodox point of view no further commentary upon the constitutionality of the New Deal legislation is needed. The President and Congress may have acted from worthy motives but their legislation failed to observe the principles of the Constitution. The Court did what it must do under the Constitution when it declared that legislation to be unconstitutional. But this simple version of the story leaves much out of account.

It is, for one thing, significant how few were the major decisions of the time in which the Court was unanimous, or nearly so. There have been many instances during the Court's history when it has been closely divided, but those decisions were, before 1935, exceptional, not usual. In the major cases of 1935-1936 votes of 5 to 4 or 6 to 3 are more common than unanimity, and in each instance of division there is a vigorous, not infrequently a bitter, dissenting opinion.

Beyond the evident division of the Justices it is noteworthy that there were two definite groups in the Court. Four members of the Court, Justices VanDevanter, McReynolds, Sutherland, and Butler, stood united against the Roosevelt legislation, just as they had, during the twenties, unitedly opposed state regulatory statutes and Congressional taxation when aimed at the wealthy, and as they had supported legislation intended to restrict civil liberties. Their point of view had long been on record and its expression in 1935-1936 is entirely consistent with that record. In the A.A.A. and Constantine cases the Old Guard was opposed by Justices Brandeis, Stone, and Cardozo. They too were on record, although that record is not quite so uncompromising. And in the Railroad Pensions case, the Coal Conservation case, and the Municipal Bankruptcy case they were joined in dissent by Chief Justice Hughes. The record of the Chief Justice was not so clearly defined as was that of the four pillars of conservatism, nor even as predictable as that of the three liberals. But, in all except two of the most doubtful cases, he voted with Brandeis, Stone and Cardozo. His waverings were, however, powerless to change the result.

It was Mr. Justice Roberts who cast the deciding vote in the 5 to 4 decisions, and, one may guess, in the Butler case, as well, for it seems a likely bet that the Chief Justice would have preferred the other side of that decision, that he went with Roberts only to prevent another 5 to 4 vote on a critical issue. Justice Roberts had been on the Court a comparatively short time but there had, before 1935, been several decisions which foreshadowed the years in which as went Justice Roberts, so went the Court. He had written the Nebbia opinion, a decision based upon a 5 to 4 vote, and his vote had been essential to the decisions of the Near and the Blaisdell cases. In the entire series of New Deal cases he was never with the minority, [43] although he agreed with Brandeis' concurring opinion in the T.V.A. case. He was also with the majority in Colgate v. Harvey and the New York minimum wage case, the two most notable decisions of 1935-1936 in which state legislative power was subjected to new or to old restrictions, both of them cases decided by a closely divided Court.

CHOICE IN INTERPRETATION

Clearly the Constitution did not mean the same thing to all of the members of the Court. It is as evident that in the cases of these years no single method of interpreting the words of that document was consistently followed. In his A.A.A. opinion Justice Roberts had made this problem of interpretation seem delightfully easy. "When an Act of Congress is appropriately challenged in the courts as not conforming to the constitutional mandate the judicial branch of the Government has only one duty; to lay the article of the Constitution which is invoked beside the statute which is challenged and to decide whether the latter squares with the former." [44] But the history of American constitutional interpretation indicates that this side-by-side comparison is only the beginning.

In the very first decade of the Court at least three methods of arriving at the meaning of the Constitution were employed. In Chisholm v. Georgia [45] the Court disregarded the available evidence as to the intent of the clause involved

[43] See also Helvering v. City Bank Farmers Trust Co., 296 U.S. 85 (1935), Helvering v. Helmholtz, 296 U.S. 93 (1935). Both cases involved the construction of a federal Revenue Act. In both Justice Roberts wrote the opinion of the Court. In the first case Justices VanDevanter, McReynolds, Sutherland, and Butler dissented. In the second the dissenters were Justices Brandeis, Stone, and Cardozo. [44] U.S. v. Butler, 297 U.S. 1, 62 (1936).

[45] 2 Dallas 419 (1793). On these cases see *supra*, 30-31.

and applied a literal interpretation. The result was an unenforced decision and the adoption of the Eleventh Amendment. In Hylton v. U.S.[46] the court followed neither the common sense nor the technical meaning of "direct tax," but gave expression to the peculiar intent of the clause in the Constitution. In Calder v. Bull[47] it applied the *ex post facto* clause not in the broad sense which might seem correct from a translation of the Latin phrase, but in the light of its technical, professional meaning.

The methods of the first decade have all, from time to time, been employed. And, with the multiplication of judicial interpretations, there has developed a great body of constitutional law which constitutes a stock-pile from which the Court can draw meanings as the need arises. The cases surveyed in the preceding chapters indicate, however, that the materials in this warehouse are not so uniform in size and shape as to be appropriate for but a single model. They are so varied as to give to the artisan a broad range of discretion. The division on the Court only emphasizes the freedom of choice allowed by the precedents.

Indeed, the freedom of choice actually used sometimes went beyond the discretionary freedom predictable from the precedents. Interpretations of the commerce clause during the preceding decade did not inevitably point to the views expressed in the Schechter, the Railroad Pensions, and the Carter cases. Nor is the Municipal Bankruptcy decision in close harmony with earlier views of the breadth of power allowable under the clause granting power to enact legislation on the subject of bankruptcies. And if the New York minimum wage act was invalidated on the authority of the Adkins decision of 1923, this conclusion was tenable only on the assumption that Justice Roberts did not mean what he said in the 1934 Nebbia opinion. Certainly there was no

---

[46] 3 Dallas 171 (1796). [47] 3 Dallas 386 (1798).

precedent for Colgate v. Harvey, and there were over fifty precedents which supported an opposite conclusion.

Sometimes, when passing upon the validity of a statute, the Court pays great deference to Congressional interpretations of the Constitution. In no decision of the years immediately preceding 1937 is this more evident than in the Humphrey case. When, in the Myers case, Chief Justice Taft held that Congress could not require Senatorial consent to the dismissal of a postmaster, he necessarily overrode the Congressional conception of an office created by Congress. In that opinion Taft went out of his way to remark that the President would be as free to remove members of administrative commissions as to remove postmasters. But in 1935 Taft's dictum was rejected and the restraint imposed upon the President by the act establishing the Federal Trade Commission sustained. It should be clear to all that the Constitution no more requires Senatorial consent to the removal of commissioners than to the removal of postmasters. The distinction of 1935 was based neither upon precedent nor upon the literal meaning of the Constitution. The opinion, written by Mr. Justice Sutherland, contains numerous references to "the intention of Congress," but one can only observe that such deference to Congressional interpretation of the Constitution is not discoverable in Mr. Justice Sutherland's opinion in the Coal Conservation case, nor is it represented in his many votes against Congressional legislation during these and his preceding years on the Court.

Unless one begins, and ends, the study of this momentous series of cases with the assumption that the decision of the Court in every cause is invariably and inevitably the true construction of the Constitution, it is impossible to characterize the actions of the Court adequately in terms of the traditional legal formulae. The decisions were dictated not by the Constitution but by the economic and political philosophy of the Justices. Four members of the Court were opposed to almost every extension of governmental authority, state as well as national, which did not accord with their conceptions of governmental functions. When this intransigent group was joined by Justice Roberts it constituted a majority. In nearly every instance where there was a choice of alternatives open to the Court, and with rare exceptions there were alternatives, that majority chose the doctrine which served to restrict the exercise of governmental powers. Where a more vigorous enforcement of the Federal Trade Commission Act was threatened by the replacement of Commissioner Humphrey by James M. Landis the Court drew a distinction which involved overruling its earlier dictum. Where, as in the A.A.A. and Municipal Bankruptcy cases, there was justification for the exercise of Congressional authority in the clauses of Article I, section 8, a principle of impotence was derived from the Tenth Amendment. Yet that amendment reserves to the states only those powers not delegated to Congress. And the decisions in the Colgate and minimum wage cases made it evident that the Court's solicitude was not for the rights of states but rather for the absence of regulation by either national or state governments.

Chapter X

RETREAT AND RECONSIDERATION

SINCE John Adams appointed Marshall to the Chief Justiceship no event has so influenced the law of the Constitution as the introduction by President Roosevelt of his plan for the reform of the federal judiciary. And no event, or series of events, has ever before produced so many changes in constitutional doctrine within so short a time. The plan was introduced on February 5, 1937. Before the end of May of that same year the Court, without any change in personnel, had reversed or modified a considerable, and extremely important, portion of its rulings of the two preceding years. And in the four subsequent terms of Court the reversals and distinctions have been so numerous and so sweeping that today much of the constitutional law of 1936 appears to belong to a different constitution. But these changes have come from interpretation, not from amendment.

After the unfavorable decisions of 1935-1936 there were criticisms of the Court's rulings, including the President's "horse and buggy" characterization of the Schechter opinion, but no open challenge to the Court's authority. In the campaign of 1936 there was some discussion of the Court's attitude, but Roosevelt again did not throw down the gauntlet, as, for example, Jackson and Lincoln had done. The Republicans, however, gave the electorate ample warning of a test to come. After winning by a much greater majority than in 1932, a majority so generally distributed that only Maine and Vermont cast electoral votes for the Republican candidate, Roosevelt, on the assumption that so long as the Court remained intransigent, there was no chance for a concerted attack upon the continuing depression, decided to attempt to alter that intransigence. The problem then became a choice between various plans of action.

THE ROOSEVELT COURT PLAN

The one finally decided upon did not, in itself, involve a challenge to the Court's power to review the constitutionality of Congressional legislation. On the excuse that the federal courts generally were behind in their dockets, and on the assumption that the number of federal judges who were more than seventy years of age contributed largely to the dissatisfaction with the workings of the law, the President proposed that he be empowered to appoint a new judge where the incumbent judge failed to retire at the age of seventy. There were other proposals involving the lower courts but this one alone affected the Supreme Court. The plan for that Court would, if accepted, have made possible the appointment of additional Justices to a total of six. The President's message made no reference to the Court's decisions invalidating the New Deal legislation. It did not, therefore, offer a clear and direct issue for discussion, although everyone in Congress understood that Roosevelt, who had had no opportunity so far to nominate any new members to the Court, wished to be able to do what Washington, Jackson, Lincoln, and Taft had done, that is to reconstitute the membership of that body so that it would read the Constitution in a more acceptable way.

While there is nothing in the Constitution to determine the size of the Court, and it had, by successive statutes, been changed from six to five to six to seven to nine to ten to seven to nine members the plan was unacceptable to a great many who had supported other legislation advocated by the President. It appeared to them to involve a direct blow at the independence of the judiciary, a defeat of the sacred traditions of American constitutionalism. And among those who opposed it were many who, like Senator Wheeler and Senator Borah, had themselves criticized the rulings of the Court and proposed constitutional amendments in some fashion limiting its final authority. As Attorney-General, now Mr. Justice, Jackson has since written, the plan was defective in that it "failed to focus attention on the real judicial offending. The fighting issues, ready-made for the President, were not seized." [1] But in spite of its very serious defects, and the plan had few merits save those given to it by the Court's decisions, the plan did muster strong support from among those who believed that the Court was rapidly endangering the possibility of dealing with the most vital problems of the day by peaceful, constitutional methods.

For five and a half months the bill was debated in the press, over the radio, in innumerable local gatherings, and in the Senate.[2] The Senate Committee on the Judiciary voted 10-8 against the bill and it was finally defeated by a vote of 70-20 in the Senate. While the constitutional traditionalism which made possible this defeat is of the first importance there were other factors which served to make that traditionalism effective. One was the announced retirement of Mr. Justice VanDevanter. Another was the death of Senator Robinson, leader in the Senate for the bill; but the most influential was "the switch in time which saved nine," the Court's almost immediate change of decision in order to avert the threat to its independence.[3]

---

[1] *The Struggle for Judicial Supremacy* (1941), 189.

[2] The longest account of the struggle is that in Joseph Alsop and Turner Catledge, *The 168 Days* (1938). This is a breezy version of the story, lacking in perspective but having the merit of being written by ringside spectators. It should be compared with Charles A. and Mary Beard's version in *America in Midpassage* (1939).

[3] Professor Corwin has recently expressed the opinion that even more important than the Court plan in inducing a change of interpretation were the

"THE SWITCH IN TIME"

This change in interpretation was heralded by three decisions given on March 29th. In the first and most important of them the Court explicitly overruled the Adkins minimum wage decision and, in all save name, overruled the New York minimum wage decision of June 1, 1936.[4] This reversal was speedier than that in the Legal Tender Cases, and it was done without the addition of new members to the court. To at least seven members of the Court the issues in the case of 1936 and that of 1937 were identical, or at least the differences were of no substantial importance. Chief Justice Hughes had dissented in the earlier case on the ground that a distinction should be drawn between the statute held invalid in 1923 and that before the Court in 1936, one which required that the minimum wage have a fair relation to the value of the labor. No other member of the Court appeared to think this distinction of importance. In 1937 the line-up of the Court was as in 1936, except that Mr. Justice Roberts shifted to the old minority. The Chief Justice's opinion evades the question of the decision in the New York case just ten months before, by saying that the broader issue was not there considered. This is a palpable evasion of the criticism contained in the dissenting opinion of Mr. Justice Sutherland. If anything, the New York statute was easier to sustain than the Washington one, although the differences are, constitutionally speaking, immaterial. And in sustaining

---

results of the election of 1936, the C.I.O. strikes in Detroit, and the willingness of Mr. Justice Roberts to learn. *Constitutional Revolution, Ltd.* (1941), 73-76. The plan would have had little support had it not been for the election of 1936, but I should be inclined to doubt whether the strikes would so much have impressed the Chief Justice and Mr. Justice Roberts had it not been for the threat contained in the President's proposal.

[4] West Coast Hotel Co. v. Parrish, 300 U.S. 379 (1937). The Washington statute here held invalid was enacted in 1913 and it had apparently been retained on the books and in some degree enforced despite the Supreme Court's rulings that such acts were unconstitutional.

the principle of minimum wages the Court modified its conception of due process to at least as great an extent as it had done in the Nebbia decision three years before.

On the same day the Court sustained unanimously the revised Farm Mortgage Act of 1935,[5] as well as the Railway Labor Act as amended in 1934.[6] Neither case represented a clear-cut doctrinal reversal of earlier decisions, but the Wright case permitted the substance of what the Radford case had forbidden and, beyond that, the opinions exhibit a less hostile attitude toward Congressional legislation than that expressed in a number of the earlier opinions.

The great change came on April 12th, for it was then that the Court handed down five decisions sustaining the National Labor Relations Act.[7] This statute provided for federal regulation and protection of labor organizations in industries affecting interstate commerce. It went far beyond any previous federal legislation, except perhaps that regulating labor relations of the railroads, and it had very generally been assumed that it would be held invalid on the authority of the principles set forth in the Pensions, Schechter, and Coal cases. Six District Courts and four Circuit Courts of Appeals had so held. The Supreme Court divided five-to-four on all of the N.L.R.B. cases except that involving an interstate bus company, where it was unanimous. To the dissenters it was a direct reversal of the recent rulings to apply the statute to the Jones and Laughlin Steel Corporation, and to the Friedman-Harry Marks Clothing Company, and a violation of freedom of the press to apply it to the Associated Press.

The clearest conception of the distance travelled by the majority, or perhaps one should say by Mr. Justice Roberts,

[5] Wright v. Vinton Branch Bank, 300 U.S. 440 (1937).

[6] Virginian Ry. Co. v. System Federation No. 40, 300 U.S. 515 (1937).

[7] National Labor Relations Board v. Jones & Laughlin Steel Corp., 301 U.S. 1 (1937), N.L.R.B. v. Fruehauf Trailer Co., 301 U.S. 49 (1937), N.L.R.B. v. Friedman-Harry Marks Clothing Co., 301 U.S. 58 (1937), Associated Press v. N.L.R.B., 301 U.S. 103 (1937), Washington, V. & M. Coach Co. v. N.L.R.B., 301 U.S. 142 (1937).

and to a lesser extent by the Chief Justice, can be had from a consideration of the case of the clothing company. This company, as Mr. Justice McReynolds pointed out in his dissenting opinion, was not a great corporation whose business materially affected the flow of interstate commerce. It employed 800 of the 150,000 workmen engaged in the manufacture of men's clothing. If Congress may regulate the labor relations of such an enterprise with its employees, it may do the same in "almost every field of human industry." But Chief Justice Hughes was evidently more concerned with the pending threat to the Court's independence than he was with the dissenters' lament for the end of state rights. "Although activities may be intrastate in character when separately considered," he says, "if they have such a close and substantial relation to interstate commerce that their control is essential or appropriate to protect that commerce from burdens and obstructions, Congress cannot be denied the power to exercise that control." In support of this proposition he cites the Schechter decision, but it would seem that, particularly in the clothing company decision, the doctrine of direct and indirect affectation there enunciated is virtually abandoned. Certainly the distinction so often made, in fact if not in doctrine, between regulations favorable to labor and those dealing with other aspects of industry, is abandoned. The rights of organization and of collective bargaining have crowded out the old liberty of contract.

Six weeks after the Labor Board Cases the Court sustained the Social Security legislation in two decisions. The Court divided five-to-four in the first of them, which involved the Unemployment Compensation Act,[8] and two dissented from the holding that the old-age assistance tax was validly imposed.[9] Together these decisions go far toward overturning the strange "dual federalism" of the Butler case. That deci-

[8] Steward Machine Co. v. Davis, 301 U.S. 548 (1937).
[9] Helvering v. Davis, 301 U.S. 619 (1937).

sion was, of course, not reversed, for the statutes did not involve precisely the same subject matter.[10] But the majority opinion of Mr. Justice Cardozo in these later cases has a close kinship to the dissent of Stone in the Butler case. The basic change is not in the character of the statutes but in the change of Hughes and Roberts from the old majority to the old minority.

In the Butler majority opinion Roberts sustained the nationalistic conception of the national tax power, the theory that Congress had the power to tax "for the general welfare," before finding that that power was limited by other grants and denials of power. In the unemployment tax case Cardozo says that "The subject matter of taxation open to the power of Congress is as comprehensive as that open to the power of the states, though the method of apportionment may at times be different." The tax here levied upon employers is an excise tax which conforms to the canon of uniformity and does not violate the Fifth Amendment. It does not coerce the states by requiring their cooperation. They may enact laws of similar kind, as nearly all had done by 1937, whereby they work together with the central government in dealing with the unemployment problem. But for them to do so did not mean, as it did to the majority in the Municipal Bankruptcy Case, that the Tenth Amendment was being violated.

Of particular interest in the old-age security case is the comment on the spending power of Congress. If the freedom of that power had been threatened by the Butler ruling, as well as the care with which the Court passed upon only one aspect of the T.V.A., this decision went far toward removing the threat. After noting that Congress may appropriate money for the general welfare, Cardozo says that the definition of the general welfare and choice of the methods of pro-

---

[10] For the distinctions between the two see Cardozo's opinion, 301 U.S. at 592.

moting it lie within the discretion of Congress, "unless the choice is clearly wrong, a display of arbitrary power, not an exercise of judgment."

A closely related point of view is to be found in the majority opinion sustaining a state unemployment compensation law passed by Alabama with the intent of participating in the benefits available under the Social Security legislation. The old argument that the tax here levied on employers and employees was not levied for a public purpose was summarily disposed of by Mr. Justice Stone. "A tax," he says, "is not an assessment of benefits. It is a means of distributing the burden of the cost of government. The only benefit to which the taxpayer is constitutionally entitled is that derived from his enjoyment of the privileges of living in an organized society, established and safeguarded by the devotion of taxes to public purposes." [11] And the category "public purpose" includes "expenditures for the general welfare." It is for the legislature, with its intimate awareness of local conditions, to determine what is most conducive to the advancement of "the public interest," but the relief of unemployment and indigence is certainly within the scope of that power.[12]

Since March of 1937 the Court has not held a single act of Congress to be unconstitutional,[13] an amazing record when compared with that for 1935 and 1936, and one which is certainly not because of an absence of cases dealing with the validity of national legislation. This reversal of the statutory mortality rate is borne out in part by the Court's record in dealing with state legislation, although there the story is not quite so easy to diagram, and it will be taken up sepa-

[11] Carmichael v. Southern Coal & Coke Co., 301 U.S. 495, 522 (1937).

[12] *Ibid.*, 514-515.

[13] The last such case was Brush v. Commissioner of Internal Revenue, 300 U.S. 352 (1937). Here the Court held that the federal income tax could not be constitutionally applied to the salary of the chief engineer of the New York City water system. The principle underlying this decision has since been overruled.

rately. The greatly changed attitude of the Court toward both state and national legislation has undoubtedly come in part from changed personnel, but it is well to remember that the cases so far considered were decided before any change was made.

THE COMMERCE POWER

There are a number of cases in which the Court has reviewed the power of Congress under the commerce clause. That the net effect of them is to strengthen and extend the interpretation given in the spring of 1937 can be quickly demonstrated.

The provisions of the Labor Relations Act have been held applicable to a fruit cannery although it secured its raw materials within the state and sent only about 37 per cent of the finished product out of state.[14] It is not necessary, said the Chief Justice, to interpret the metaphor of a "stream of commerce" as applying only where there is a continuous flow of raw materials into and of products out of the state. Congress possesses power to prevent the obstruction or burdening of interstate commerce. And in Consolidated Edison Company v. N.L.R.B.[15] it was held that the commerce clause was broad enough to allow Congress to regulate the labor practices of the company which supplied New York City with electrical energy. The company did not sell for resale outside of the state, but it did supply power and light upon which most of the interstate and foreign commerce in the New York area depended. If the operations of the company were to be stopped, "the terminals and trains of three great interstate railroads would cease to operate; interstate communication by telegraph, telephone, and radio would stop; lights maintained as aids to navigation would go out; and

[14] Santa Cruz Fruit Packing Company v. N.L.R.B., 303 U.S. 453 (1938).

[15] 305 U.S. 197 (1938). See also N.L.R.B. v. Fainblatt, 306 U.S. 601 (1939) where the provisions of the act were held applicable to the labor relations of a small processor.

the business of interstate ferries and of foreign steamships whose docks and lines are operated by electric energy would be clearly impeded." Congress may constitutionally avoid these consequences by providing for the prevention of labor disputes in the industry.

It is significant that these broad interpretations of the commerce power were given in cases involving acts seeking to promote the interests of organized labor, a field in which the Court had previously been most inclined to read the commerce clause with nearsighted vision. And no case more sharply divides the new from the older interpretation of that clause than United States v. Darby Lumber Company.[16] Here the Court unanimously sustained the Fair Labor Standards Act of 1938, an act prohibiting the shipment in interstate commerce of certain products produced under labor conditions, as respects both wages and hours, which fail to conform to the standards established by the act. Clearly this statute is as much a regulation of manufacturing as that held unconstitutional twenty-three years earlier in the first Child Labor Case. But here the Court follows the line earlier taken by Holmes in his dissenting opinion. Congress does not have power to regulate manufacture as such but it has power to regulate commerce. "While manufacture is not of itself interstate commerce the shipment of manufactured goods interstate is such commerce and the prohibition of such shipment by Congress is indubitably a regulation of commerce." The Court will not inquire into the purpose or motive of the act beyond ascertaining that it is to deal with the conditions of commerce. The distinction emphasized in Hammer v. Dagenhart between the Congressional power to prohibit commerce in articles in themselves harmful and the inability to prohibit the sending of harmless objects, is dismissed as

[16] 312 U.S. 100 (1941). The case immediately following, Opp Cotton Mills v. Administrator, 312 U.S. 126 (1941) deals with the same statute largely in terms of the delegation of powers principle and will be considered later in this chapter.

"novel when made and unsupported by any provision of the Constitution" and one that has "long since been abandoned." Hammer v. Dagenhart was explicitly overruled.

With these decisions may be mentioned the cases dealing with the Norris-La Guardia Act regulating the issuance of injunctions in labor disputes.[17] These rulings, while upholding the general scope of the act and the validity of its procedural requirements, leave its meaning to be determined largely by the further process of interpretation.

Almost as notable as the labor act cases are those sustaining Congressional authority to deal with the problems of agriculture and of marketing under the commerce power. Three major statutes were involved, the Tobacco Inspection Act of 1935, the Agricultural Adjustment Act of 1938, and the Agricultural Marketing Agreement Act of 1937. The first authorized the regulation of auction markets where tobacco moving in interstate commerce was sold. The Secretary of Agriculture was authorized to establish uniform standards and classifications of the tobacco. This was sustained in Currin v. Wallace [18] over the protest that the transactions were local in character. The Agricultural Adjustment Act of 1938 was upheld in Mulford v. Smith [19] so far as it involved the fixing of marketing quotas for flue-cured tobacco. This act, like the Tobacco Inspection Act, went into effect after a favorable vote of two-thirds of the growers had been secured in a referendum held among the producers concerned. The quota was enforced by a penalty equal to fifty per cent of the market price of the excess. In an opinion by Mr. Justice Roberts, author of the opinion invalidating the first A.A.A., the Court holds that Congress has not here attempted to control production. It did not limit the acreage cultivated or the amount of tobacco grown. It merely restricts the amount

---

[17] Lauf v. Shinner & Co., 303 U.S. 323 (1938), New Negro Alliance v. Sanitary Grocery Co., 303 U.S. 552 (1938).

[18] 306 U.S. 1 (1939).

[19] 307 U.S. 38 (1939).

which can be marketed at the point which constitutes "the throat where tobacco enters the stream of commerce."

The Rock Royal and Hood Cases[20] involved the Marketing Agreement Act, and more immediately orders issued by the Secretary of Agriculture fixing the price that handlers or distributors of milk in the New York and Boston areas must pay to the producers. Here, as in the acts in the Currin and Mulford cases, the problem being dealt with was not that of transportation but that of surplus production and a demoralized market. The technique of milk control was different, but the constitutional issues were the same. In sustaining Congressional power under the commerce clause the Court pointed out that most of the milk consumed in both of these great metropolitan centers came from out of state. This was sufficient to justify regulation by the only power which could regulate, the federal government. But to Mr. Justice McReynolds, with whom Mr. Justice Butler concurred, this holding was clearly a violation of "ancient doctrine" recently restated in the Schechter opinion. Congress does not have

> authority to manage private business affairs under the transparent guise of regulating interstate commerce. True, production and distribution of milk are most important enterprises, not easy of wise execution; but so is breeding the cows, authors of the commodity; also, sowing and reaping the fodder which inspires them.[21]

In 1936 the Bituminous Coal Act was held invalid because of its labor provisions. Although the statute contained a separability clause, the majority of the Court ruled that the price-fixing clauses were inseparable from the labor provisions and declared the entire act void without passing upon the sections dealing with prices. In 1937 Congress enacted a new statute, omitting the labor sections, but providing for

[20] U.S. v. Rock Royal Cooperative, 307 U.S. 533 (1939), H. P. Hood and Sons v. U.S., 307 U.S. 588 (1939).

[21] 307 U.S. at 582. Justice Roberts and Chief Justice Hughes dissented in part but not on commerce clause grounds.

price fixing and the regulation of competition. This act was sustained under the commerce power.[22] Citing the *dissenting* opinion of Cardozo in the Carter Case, Mr. Justice Douglas said that "The fixing of prices, the proscription of unfair practices, the establishment of marketing rules respecting such sales of bituminous coal constitute regulations within the competence of Congress under the commerce clause." A tax of 19½ per cent was imposed by the act upon producers who were not code members. Douglas acknowledges that "clearly this tax is not designed merely for revenue purposes. In purpose and effect it is primarily a sanction to enforce the regulatory provisions of the act." But Congress may employ the power of taxation "as a sanction for the exercise of another power which is granted it." The authority to impose the regulations comes from the commerce clause; the penalty-tax is primarily a sanction to enforce those provisions.

Several further extensions of the commerce power may be more briefly mentioned. In sustaining the registration provisions of the Public Utility Holding Company Act of 1935 the Court found that the defendant companies were operating in several states and their contracts of sale involved use of the mails and of the instrumentalities of interstate commerce.[23] Congress is accordingly entitled to prohibit the use of the mails or of interstate commerce to those refusing to comply with a valid regulation. The federal police power was slightly broadened by the decisions sustaining the Filled Milk Act of 1923 [24] although there was little difficulty in demonstrating to the satisfaction of all members of the Court save Mr. Justice McReynolds that the prohibition of shipments in interstate commerce of skimmed milk or cream compounded with any fats or oil other than milk fat so as to resemble milk or cream was similar to prohibitions upheld before 1937.

[22] Sunshine Anthracite Coal Co. v. Adkins, 310 U.S. 381 (1940). Justice McReynolds alone dissented.

[23] Electric Bond & Share Co. v. S.E.C., 303 U.S. 419 (1938).

[24] U.S. v. Carolene Products Co., 304 U.S. 144 (1938).

A decision carrying the federal power over "navigable" rivers beyond previous principles was that in which the Water Power Act of 1920 was held applicable to the construction of a dam on the New River in Virginia.[25] Since the time of Gibbons v. Ogden the Court had been inclined to sustain federal regulation of commerce on the nation's waterways even when the stream or lake was not itself in more than one state. The New River did flow through two states but in its upper reaches it was hardly navigable for commercial purposes, although a few light craft had been pushed and hauled through its shallower stretches. With Justices Roberts and McReynolds dissenting, the Court held that since the stream could be made navigable by improvements, the authority of the Federal Power Commission was supreme over the building of dams on the river. In an opinion handed down a few months later this ruling was further extended in a case involving the power of Congress to authorize a dam across the upper Red River, well above the navigable portion of that stream, for purposes of flood control.[26]

> . . . we now add that the power of flood control extends to the tributaries of navigable streams. For just as control over the non-navigable parts of a river may be essential or desirable in the interests of the navigable portions, so may the key to flood control on a navigable stream be found in whole or in part in flood control on its tributaries.[27]

OTHER POWERS OF CONGRESS

Any lingering doubts about the virtually unlimited scope of the spending power were removed by two decisions. In Alabama Power Co. v. Ickes [28] the Court refused to issue an injunction to restrain the federal authority from making P.W.A. grants to municipalities for the construction of elec-

[25] U.S. v. Appalachian Electric Power Co., 311 U.S. 377 (1940).
[26] Oklahoma ex. rel. Phillips v. Atkinson, 313 U.S. 508 (1941).
[27] *Ibid.*, at 525-526. [28] 302 U.S. 464 (1938).

tricity distribution systems. On the authority of the Mellon cases [29] it was said that the plaintiff companies had no standing in court to question the propriety of a federal loan. The municipalties were constitutionally empowered to establish publicly owned plants. In the absence of a contract so stipulating the company had no constitutional right to be free of competition. A year later the Court was asked to rule that the Tennessee Valley Authority was exceeding the delegated authority of the federal government and depriving persons of property without due process of law in competing with the private sale and distribution of electric power. The Court sustained the lower court which had dismissed the petition for an injunction.[30] None of the companies was operating under a charter granting it freedom from competition. The companies had suffered no legal damage and were without standing to challenge the validity of the government's program in the Tennessee Valley area. Evidently objections to public competition are now political questions. They are, that is to say, beyond the jurisdiction of the courts, and are to be passed upon by Congress or by executive agencies.

An attempt to have the municipal bankruptcy provision of the Federal Bankruptcy Act of 1937 held contrary to the Tenth Amendment met with failure, although Justices McReynolds and Butler contended that the decision in the Ashton case in 1936 applied as well here as to the act there held invalid.[31] The monetary provisions of Article I were held to justify the Gold Clause invalidation, even when the contract provided for payment in foreign coin.[32] And the police power under the tax clause was held applicable to the regulation of the sale of firearms, despite the guarantee in the Second Amendment of the right to keep and bear arms.[33]

[29] *Supra*, 190. [30] Tennessee Electric Power Co. v. T.V.A., 306 U.S. 118 (1939).
[31] U.S. v. Bekins, 304 U.S. 27 (1938).
[32] Guaranty Trust Co. v. Henwood, 307 U.S. 247 (1939), Bethlehem Steel Co. v. Zurich Ins. Co., 307 U.S. 265 (1939).
[33] Sonzinsky v. U.S., 300 U.S. 506 (1937), U.S. v. Miller, 307 U.S. 174 (1939).

That provision was intended to enable citizens to protect themselves against unjust government, to take part in militia service, not to safeguard criminals whose profession requires the use of sawed-off shotguns or sub-machine guns.

In one of the last decisions of the 1940 term the Court held that Congress has power to regulate primary elections at which nominations for Congressional office were made.[34] To the extent that the Newberry case [35] had held that primaries are not elections, so far as the national power is concerned, it was disregarded. The fact that primaries had come into existence since 1789 was no more determinative of the Congressional power over the free election of its own members than the fact that telephone, telegraph and wireless communication were not contemplated by the fathers, limited the scope of the commerce clause. Primaries have become an integral part of the process of election and the power of Congress applies as effectively to protecting the right of qualified persons to vote for members of the national legislature in that stage of the election as it does to securing the same right in the final stage.

THE REVOLUTION IN DUE PROCESS

The cases dealing with state legislation contain the more significant discussion of due process, but there are a number of cases involving Congressional legislation which indicate how materially the conception of due process has been altered since 1936. Probably the most definite principle recently expressed in this connection is that equal protection of the laws is not included within the Fifth, as it is within the Fourteenth Amendment, and that, therefore, Congress has a greater freedom of classification than is allowed the states.[36] But this

[34] U.S. v. Classic, 313 U.S. 299 (1941).
[35] Newberry v. U.S., 256 U.S. 232 (1921).
[36] Steward Machine Co. v. Davis, 301 U.S. 548, 584 (1937).

was not an entirely new pronouncement and the history of constitutional adjudication in the last thirty years indicates that due process alone can include and has included all that is needful, if the Court is disposed to apply it with a jealous regard for the rights of private property and the once sacred liberty of contract.

A fair measure of the difference between the pre-1937 and the post-1937 interpretations of due process can be had by comparing the attitude of suspicion and distrust found in the Railroad Pension opinion with that of deference toward Congressional intentions exhibited in the cases interpreting the scope of the Labor Relations Act. In the first a pension scheme for railroad employees was scornfully dismissed as a meddlesome piece of social welfare tinkering. In the second the Court defers to Congress' finding that when Congress interfered with the rights of employers to hire and fire as they saw fit, and with the rights of employees to organize in many groups or to refuse to organize at all, it was doing so in order "to protect commerce against threatened industrial strife." [37] If Congress has power to deal with the subject, that is to say, then the Court will allow great freedom to Congress in its choice of means for dealing with that subject. The opinion of Chief Justice Hughes in Currin v. Wallace is further illustrative of those in recent cases where the due process issue has been raised:

> It is of the essence of the plenary power conferred that Congress may exercise its discretion in the use of the power. Congress may choose the commodities and places to which its regulation shall apply. Congress may consider and weigh relative situations and needs. Congress is not restricted by any technical requirement but may make limited applications and resort to tests so that it may have the benefit of experience in deciding upon the continuance or extension of a policy which under the Constitution it is free to adopt. As

[37] N.L.R.B. v. Mackay Radio & T. Co., 304 U.S. 333, 347 (1938).

to such choices, the question is one of wisdom and not of power.[38]

In the last few years the Court has been inclined to look with suspicion upon some of the administrative techniques used in enforcing and applying the acts of Congress but it has not found that any of the acts themselves provided or required unconstitutional procedures. The battle has become one primarily over administrative rather than constitutional law, if a somewhat tenuous distinction in nomenclature may be drawn. There is much evidence to indicate the increasing importance of that field of public law which deals with the powers and procedures of administrative boards and agents, and in this field it is probable that due process will play an important role, more important, in all likelihood, than in discussions concerned with the constitutionality of statutes.[39]

DELEGATION OF DISCRETIONARY AUTHORITY

After the N.I.R.A. was held unconstitutional on the basis of the delegation of powers principle and the Bituminous Coal Act was invalidated partly for that reason, the Court had established another area in which it would have the choice long enjoyed when interpreting the commerce and due process clauses. It had alternative precedents to choose from, and legislation could be justified or condemned with equal authority, depending upon the decision of the Court. Since 1937 only the pre-1935 line has been utilized. And in sustaining some of the legislation challenged on this ground the Court has gone far in allowing to Congress the right to delegate to administrative agencies and to private groups

[38] 306 U.S. 1, 14 (1939). Cf. U.S. v. Rock Royal Cooperative, 307 U.S. 533, 570-573 (1939).

[39] For a recent comprehensive collection of cases with helpful notes on administrative due process, cf. Walter Gellhorn, *Administrative Law: Cases and Comments* (1940), chs. IV-IX.

power to make decisions affecting a great many aspects of economic enterprise.

Both the Tobacco Inspection Act and the second Agricultural Adjustment Act were challenged on the delegation of legislative powers ground. The Court held, however, that Congress had not abdicated its legislative powers but had laid down the policies and established the standards upon which the administrative agents must act.[40] The referendum held among tobacco growers to determine whether the first act would be effective was valid since this vote did not legislate a code into existence. "Congress has merely placed a restriction upon its own regulation by withholding its operation as to a given market 'unless two-thirds of the growers voting favor it.'"

Mr. Justice Roberts, who wrote the majority opinion in Mulford v. Smith, dissented in the cases sustaining the Agricultural Marketing Agreement Act, partly upon the delegation ground. He argued at length that the statute unconstitutionally delegated to an executive officer "authority to impose regulations within supposed limits and according to supposed standards so vague as in effect to invest him with uncontrolled power of legislation."[41] The Secretary of Agriculture, he said, was given authority to determine what commodities shall be regulated, in what areas they are to be regulated, the period of regulation, and the character of the regulations to be imposed. Under the principles set forth in the Panama Oil and Schechter cases such delegation should be held contrary to Article I, section 1, of the Constitution.

In sustaining the act against this charge Mr. Justice Reed first announces the general principle to be observed:

> In dealing with legislation involving questions of economic adjustment, each enactment must be considered to determine whether it states the purpose which the Congress

---

[40] Currin v. Wallace, 306 U.S. 1, 15 (1939), Mulford v. Smith, 307 U.S. 38, 48, 49 (1939). [41] H. P. Hood & Sons v. U.S., 307 U.S. 588, 604 (1939).

> seeks to accomplish and the standards by which that purpose is to be worked out with sufficient exactness to enable those affected to understand these limits. Within these tests the Congress needs specify only so far as is reasonably practicable.[42]

Unlike the N.I.R.A. this Act was not couched in "the most general terms." The aim is to restore parity prices; the procedure to be followed is described; and the list of commodities to which it may be applied enumerated. "The Act authorizes a marketing agreement and order to be issued for such production or marketing regions or areas as are practicable. A city milk shed seems homogeneous. This standard of practicality is a limit on the power to issue orders. It determines when an order may be promulgated." Nor did Congress delegate to the producers the power to put an order into effect. Congress had the power to put the order into effect without their approval. "A requirement of such approval would not be an invalid delegation."

It is clear that the majority viewed more leniently the restrictions upon the delegation of authority to administrative agents than it had done in the Panama Oil and Carter Coal cases. The point of view of Reed is comparable to that of Cardozo's dissent in the Panama Oil case:

> Discretion is not unconfined and vagrant. It is canalized within banks that keep it from overflowing . . . the separation of powers between the Executive and Congress is not a doctrinaire concept to be made use of with pedantic rigor. There must be sensible approximation, there must be elasticity of adjustment, in response to the practical necessities of government, which cannot foresee today the developments of tomorrow in their nearly infinite variety.[43]

A still more recent expression of this attitude is found in the opinion of Mr. Justice Stone for a unanimous Court in one of the cases sustaining the Fair Labor Standards Act. In

[42] U.S. v. Rock Royal Cooperative, 307 U.S. 533, 574 (1939).

[43] Panama Refining Co. v. Ryan, 293 U.S. 388, 440 (1935).

answering the argument that the standards prescribed in the act for fixing the minimum wage between 30 and 40 cents per hour are too vague and indefinite, and that Congress did not prescribe the relative weight to be given to the various factors involved, Stone says that Congress did all that was necessary.

> The Constitution, viewed as a continuously operative charter of government, is not to be interpreted as demanding the impossible or the impracticable. The essentials of the legislative function are the determination of the legislative policy and its formulation as a rule of conduct. Those essentials are preserved when Congress specifies the basic conclusions of fact upon ascertainment of which, from relevant data by a designated administrative agency, it ordains that its statutory command is to be effective.[44]

If, then, Congress prescribes the policy, and enumerates the facts or factors which are to be taken into consideration by the agency, and if the act is so drawn that "Congress, the courts, and the public can ascertain whether the agency has conformed to the standards which Congress has prescribed," it has exercised its power of legislating. Just as Congress may accept and act "upon the advice of experts as to social and economic conditions," so it may make the effect of its acts depend upon "the administrative judgment as to the relative weights to be given to these factors in each case when that judgment in other respects is arrived at in the manner prescribed by the statute."

In spite of the breadth of discretion which these rulings and statements appear to make allowable, it is also evident that the Schechter case has not been overruled. It stands as a warning to Congress and a weapon available to the Court. But so long as the Court abides by the principles more recently expressed, the shotgun-behind-the-door should have the desirable effect of causing Congress to consider more

---

[44] Opp Cotton Mills v. Administrator, 312 U.S. 126, 145 (1941).

carefully the terms of its legislation, without seriously impairing its ability to deal with the problems confronting it.

STATE LEGISLATION AND THE NEW DUE PROCESS

It is evident that the decisions of the Court since the spring of 1937 have resulted in a considerable extension of national power. A mechanical theory of federalism might, if applied here, produce the conclusion that the Court has been correspondingly unsympathetic with state legislation. This would be a misleading assumption, although it is true enough that there are a few areas in which the states could previously legislate which are now closed to them. But it is also true that there are other, and not less vital, areas from which the states were excluded before 1937 and in which they now function. Much of the recent legislative expansion has been at the expense of that "twilight zone" from which the Court formerly excluded the operation of both national and local statutes.

Statistics may help to suggest the nature of the change. It will be remembered that since the spring of 1937 no act of Congress has been held unconstitutional. The figures for state legislation are not so striking. Between February 5, 1937 and June, 1941, state legislation was invalidated in 26 cases. This figure is smaller than that for the preceding four and a half years, when it was 37, but it is not a remarkable one. When broken down, however, it takes on a greater interest and significance. For of the 26 cases 12 involved the protection of civil liberties. Only two of the 37 cases in the preceding years were of that kind. In that period, moreover, there were 12 cases in which the Fourteenth Amendment was utilized in order to hold unconstitutional statutes interfering with the rights of property. Since 1937 there have been but two such cases, and the last of these was decided in January, 1938. The transformation of that amendment, and particularly of the due process clause therein, constitutes a change in constitutional law which promises to be one of the major effects of the Court battle.

When Mr. Justice Roberts changed sides and the new majority sustained the State of Washington's minimum wage law [45] the modification of due process was begun. But even though this case explicitly overruled the Adkins decision of 1923, and in effect overruled the New York decision of 1936, it might have brought a change no greater than that of the Nebbia decision in 1934.[46] In spite of what Roberts said in that opinion about prices he voted with the 1934 dissenters in the 1936 decision. While Nebbia came as an almost isolated instance, the West Coast Hotel case was only the opening move in the Court's strategic retreat produced by the Roosevelt Court bill. That this retreat went farther than was at first intended is highly probable.

A few weeks after the wage decision a bare majority held that a Georgia statute allowing mutual insurance companies to act through salaried resident employees but excluding stock companies from the same privilege was contrary to the equal protection clause.[47] The significance of the decision is not so much in the difference between Mr. Justice McReynolds's statement that there is here arbitrary and unwarranted discrimination, and Mr. Justice Robert's dissenting view that the classification had not been shown to be arbitrary with sufficient clearness to overcome the normal presumption of validity. It is rather in the fact not known in May of 1937 that this was to be the last case, for at least four years, in which the equal protection clause was to be employed for the protection of property rights. During those years the prediction of Miller in the Slaughter House opinion concerning the application of that clause was substantially correct.

On January 31, 1938, the Court decided the case of Con-

---

[45] West Coast Hotel v. Parrish, 300 U.S. 379 (1937). [46] *Supra,* 169.
[47] Hartford Steam Boiler Co. v. Harrison, 301 U.S. 459 (1937).

necticut General Life Insurance Co. v. Johnson.[48] Before 1937 this decision would have attracted little attention. Even in 1938 it would probably have been considered a run-of-the-mill affair had it not been for the lone-wolf dissent of the newly appointed Mr. Justice Black. The majority held a California tax statute as applied to a foreign insurance company doing business in California (the subject of the tax being reinsurance premiums paid in Connecticut by companies doing business in California and on California risks) contrary to the due process clause. Mr. Justice Black paid relatively little attention to the argument of the majority, for his principal contention was that the word "person" in the Fourteenth Amendment was not intended to include corporations, and, therefore, the statute could not possibly be held contrary to the due process clause. "The history of the Amendment proves that the people were told that its purpose was to protect weak and helpless human beings and were not told that it was intended to remove corporations in any fashion from the control of state governments." [49] The Court should correct its sixty years of error, as it had just corrected another error by overruling the Adkins decision.

Justice Black's plea for the abandonment of an interpretation which had resulted in so many decisions holding state acts unconstitutional produced a good deal of surprise, and a great deal of scorn from the legal profession. Many of those who had long been critics of the due process rulings of the Court were unwilling to accept his argument. To most of them it appeared that he would have been on firmer historical and legal ground had he argued against a substantive conception of due process rather than attempt to confine the term "person" to natural persons, when it had, long before 1868, frequently been applied to artificial, corporate persons as well. But perhaps Black did not take that line because he

[48] 303 U.S. 77 (1938).
[49] *Ibid.*, 87. Cf. the discussion on this point, *supra*, 97-98.

wished to see a broader application of due process in civil liberties cases, and to this end a substantive interpretation was essential. At any rate he apparently gave up his crusade for a narrower interpretation of "person" almost immediately, and since January, 1938, he has joined in taking jurisdiction of many causes which could not have been considered by the Court had it accepted the argument of his dissenting opinion.

But if Black lost on the ground that he chose for the opening battle, his campaign was not lost. Not since the case in which he then dissented have the due process or equal protection clauses been employed in holding invalid an act interfering with rights of property. They have, on the other hand, been more frequently applied for the protection of civil liberties than in any preceding period.

Aside from the minimum wage case the most striking reversal involving the Fourteenth Amendment came in Madden v. Kentucky.[50] This had to do not with due process or equal protection but with the privileges and immunities clause, and it expressly overruled Colgate v. Harvey. Kentucky imposed on its citizens a tax of fifty cents per hundred dollars on bank deposits outside of the state, while taxing those in the state ten cents per hundred dollars. The Court found that this classification did not violate the due process or equal protection clause, and that no national privilege or immunity was involved.

It was pointed out in the last chapter that the problem of taxation where questions of interstate jurisdiction arose had come to be discussed largely in terms of due process. That too has apparently gone the way of the 1935 interpretation of privileges and immunities. Thus in Curry v. McCanless [51] the majority ruled that the multiple taxation of intangibles does

---

[50] 309 U.S. 83 (1940). Roberts and McReynolds, JJ. dissented.

[51] 307 U.S. 357 (1939). Mr. Justice Butler dissented in an opinion with which the Chief Justice and Justices McReynolds and Roberts concurred.

not necessarily deny due process. Mr. Justice Stone for the majority says that "all subjects over which the sovereign power of a state extends are objects of taxation . . . there are many circumstances in which more than one state may have jurisdiction to impose a tax." It does not follow that the Fourteenth Amendment, even with the majority disposed as at present, cannot be made the basis for holding invalid any instance of multiple taxation, but it is clear that the present point of view on the subject greatly enlarges the tax jurisdiction of the states, as it decreases the scope of the Court's veto.

Another modification of due process in the tax field was set forth in the case sustaining a Wisconsin act of 1935 imposing a tax on corporate dividends received in 1933 at rates different from those applicable in that year to other types of income.[52] Three members of the Court believed, not without justification, that the decision invalidating retroactive gift taxes required that this act be held invalid. But the majority found that here the taxpayer would have received the dividends whether he knew they were to be taxable or not, and was not therefore deprived by the retroactive tax of any opportunity to avoid the tax.

In a limited space it is impossible to indicate adequately the extent to which property due process has been modified. It is not only in tax cases,[53] although here the change is apparent and may be far-reaching in its effects. Statutes allowing peaceful picketing,[54] providing for state unemploy-

---

[52] Welch v. Henry, 305 U.S. 134 (1938).

[53] For some other due process tax cases of the period see First Bank Corp. v. Minnesota, 301 U.S. 234 (1937), Great A. & P. Co. v. Grosjean, 301 U.S. 412 (1937), Felt & Tarrant Mfg. Co. v. Gallagher, 306 U.S. 62 (1939), Dixie Ohio Express Co. v. St. Comm., 306 U.S. 72 (1939), Chesebro v. Los Angeles Cty. Flood Control, 306 U.S. 459 (1939), Graves v. Elliott, 307 U.S. 383 (1939), Newark Fire Ins. Co. v. St. Bd. of Tax Appeals, 307 U.S. 313 (1939), Pearson v. McGraw, 308 U.S. 313 (1939), Ford Motor Co. v. Beauchamp, 308 U.S. 331 (1939), Whitney v. Tax Comm., 309 U.S. 530 (1940), Wisconsin v. J. C. Penney Co., 311 U.S. 435 (1940). Here four Justices dissented, arguing that the Connecticut General Life Insurance Co. decision required a ruling of invalidity.

[54] Senn v. Tile Layers Union, 301 U.S. 468 (1937).

ment insurance in accordance with the federal Social Security Act,[55] and exempting agricultural activities from the criminal provisions of an anti-trust act,[56] have all been sustained. In the first two of these cases four Justices vainly argued that the old order was being overthrown, that the Constitution was being changed by interpretation. In the third case only McReynolds of the four dissenters remained to protest against the overruling of the Conolly case.[57] And when, in April, 1941, the Court sustained a statute fixing maximum rates for employment agencies, it did so unanimously.[58] Mr. Justice McReynolds, habitual dissenter of the preceding three years, as well as the most frequent dissenter the Court has ever known, and the last of the conservative majority which dominated the Court between 1923 and 1937, was no longer present to protest against the overruling of Ribnik v. McBride.[59]

The new majority's attitude of hands-off in property due process cases is well expressed in one of Mr. Justice Frankfurter's opinions. A Virginia statute prohibited contracts of insurance within the state except through regularly constructed and registered agents and forbade local agents to share more than half of their commission with non-resident brokers. This, said Mr. Justice Roberts for the three dissenters, is an attempt "by Virginia to compel a non-resident to pay a resident of Virginia for services which the latter does not in fact render and is not required to render." [60] Justice Frankfurter replied:

> The mere fact that state action may have repercussions beyond state lines is of no judicial significance so long as the action is not within that domain which the Constitution forbids . . . It is equally immaterial that such state action

[55] Carmichael v. Southern Coal & Coke Co., 301 U.S. 495 (1937).
[56] Tigner v. Texas, 310 U.S. 141 (1940). [57] *Supra,* 164.
[58] Olsen v. Nebraska, 313 U.S. 236 (1941). [59] *Supra,* 167.
[60] Osborn v. Ozlin, 310 U.S. 53, 69 (1940).

may run counter to the economic wisdom either of Adam Smith or of J. Maynard Keynes, or may be ultimately mischievous even from the point of view of avowed state policy. Our inquiry must be much narrower. It is whether Virginia has taken hold of a matter within her power, or has reached beyond her borders to regulate a subject which was none of her concern because the Constitution has placed control elsewhere.[61]

THE EXPANSION OF CIVIL LIBERTIES

This hands-off attitude has not, however, been characteristic of the civil liberties cases. There the Court has shown less deference to legislative majorities than ever before. Nine of the twelve [62] rulings of unconstitutionality depended upon an interpretation of the Fourteenth Amendment which was not explicitly accepted until 1931.[63] In 1937 the Court, with only Mr. Justice Butler dissenting, held that the rights of the first ten amendments are not automatically protected by the Fourteenth. Only those rights which are "of the very essence of a scheme of ordered liberty" are included within the liberty there guaranteed.[64] This excludes various traditional procedural rights, but includes some substantive rights not listed in any eighteenth-century bill of rights, and probably in none of the nineteenth. Some of the older rights, furthermore, have been given a broader interpretation.

[61] *Ibid.*, 62. Cf. Railroad Comm. v. Rowan & Nichols Oil Co., 310 U.S. 573 (1940). Here the same three dissenters contended that the majority was not following Thompson v. Consolidated Gas Corp., 300 U.S. 55 (1937), the last of the pre-February 5, 1937, property-due process cases. Justice Frankfurter's majority opinion is particularly interesting for its attitude of deference to the findings of administrative agencies.

[62] This number does not involve such cases as Chambers v. Florida, 309 U.S. 227 (1940) and White v. Texas, 310 U.S. 530 (1940), where the validity of a statute was not involved.

[63] Lindsey v. Washington, 301 U.S. 397 (1937) was an *ex post facto* case, and Lane v. Wilson, 307 U.S. 268 (1939) involved an Oklahoma registration law seeking to attain the objective of the old Grandfather Clause act. This statute was held contrary to the Fifteenth Amendment.

[64] Palko v. Connecticut, 302 U.S. 319, 325 (1937).

Thus the freedom of the press has recently been held to include the right to distribute pamphlets and handbills free from interference by municipal authorities.[65] The local governments have, said the Court, the duty to keep their communities' streets open and available for movement of people and property,[66] but in doing so they may not make such regulations a means of exercising previous administrative control over freedom of expression. Either a licensing system or absolute prohibition of distribution is invalid, and the purpose to keep the streets free of litter is insufficient to prohibit the distribution of pamphlets or sheets discussing religious or public questions.

Cantwell v. Connecticut[67] and Hague v. C.I.O.[68] invalidated somewhat similar municipal regulations. The first was one of the several recent cases involving the activities of the sect known as Jehovah's Witnesses. Members of this group refuse to apply for permits to carry on their activities on the principle that any such acknowledgment of an earthly power would be an act of disobedience to God's commandments. When three members of this sect were found guilty of violating a statute prohibiting any person from soliciting contributions for a religious or charitable cause without the previous approval of the local secretary of the public welfare council, the Court found that the act violated the rights of free speech and freedom of religion protected by the due process clause. In the Hague case a municipal ordinance prohibiting public assemblies without a permit from the director of public safety was held to deny the rights of freedom of speech and of peaceable assembly. A peculiar feature of this decision was that the majority could not agree whether

---

[65] Lovell v. Griffin, 303 U.S. 444 (1938), Schneider v. Irvington, 308 U.S. 147 (1939).

[66] Cf. the still more recent case, Cox v. New Hampshire, 312 U.S. 569 (1941), sustaining the right to regulate parades. Here members of Jehovah's Witnesses had refused to apply for a permit to parade.

[67] 310 U.S. 296 (1940). [68] 307 U.S. 496 (1939).

only the due process clause, or the privileges and immunities clause as well, had been infringed. Justices Roberts and Black, with whom the Chief Justice concurred in part, thought that the latter clause was involved in that citizens had been denied the right to discuss the National Labor Relations Act, this being a right of national citizenship.[69]

Evidence that the "clear and present danger" test stated by Justice Holmes in the Schenck case [70] might again be used as a criterion by the Court is found in Herndon v. Lowry.[71] Herndon was a negro and an organizer for the Communist Party. Convicted under the Georgia laws for inciting insurrection, he was freed by a five-to-four vote of the Supreme Court on the grounds that he had been deprived of the freedom protected by the Fourteenth Amendment. There was no evidence that his activities had constituted a "clear and present danger," an incitement to revolution. The statute, moreover, is so vague in its terms as to furnish no "sufficiently ascertainable standard of guilt." Neither here nor in the earlier DeJonge case did the Court hold a statute invalid for making membership in the Communist Party a crime. In both instances the Court restricted its decision to ruling upon the application of the statutes to the particular acts and circumstances involved.

Missouri's refusal to admit negroes to a state-supported law school, even though the state offered to pay the fees of negroes at such a school in one of the adjacent states, was found to deny equal protection of the laws.[72] States may re-

---

[69] In Edwards v. California, 62 Sup. Ct. 164 (1941) the Court unanimously held unconstitutional a statute penalizing bringing or assisting to bring into the state any indigent person. Five Justices thought the act a violation of the commerce clause but Justices Douglas, Black, Murphy, and Jackson thought it a violation of the privileges and immunities of national citizenship.

[70] Schenck v. U.S., 249 U.S. 47 (1919).

[71] 301 U.S. 242 (1937). Cf. Lanzetta v. New Jersey, 306 U.S. 451 (1939) in which a statute making it a crime for a person not engaged in any lawful occupation, and who has previously been convicted of a crime, to be a known member of any gang was held to deny due process because it was vague and uncertain.

[72] Missouri *ex rel.* Gaines v. Canada, 305 U.S. 337 (1938).

quire segregation of the races in the schools, but they must provide separate and, theoretically, equal facilities for those denied admission to the schools for whites.

The two cases[73] in which statutes prohibiting picketing and prohibiting the carrying of banners or signs by picketers were held to deny due process of law certainly add a content to the Fourteenth Amendment not planned for in 1868, as they also reflect a point of view which would have been unacceptable to the majority in 1935. But, said Mr. Justice Murphy,

> In the circumstances of our times the dissemination of information concerning the facts of a labor dispute must be regarded as within that area of free discussion that is guaranteed by the Constitution. . . . Abridgment of the liberty of such discussion can be justified only where the clear danger of substantive evils arises under circumstances affording no opportunity to test the merits of ideas by competition for acceptance in the market of public opinion.[74]

Statutes prohibiting all picketing, or the display of any signs or banners, take no account of the circumstances of the case and interfere with the means employed by workers to discuss the labor controversies in which they are involved.

A few days after these rulings the Court handed down its decision in the much discussed flag salute case.[75] Here, with only Justice Stone dissenting, a statute requiring children attending public schools to salute the flag was sustained. The presumption of constitutionality, so repeatedly applied in the property-due process cases of the preceding three years, was here applied to a statute which had the effect of preventing children belonging to the sect of Jehovah's Witnesses from attending public schools. The Court which, only two weeks before, had overruled legislative judgment in the

[73] Thornhill v. Alabama, 310 U.S. 88 (1940), Carlson v. California, 310 U.S. 106 (1940). [74] 310 U.S. at 102, 104-105.

[75] Minersville School District v. Gobitis, 310 U.S. 586 (1940).

Cantwell and anti-picketing cases, refuses to do so here since to do so "would amount to no less than the pronouncement of a pedagogical and psychological dogma in a field where courts possess no marked and certainly no controlling competence." Children may not be required to attend the public schools, "but it is a very different thing for this Court to exercise censorship over the conviction of legislatures that a particular program or exercise will best promote in the minds of the children who attend the common schools an attachment to the institutions of their country."

Just how close was the connection between this decision and the crisis fervor produced by the successful march of the Nazi army into the Low Countries and France only the events and decisions of the next few years can determine. Certainly it seems out of line with the opinions which went before.

TAXATION OF GOVERNMENTAL INSTRUMENTALITIES

Aside from the civil liberties cases most of the rulings of unconstitutionality have come in cases involving the problem of federalism. But only one of these has to do with the taxation of government instrumentalities, a doctrine so productive of such decisions in earlier periods. There are several cases of 1937 and 1938 which indicated that the Court was modifying somewhat the rigor of its previous rulings.[76] In one of these cases Mr. Justice Black, although concurring in the result, contended that what was needed was a review and reexamination of the entire doctrine on which the Court was here proceeding.[77] This radical revision began less than a year later in Graves v. New York.[78] After an examination of the doctrine's history which is more ingenious than realis-

---

[76] James v. Dravo Contracting Co., 302 U.S. 134 (1937), Helvering v. Mountain Producers Corp., 303 U.S. 376 (1938), Helvering v. Gerhardt, 304 U.S. 405 (1938). [77] 304 U.S. 405, 424-430 (1938). [78] 306 U.S. 466 (1939).

tic the older cases were overruled "so far as they recognize an implied constitutional immunity from income taxation of the salaries of officers or employees of the national or a state government or their instrumentalities."

This decision presumably applies to more than the line of cases descending from Dobbins v. Erie County and Collector v. Day,[79] but it leaves intact the progeny of Weston v. Charleston.[80] The income from some sixty-odd billions of national, state and local securities continues to be immune from taxation by the other member of the federal system. It is likely that further modifications will be made in this doctrine which has long been an unjustifiable gloss upon the principles of federalism.

STATE TAXES AND THE COMMERCE CLAUSE

Almost all of the remaining cases in which state acts have been held unconstitutional by the Court since 1937 were decided under the commerce clause [81] and every one of the seven commerce cases involved a state tax which in some fashion interfered with interstate commerce or extrastate business. These acts were among those which have demonstrated of recent years a tendency toward the erection of barriers to interstate trade, or, as has been said with extravagant alarm, toward the Balkanization of the United States. That unhappy condition does not seem just around the corner, but the search by the states for new sources of revenue in an age when business continues to transcend state lines has produced problems to which the solution is not yet

[79] In Pittman v. Home Owners Loan Corp., 308 U.S. 21 (1939), the Court held that Congress could exempt the mortgages held by the H.O.L.C. from state taxation. In O'Malley v. Woodrough, 307 U.S. 277 (1939) the imposition of a federal income tax upon the salary of a federal judge appointed after the new tax provision went into effect was sustained. [80] *Supra*, 50.

[81] The once deadly contract clause accounted for two cases, Indiana v. Brand, 303 U.S. 95 (1938), and Wood v. Lovett, 313 U.S. 362 (1941).

clear.[82] Some examples of the Court's rulings will illustrate certain of the difficulties.

A California tax upon those motor "caravans" brought into the state[83] and a Florida "inspection" tax upon imported cement[84] were both found to discriminate against interstate commerce. A similar ruling was unanimously reached as against a Washington occupation tax measured by gross receipts and here levied against a stevedoring company engaged in loading and unloading vessels in interstate and foreign commerce.[85] With Mr. Justice Black dissenting, a "privilege" tax upon gross income was held to violate the commerce clause when imposed upon a company engaged in both interstate and local business.[86] And the Court was unanimous in invalidating a tax of $250 imposed on out-of-state merchants displaying samples in hotel rooms for the purpose of securing retail orders.[87]

An Indiana gross income tax was invalid when applied to a company which sold eighty per cent of its products in interstate and foreign commerce.[88] The tax as here applied made no distinction between the sources of the company's receipts, and by taxing receipts from business derived from out-of-state, exposed the company to double taxation, which constitutes a burden on that commerce. The Court also found that the New York City sales tax could not validly be imposed on sales of fuel oil, when the oil had been imported from abroad, kept under bond and refined by the company, later to be withdrawn from bond and sold in New York harbor to for-

---

[82] See the articles on this subject included in *Law and Contemporary Problems,* VIII, No. 2 (Spring, 1941).

[83] Ingels v. Morf, 300 U.S. 290 (1937). An amended statute, which the Court found did not discriminate against interstate commerce, was sustained in Clark v. Paul Gray, Inc., 306 U.S. 583 (1939).

[84] Hale v. Bimco Trading Co., 306 U.S. 375 (1939).

[85] Puget Sound Stevedoring Co. v. Tax Comm., 302 U.S. 90 (1937).

[86] Gwin, White & Prince v. Henneford, 305 U.S. 434 (1939).

[87] Best & Co. v. Maxwell, 311 U.S. 454 (1940).

[88] J. D. Adams Mfg. Co. v. Storen, 304 U.S. 307 (1938).

eign-bound vessels.[89] But in contrast to this ruling it held that the same tax was not a violation of the commerce clause when applied to sales of coal brought from Pennsylvania and sold in New York to public utility and steamship companies.[90] The effect of the tax upon interstate or foreign commerce was found to be incidental and to require companies engaged in such commerce to bear no more than "their just share of state tax burdens."

Still more recently a closely divided Court sustained a state tax on foreign corporations measured by dividends declared by the corporation out-of-state, to the extent that the income was derived from property located in and business done in the state.[91] This case was discussed in terms of the due process rather than the commerce clause. It may indicate the return of due process to the field of intra-state taxation, but that is not yet a likely bet, for, of the minority of four, two, Chief Justice Hughes and Justice McReynolds, have since retired.

That the present Court is disposed to go far in sustaining state taxation of extraterritorial values is again indicated in the Nelson cases.[92] Here the Iowa use tax, a complement to the retail sales tax, was sustained in its application to foreign corporations. These corporations were required to act as the agent of the state in collecting the tax on goods sold through their mail order departments to local buyers, although the mail order departments were located outside the state.

But what may prove to have been the most significant expression of principle as regards such taxes came in the recent Arkansas gasoline tax case. The act forbade the entry into

[89] McGoldrick v. Gulf Oil Corp., 309 U.S. 414 (1940).

[90] McGoldrick v. Berwind-White Coal Mining Co., 309 U.S. 33 (1940). The Chief Justice dissented in an opinion with which Justices Roberts and McReynolds concurred.

[91] Wisconsin v. J. C. Penney Co., 311 U.S. 435 (1940).

[92] Nelson v. Sears, Roebuck & Co., 312 U.S. 359 (1941), Nelson v. Montgomery Ward Co., 312 U.S. 373 (1941). Justice Roberts dissented for himself and the Chief Justice.

the state of any automobile or truck carrying over twenty gallons of gasoline to be used by that vehicle until the state tax of six and one-half cents per gallon had been paid. In McCarroll v. Dixie Greyhound Lines, Inc.[93] the majority found this to be an invalid burden upon interstate commerce. The buses of this company passed through a corner of the state en route from Memphis to St. Louis, and ordinarily carried enough gasoline for the entire trip, over three-fourths of which was in Missouri. The tax, said Mr. Justice McReynolds, had no reasonable relation to the use of the Arkansas highways.[94] Justices Black, Frankfurter, and Douglas dissented in a joint opinion. They found that the tax need place no burden upon interstate commerce. But their opinion is not primarily an expression of sympathy with state taxation, for it goes on to invite the intervention of Congress. In their view the problem here presented is only one aspect of a situation for which a single national rule is needed, and the Court cannot supply that rule.

> Judicial control of national commerce—unlike legislative regulations—must from inherent limitations of the judicial process treat the subject by the hit and miss method of deciding single local controversies upon evidence and information limited by the narrow rules of litigation. Spasmodic and unrelated instances of litigation cannot afford an adequate basis for the creation of integrated national rules which alone can afford that full protection for interstate commerce intended by the Constitution.[95]

Whether a majority of the Court will come to accept this self-denying view of the Court's role as umpire of the federal system, and whether Congress will accept the invitation, remains to be seen. Even if Congress did act its legislation

---

[93] 309 U.S. 176 (1940).

[94] A curiosity of the case is that there is a concurring opinion by Justice Stone with which the Chief Justice, and Justices Roberts and Reed, concur. The opinion of the Court is thus an expression of the opinion of Justice McReynolds alone, since Justice Murphy took no part.

[95] *Ibid.*, 188-189.

would have to be interpreted and applied to a great number of divergent statutes and situations. In this process the Court would continue to function as umpire, although the rules of the game would be based upon the Congressional declaration of policy. And in the absence of such action by Congress the Court will apparently continue to exhibit a reluctance to act as a censor of the righteousness of state legislatures seeking to tax business which spreads over more states than one.

There is an alternative to either of these methods of dealing with the problem of interstate tax barriers for which there is good historical precedent. The situation in state taxation is now similar to that in railroad regulation just prior to the Wabash decision.[96] Either the equivalent of the Wabash ruling—or, as now seems more likely, the exact opposite—may produce Congressional action, not simply in the form of a statute laying down general principles to be followed by the courts, but by a statute establishing a tax commission which, under general principles established by Congress, would have the duty of working out a division of revenue sources among states and between states and nation, perhaps laying its orders before Congress for approval or disapproval, as in England. The problems are so complex, so technical, so much matters of expediency rather than constitutionality, and so constantly shifting, that it may well be doubted whether anything less than such an expert and specialized tribunal will serve the purpose. States might be represented on such a commission, at least in an advisory capacity. Under the recent rulings such a scheme seems to be constitutionally defensible. As the history of the Interstate Commerce Commission indicates, the work of the courts in relation to such a plan would not end with a holding of constitutional validity.

---

[96] *Supra,* 90.

THE NEW CONSTITUTIONAL LAW

We are too close to the events of 1937-1941 to make it possible for us to determine the lasting effects of the decisions then handed down. There are, however, a number of tendencies outlined by those cases, tendencies which will apparently influence, if not determine, the law of the Constitution for some years to come.

Viewed in terms of governmental power, the most notable change from the doctrine of 1935-1936 is the great increase in the scope of Congressional authority under the commerce clause. The distinction between commerce and production is perhaps not entirely gone, but the conception of commerce as transportation has departed. Rather does the term now have a meaning nearer to that frequently used in the titles of schools or colleges of commerce, and there it ordinarily signifies business. Commerce among the states means, and should mean, business among the states. Transportation is one aspect of commerce, but only one. This conception of commerce does not extend the national commerce power to all economic enterprise, but it does not exclude it from that which involves more states than one. And it is obvious that an ever increasing proportion of business is of that character. It should be remembered, moreover, that a large part of agricultural enterprise is now safely within the commerce rubric. The regulation of agricultural marketing may be classifiably different from the regulation of production, but the farmer who wishes to sell all of the crop he has grown will find the restrictions contained in recently sustained legislation a deterrent as effective as one more immediately affixed to production. Similarly the tax imposed by the Bituminous Coal Act of 1937 can achieve the regulatory effects sought under the earlier Coal Conservation Act.

National control over the building of dams, whether for the development of power, the prevention of floods, or the conservation of water reserves for irrigation, no longer is limited to great interstate streams or to those in fact navigable. Potential navigability is a broad concept, capable, in sympathetic hands, of being applied to many small rivers, or to those which, without damming, would become dry beds in rainless seasons. And the tributaries of navigable streams include a large proportion of the nation's waterways.

The recent interpretation of the taxing-spending power may prove to be of even more far-reaching significance than the broader conception of the commerce power. Acceptance of the principle that the power to levy taxes to provide for the general welfare is a separate grant does not inevitably produce a verdict of constitutionality, as the first A.A.A. decision demonstrated. But the effect of this acceptance is likely to bolster the national authority. And when it is read in the light of the Social Security and other recent decisions its potential scope appears great indeed. Limitations upon the spending power may be devised, but under the second T.V.A. and the P.W.A. ruling, that power appears to be virtually boundless. These decisions make constitutionally possible a great increase in governmental ownership and operation, as well as the expansion of national subsidies to state and local publicly owned enterprise. With national subsidies, some measure of national supervision is almost inevitable.

The partial removal of old limitations upon inter-governmental taxation of public instrumentalities will at least increase the subject matter open to taxation by both national and state governments. It is not now apparent just how far this doctrine will be carried, and precisely what will be the effects upon the federal distribution of powers.

With the belated recognition that a primary election is a part of the governmental process the Court has begun to make possible some federal control of state restrictions upon the suffrage. Again, it is not yet clear what will be the scope under the effect of the recent ruling. But the Classic decision may have far-reaching importance, particularly in those states where the primary is the real election. Such a decision as that in Grovey v. Townsend,[97] although not overruled by the Classic case, appears inconsistent with the later view. The later decision holds that a primary for the election of Congressmen is part of the election, while the earlier ruling is based upon the premise that all primaries are private affairs. Congress and the federal courts will probably limit the right of the states to restrict the suffrage to favored groups.

The Hot Oil and Schechter decisions of 1935 challenged the foundation upon which a large proportion of regulatory legislation is erected. It has long been impossible to provide in statutes for all details or all contingencies. The N.I.R.A. did, to be sure, go very far in delegating authority, but it may be doubted whether it was so much the broad delegation as the spectacularly ambitious character of the statute which produced the decision of invalidity.[98] Had the Court believed the act to be substantively constitutional, it might have been able to accept the procedure there provided. Certainly the amount of delegation involved was far less than that contained in a number of Congressional acts passed during World War I. And, as has been previously remarked, the doctrine of the Schechter opinion, so far at least as the delegation of powers principle is concerned, has not been reversed. That doctrine may again be used against a regulatory statute when a majority of the Court views with alarm its substantive policy.

In the meantime the allowable range of discretion is great. It is difficult, probably impossible, to state the bounds of the allowable quantitatively. Both the dissenting opinion of Justice Roberts in the Hood case and the various majority opinions surveyed above indicate, however, that the Court is now disposed to find that Congress does all that is neces-

[97] 294 U.S. 699 (1935). *Supra*, 150.

[98] Cf. Corwin, *Constitutional Revolution, Ltd.*, 49.

sary when it lays down general standards and establishes statutory objectives. Neither the objectives nor the standards need be stated in exact terms, nor need categories be used which are capable of precise measurement.

While the increase in Congressional power has been apparent to the proverbial man on the street, the accompanying broadening of the states' powers has not been generally understood. This extension has taken place not at the expense of Congressional authority but at the expense of the former no-man's land of due process. Since due process and equal protection have shed almost all of the meaning written into them between 1873 and 1936, that territory into which no legislature might safely venture has apparently vanished. It is apparently gone, that is to say, so far as concerns legislation regulating wages and hours, industrial relations and employment agencies, financial relations and extra-state taxation, monopolies and cooperatives. The categories used during the twenties for a discussion of the state police power are now largely inappropriate, so far at least as concerns legislation affecting property rights. It has been four years since a statute of that kind was set aside as contrary to due process or equal protection. No one can safely predict whether old style due process will some day be revived, but the omens do not now indicate such a revival.

What has been said applies to substantive due process. Procedural due process is not gone. Its importance may even be on the increase, particularly in the field where the courts are reviewing the actions of administrative officers and commissions.

Nor has all of substantive due process vanished. That concept is no longer employed as a constitutional justification for declaring unconstitutional legislation affecting property rights. Since 1937 it has been more frequently the basis for holding interferences with civil liberties invalid than in any previous period of our history. The no-man's land wherein neither the state nor national legislatures may venture for the purpose of limiting the guarantees of the bills of rights has been expanded. This tendency will probably not be continued during time of war, but its recent expansion is one of the real achievements of the reformed Court. It has greatly weakened the old charge that the Court was more zealous to protect the vested rights of the wealthy than the civil rights of the less privileged and the less orthodox.

It is not correct to say, as some critics of the recent decisions have said, that any tax law is now constitutional. The cases invalidating extra state taxation constitute a large proportion of the post-1937 decisions of unconstitutionality. True, the Court has been less suspicious of such attempts to reach values or transactions which transcend state lines than was previously the case. And when it has held such legislation invalid it has employed the commerce rather than the due process clause. The present situation is undoubtedly a serious as well as a complex one. Undoubtedly the states have sought to protect, to discriminate in favor of, local interests, as well as to reach legitimate sources of revenue. That discrimination would not justify a return to due process analytics. The judicial leniency and the use of the commerce clause in recent cases may both indicate the need for and the possibility of Congressional action. We need the kind of general rule which only Congress can formulate and establish. Piecemeal, after-the-fact review by the Court in the absence of such legislation will probably continue to prove unsatisfactory except to those who have confidence in the efficacy of dialectic.

Chapter XI

THE FUNCTION OF JUDICIAL REVIEW

IT WAS suggested in the introductory chapter that judicial review is our most characteristic, because our most unique political institution. It was further suggested that there must be a connection between this institution and the amazing longevity of the American Constitution. The expansion of that Constitution has been accomplished only in small degree by formal amendment. Adjustments made necessary by the vast changes in American life have been accomplished largely through interpretation. And the final interpreter has been the Supreme Court. To a much greater degree than was foreseen by the authors of the Constitution the Court has moulded the governmental processes, the social and economic practices, the very folkways of the country.

THE COURT AS PRODUCT

But if the Court has been a controlling force in American life, it has also been a product of that life. It was no independent agent above and apart from the culture of the country to which its decisions applied. In Mr. Dooley's famous phrase, the Supreme Court "follows th' eliction returns." In more academic, as well as more inclusive, language it may be said that the Court has always expressed the major movements in American history. Not just the election returns, and not just the economic transformations, but the totality of change which has produced the patterns and climates of opinion.

These generalizations are, I believe, profoundly correct, but they are not of themselves adequate. For the Court has not always followed the most recent election returns; sometimes the returns were those of a previous generation. The political or economic or cultural ideas expressed in decisions and opinions have not infrequently been those of a bygone era, as they have sometimes been representative of a contemporary minority. For this reason the Court has often operated as a conservative force, moving at a slower pace than the development of American civilization would have warranted. In certain notable instances, indeed, the Court was so far from being in harmony with the movement of American history that its decisions threatened the continued existence of that constitutional government which it desired to perpetuate. The basic character of judicial review may be clear but the history of its operation can not be inclusively presented in a simple formula.

Statistics suggest the magnitude of the problem even though they do not furnish clues to many of its most significant aspects. Between the first term of the Court in February of 1790 and the term ending in June of 1941 the Court considered the constitutionality of national and state legislation in more than two thousand cases. In 79 cases Congressional statutes were held to violate the Constitution, and it ruled against the validity of state legislation in 658 cases.

That this bulk of constitutional litigation is much greater than the fathers anticipated seems reasonably certain. I do not mean to imply that the courts usurped the power to pass upon conflicts between statute and Constitution. If the federal courts are granted no such powers the omission was apparently the product of an assumption that such a grant was not necessary. But the debates in the Convention also indicate that the framers believed that the role of the courts would be confined to setting aside explicit violations of the Constitution. The judiciary would not be concerned with the policy, the reasonableness or arbitrariness, the wisdom of legislation. It was Hamilton, the author of a plan which the Convention did not so much reject as ignore, not Madison or Wilson, or any of the score of men whose ideas were combined in the finished document, who advocated a broader sphere for the judiciary. And he did not do so until over six months after the Convention had adjourned. It was his theory, not that of Madison, which Marshall wrote into the law of the land. It was Hamilton and Marshall who were responsible for developing a Rousseauan conception of the general will safeguarded by an almost Platonic council, although the labors of that council were to be carried on not by resort to the stars, but by appeal to the spirit of the written Constitution.

What has just been said concerning the paternity of judicial review as it developed after 1801 may appear inconsistent with the previous statement that the Court's interpretation of the Constitution has been expressive of the course of American history. Is judicial review itself but a left-over from the Federalism that Jefferson defeated at the polls in 1800? I think not. For not even the genius of Hamilton and the ascendancy of Marshall could have established judicial review on this pattern had the seed not been suited to the soil. Modern judicial review is a product of many forces, but foremost among them must be reckoned a profoundly conservative strain in the American political character, as well as that abiding distrust in the officers of government vested with positive powers, which has long been one of our deepest feelings about government. Judicial review of the Hamilton-Marshall pattern was not foreordained by the events of the Revolution, the Confederation, or the Federalist era. Given the circumstances and the convictions of the day, some kind of judicial review was certain. Had Jefferson rather than Adams appointed a Chief Justice, it would probably have been judicial review of a more limited scope. The Supreme Court would have declared legislation, both state and national, contrary to the Constitution, but it is extremely improbable that it would have begun so early the exercise of powers akin to those of the rejected council of revision.

Had Jefferson appointed the Chief Justice in 1801 the Court would probably have been less nationalistic during the next three decades, and it is likely that the contract clause would not have become quite so formidable a bulwark against state regulatory and tax statutes. But the development of judicial review in the states supports the view that in 1788 Hamilton seized upon a conception in harmony with the trend of institutional development in the country of his adoption, whereas in the Federal Convention he had demonstrated his desire to see established a system entirely out of keeping with American traditions or ideals. This view is further supported by the failure of the Jacksonian Justices to repudiate the powers acquired under Marshall, and the continued expansion of judicial control long after manhood suffrage had become the universal rule.

THE COURT AND POLITICS

The intimate relation of the Court's decisions to the course of political controversy is additional evidence that the Court has never been more than temporarily divorced from the major currents of American life. As every reader of Mr. Charles Warren's admirable *The Supreme Court in United States History* knows, the Court has been a center in many political storms. The revisionary power has not been carried on in conditions of peaceful isolation. It is an illuminating paradox of American development that while there has been a general acceptance and approval of judicial review and of its expansion, there has at times been strong, even bitter criticism.

Jefferson's opposition to the Judiciary Act of 1801 and his denunciation of Marshall's doctrines have been cited.[1] He never regarded the Court as a final constitutional authority,[2] nor did Jackson[3] nor Lincoln. Jackson refused to support the Court's decision in the Cherokee Indian case. Lincoln, in one of his debates with Douglas, declared that if he were in Congress he would vote to prohibit slavery in the territories, in spite of the Dred Scott decision. And in his First Inaugural Address, he said that "if the policy of the government upon vital questions affecting the whole people is to be irrevocably fixed by decisions of the Supreme Court . . . the people will have ceased to be their own rulers, having to that extent practically resigned their government into the hands of that eminent tribunal."

Since 1861 the finality of the Court's decisions has been generally acquiesced in, but that has not meant an end to the criticism of decisions, or to proposals for controlling the way in which the Court should exercise its powers. Theodore Roosevelt, primarily because of the invalidation of so many state, and some national, statutes dealing with problems of social and economic reform, even advocated the recall of judicial decisions, although in 1912 he would have applied this principle only to the state courts. "I contend," he said, "that the people, in the nature of things, must be better judges of what is the preponderant opinion than the courts,

[1] *Supra,* 31, 48.

[2] "The constitution has erected no such single tribunal, knowing that to whatever hands confided, with the corruptions of time and party, its members would become despots. When the legislative or executive functionaries act unconstitutionally, they are responsible to the people in their elective capacity. The exemption of the judges from that is quite dangerous enough." *Writings* (Ford ed.) X, 170-171.

[3] Richardson, *Messages and Papers of the Presidents,* II, 581-582.

and that the courts should not be allowed to reverse the political philosophy of the people." [4]

The plain fact is that every determined President who has been faced with a hostile majority in the Court has criticized its decisions, and Jefferson, Jackson, and Lincoln challenged its final authority. The second Roosevelt did not go so far as did they, but his proposal for a contingent enlargement of the Court was in an old tradition. There had been many plans before for limiting or controlling the power of the Court,[5] but President Roosevelt's followed none of them in detail, although it was in part similar to that contained in a bill which passed the House but failed to carry the Senate in 1869.

I have said that it is a paradox of American history that the Court's finality of decision has in general been upheld by popular support, whereas at times the Court has been denounced as a tool of special interests. It is perhaps a more striking paradox that it has grown and flourished upon partisan criticism. Had it been kept aloof and sacrosanct, like some ark of the convenant too holy to be mentioned save in reverential terms, it would never have gained the position of primacy that it secured. The Court has been frequently attacked, but, over the long haul, it has grown in power and prestige, both because of the criticism and of the publicity, the prominence thus given to its activities. The criticism has aided in keeping its decisions consistent with national development, and the prominence did much to make a position on it attractive to ambitious and dynamic men.

The Court's relation to the course of American politics is not seen in controversy alone. Its membership has been largely drawn from those who have been active in some

---

[4] Cited in C. G. Haines, *The American Doctrine of Judicial Supremacy* (2d ed. 1932), 483. See chapters X, XII, XVI-XVII, for material dealing with controversies over the judicial power. [5] Haines, *op. cit.*, ch. XVII.

sphere of partisan activities. The day Washington signed the Judiciary Act of 1789 he sent to the Senate his list of nominations for the six Justiceships then provided for the Supreme Court. Although political parties were already emerging, he made no attempt to balance the membership of the Court between them. All of the first six, as well as the four whom he subsequently nominated, were Federalists. He wished to have the Court represent the party which had drafted the Constitution and worked for its adoption. That document was to be interpreted by its friends. With rare exceptions, his example has been followed by every President since his time. John Adams appointed Federalists; Jefferson and his three successors appointed Democratic Republicans; Jackson appointed Democrats. From 1829 to 1861 the only man not a Democrat appointed to the Court was Benjamin R. Curtis of Boston, a Whig appointed by a Whig President. Lincoln began the appointment of Republicans in 1862. By 1869 the Court contained a majority of Republicans and that majority remained until 1939. The Court has steadily reflected the complexion of the dominant political party. The Presidents and the Senate have sought for judges of a congenial point of view.

It is of course true that not all of these men had been active in politics before they went to the Supreme Court. But it is true that every one of the eighty-three Justices has held some public office prior to taking his seat on the supreme bench, and only ten of them had held no public office other than a judgeship. In the present Court (1942) only two members, Mr. Justice Black and Mr. Justice Murphy, had served previously in a judicial capacity, in each instance consisting of a short term as a municipal court judge. Of the eleven Chief Justices in the Court's history, including Chief Justice Stone, only four had ever held any judicial office before their first appointment to the Supreme Court, and the combined services of these four made but thirty-two out of a total of one hundred and fifty-two years. Not one of the Chief Justices who presided over the Court between 1801 and 1910 had any previous judicial experience of any kind.

These facts indicate that the Presidents have long realized that the principal work of the Court was not that ordinarily assigned to the courts of law. Its great task was one of statesmanship. And for the performance of this task learning in the common law was largely irrelevant. For, as the Court has become more and more concerned with questions of statutory construction and of constitutionality, its work has been progressively less that of the ordinary kind of private litigation.

The nature of the task performed by the Court for over a century makes the traditional, legalistic interpretation of judicial review quite misleading. Bryce, to take an eminent exponent of this view as an example, apparently saw the power of passing upon the validity of legislation as simply "to declare and apply the law." The principles of the law of agency he found pertinent and satisfying. For, he said, the Court does not pass upon the policy or reasonableness of legislation; it is concerned only with the authority delegated to the Congress, or not prohibited to the States, by the document which embodies the will of the people. And the only criterion, apart from the decisions of the Court, of correctness in the interpretation of the Constitution is the "general opinion of the [legal] profession." A "bad decision of its meaning" is one "which the general opinion of the profession condemns." [6] Tocqueville's earlier observation that judicial review gave to the judges "immense political influence"

---

[6] *The American Commonwealth* (1888 ed.) I, 247-248. Thomas Reed Powell's "The Logic and Rhetoric of Constitutional Law," *Journal of Philosophy, Psychology and Scientific Method,* XV, 654 (1918), *Selected Essays on Constitutional Law,* I, 474, is an excellent corrective to this theory of constitutional interpretation.

is illustrative of his deeper understanding of the role played by the American courts.[7]

In adapting the written Constitution to the changing circumstances of American life [8] the Court has always operated within a broad area of discretion. Since the earliest years the test of constitutionality has not been the words of the Constitution alone. They are the starting point but most cases are not decided by them. For most constitutional causes are not concerned with terms of precise meaning; they involve one or more of a few general phrases. The greater number of such cases, that is to say, have been decided in terms of the commerce, the contract, and the due process and equal protection clauses. The first of these was and is incapable of exact definition. The others were so expanded by the Court that precision in application gave way to latitudinarianism. When the Court began to interpret the spirit of the Constitution, and particularly when, in 1810, it began to incorporate the "principles of natural justice and the fundamental laws of every free government" into the contract clause, it had embarked upon a voyage for which the black letter Constitution was only a general guide to navigation. And the record of modifications in interpretation and of overruled decisions does not begin with the year 1937.[9]

THE COURT AS UMPIRE

This breadth of discretion within which the Court determines the meaning of the Constitution is easily seen when

---

[7] Cf. C. G. Haines, "James Bryce and American Constitutional Federalism," in Robert C. Brooks (ed.), *Bryce's American Commonwealth: Fiftieth Anniversary* (1939).

[8] For an analysis of the relationship between the changes in economic organization and the Court's decisions see the brilliant essay of Max Lerner, "The Supreme Court and American Capitalism," 42 *Yale Law Journal* 668 (1933), *Selected Essays on Constitutional Law,* II, 154.

[9] Cf. Malcolm P. Sharp, "Movement in Supreme Court Adjudication—A Study of Modified and Overruled Decisions," 46 *Harvard Law Review* 361, 593, 795 (1933).

one reflects upon the Court's work as umpire of the federal structure. Now that the Eighteenth Amendment has been repealed the only amendment which has added to the power of Congress is the Sixteenth, one made necessary only by the unfortunate income tax decision in 1895.[10] There is not a word in the Constitution about banks, or a paper currency, or the acquisition of new territories, or the conservation of natural resources, or establishing agricultural experiment stations, or loaning money to railroads, or preventing starvation among the victims of economic depressions, or, for that matter, of communication through the use of steamboats, railroads, the telegraph, the telephone, and the radio. Had the Court set itself against the exercise of power over these and many other subjects by the national government, had it insisted upon a narrow interpretation of the finance and commerce clauses, either the Constitution would have been many times amended, or it would have been replaced, or the Court would have suffered defeat.

Until very recently the Court had been least successful, in its capacity as federal referee, when issues of social reform were involved. This was foreshadowed in the disastrous Dred Scott decision, and it is evident in some of the later cases involving labor statutes. In the same year, for example, that the Court found a labor union boycott to be a violation of the Sherman Act, an act dealing with commerce among the states, it held, in the Adair case, that there was no connection between an employee's membership in a labor organization, and the carrying on of interstate commerce.[11] In one case an act was applied as against labor unions, in the other an act protecting labor unions was declared unconstitutional. A distinction between the two sets of facts can, as usual, be found. But to a labor union member, or to those working for the

---

[10] The Reconstruction Amendments do contain grants of power to Congress but those grants have been of slight effectiveness, in part because of the Court's decisions. [11] *Supra,* 117, 119.

advancement of labor unions, it seemed that here, as later, the Court saw fit so to draw the distinction as to exclude labor from the benefits of the Constitution. The child labor cases gave support to the same attitude.

Criticism of the Court's rulings as federal umpire has not been confined to those dealing with slavery, or the power of Congress under the Reconstruction Amendments, or labor legislation. Particularly during the era of Marshall, although not then only, was the fierce antagonism produced by sectional interests and doctrinaire faith in states' rights directed against decisions sustaining Congressional authority. But, in the long-run view, the Court appears most accurately to have expressed the trends of American development when it sustained the action of Congress.[12]

So far as concerns the separation of governmental powers there have, since the Court established its own position of primacy as an interpreting body, been relatively little constitutional litigation and rare decisions resulting in popular condemnation or applause. Most of the cases have been of a non-spectacular character. But some of the recent rulings, especially those dealing with the removal power and with the delegation of legislative powers, indicate that this part of constitutional law may be far more prominent in the future than it has been in the past.

THE COURT AS CENSOR

From Fletcher v. Peck in 1810 until 1937 the stream of cases in which the Court gave protection to the rights of persons grew rapidly in volume. But the vast majority of these cases, be it remembered, dealt with property rights,

[12] For a recent article harshly critical of the Court's interpretation of Congressional powers in the sphere of federalism, as well as in that pertaining to the rights of persons, see Henry W. Edgerton, "The Incidence of Judicial Control over Congress," 22 *Cornell Law Quarterly*, 299 (1937), *Selected Essays on Constitutional Law*, I, 793.

with protecting, that is, against legislative regulation of economic interests, and not with civil rights. Had judicial review been concerned primarily with civil rights, with the protection against bills of attainder and *ex post facto* laws, against restrictions upon the freedom of speech or religion, or against statutes denying a free and open trial, the Court would have had little to do. Before 1865 there was but a single case in which an act was held invalid because it violated a civil right. The later expansion of due process somewhat extended the work of the Court in this respect, but it did not, before 1937, fundamentally alter the balance. In the period of Chief Justice Taft there were 70 cases in which the due process and equal protection clauses were the justification for holding state statutes regulating or taxing property interests unconstitutional. There were only seven cases in which the Court invalidated state legislation because of interference with civil liberties.

It has been indicated that there have been but few cases in which Congressional action has been found to be in conflict with the Bill of Rights. Not yet, for example, has a national statute been found to infringe that most vital of rights, freedom of speech. It may be that, had it not been for the presiding watchfulness of the Court, more statutes like the Sedition Act of 1798, aimed at opposition criticism of the party in power, would have been enacted. I doubt it, but my doubt is incapable of proof. What is certain is that the Sedition Act was not held invalid. It never came to the Supreme Court, although some of the members of that Court, on circuit duty, enforced it with rigor and enthusiasm. And the Congressional limitations upon civil rights enacted during the Civil War and the World War were in no instance invalidated. During the World War the Espionage and Sedition Acts were sustained and enforced. In the years following that War, when the Red-hunt was on, the only statutes held unconstitutional which discriminated against radicals or aliens were those requiring teaching in English in the schools.

The members of the Court are not on, or from, Olympus and they are affected, as are Congressmen, by the strong feeling engendered in times of crisis. It is at such times that civil liberties are in greatest danger. The history of judicial review does not furnish the evidence to indicate that the Supreme Court will, in periods of intense feeling or of hysteria, afford a sanctuary to those whose views run counter to the popular will.[13] Nor, at least until very recently, have those rights of persons or of groups which have not been accepted as legally respectable always been sustained, even in the piping times of peace. The rights of those accused of crimes were much more likely to be protected than were the rights of those who advocated a more equal social order.

There have, then, been comparatively few cases in which civil rights have been protected and hundreds in which the vastly expanded contract and due process clauses were given as the justification for invalidating acts regulating or taxing property. John Marshall, under the influence of Hamilton, distrusting the new democracy, and anxious to bring security to speculators in land as well as to owners of more conservative business enterprise, carried his interpretation of the contract clause beyond the intent of the framers and the requirements of his time. After state reservation clauses had confined his doctrine, another and more elastic device for invalidating statutes hazardous to vested rights was fashioned out of the due process clause.

A considerable number of the decisions under the expanded version of due process, as well as the income tax case, and those in which labor legislation was dealt with under the commerce clause, undoubtedly are expressive of an extreme *laissez faire* philosophy. The point of view succinctly stated by Justice Brewer when he wrote that "the paternal theory

[13] See Z. Chafee, Jr., *Free Speech in the United States* (1941).

of government is to me odious" [14] was responsible for the enunciation of numerous constitutional limitations upon the regulatory power. Had Field, Fuller, Brewer, Peckham, and others of this persuasion agreed with the point of view best exemplified by Holmes, their personal opposition to the newer trends in legislation would have had no greater constitutional effect than Holmes' scepticism about social reformers.[15] But to them Holmes' view that a judge should not read his own social philosophy into the Constitution was a simple evasion of judicial duty, for in their judgment the Constitution spoke with the voice of "rugged American individualism." Whether this doctrine had ever been so generally accepted as these Justices apparently believed is highly doubtful. The debates in the Federal Convention do not indicate that it was there the assumed basis of constitutional construction. And certainly it was no longer, if it had ever been, the accepted theory of legislative action by the time that it was expounded and implemented by the Court. The evidence is not yet sufficiently abundant to warrant a dogmatic statement, but it now appears that the economic and social individualism of the seventies and eighties was created by that generation rather than inherited from the founders. It was the creed of a minority which, like the Federalists of two generations before, was fast losing out at the polls.

What has just been said is not intended to imply that in all of the constitutional decisions of this era the Court expressed the attitude of a minority in opposition to the currents of the time. It is only in dealing with certain kinds of

---

[14] Dissent in Budd v. N.Y., 143 U.S. 517, 551 (1892).

[15] In 1915 Holmes wrote: "The social reformers of today seem to me so far to forget that we can no more get something for nothing by legislation than we can by mechanics as to be satisfied if the bill to be paid for their improvements is not presented in a lump sum." *Collected Legal Papers* (1921) 305. For other examples of his economic conservatism see *Holmes-Pollock Letters* (ed. by M. D. Howe, 1941) I, 152, 163; II, 25.

legislation that this point of view emerges. But a sufficient number of these issues were either intrinsically dramatic or were so tied up with current political controversy that they brought the doctrine and the decisions of the Court into public attention and made it appear to many that the Justices were encouraging an intransigent minority to resist and to continue to be bitter against change by putting the stamp of approval upon this minority's ideology.

To the extent that the Court did this, and it can hardly be doubted that a good many of its decisions can be so described, it was failing to fulfill its historic function. It was making the way of constitutional government more difficult. It was promoting national division rather than national unity. But at its worst the Court was working from inside, not outside the machine. It did speak for at least a minority view and frequently for the attitude of a very large, as well as a powerful, minority.

A slightly different way of describing the opposition of the Court to regulatory legislation is by saying that it refused to accept the full consequences of the industrial revolution. The statutory history of this country after the introduction of the technological changes made possible by the age of invention is similar to that of every country which has experienced those transformations.

This judicial reluctance to accept the legislation which followed alterations in social, economic, and political processes culminated in the slaughter of 1935-1936. The Court was then dealing primarily with national legislation, but, while acting as federal umpire, it applied the point of view repeatedly given expression during the preceding decades when the statutes before it were chiefly those of states and when, in most instances, the federal problem was not involved. That distrust, if not hatred, of "paternalism" which had served to curb state attempts to deal with economic and social problems was now turned against the Congressional attempt to mitigate the plight of the millions who were caught by the downswing of the depression. For a short, but almost disastrous, period, the majority of the Court "imputed to our fundamental law their own too narrow construction of it, their own theory of its purposes and its spirit and sought thus . . . to restrict its great liberty." [16]

Viewed in terms of historical comparisons the Court in 1935-1936 was doing much what it had done in Dred Scott, in 1895-1898, and in the decade of the 'twenties. The majority of the Justices shut their eyes to the injunction of Marshall: "we must never forget that it is a *constitution* we are expounding." [17] They ignored the purpose behind many of the grants of power and magnified some of the restraints beyond recognition. The Constitution which, in Justice Matthews' fine phrase, "was made for an undefined and expanding future" [18] was interpreted as though it were a private contract or a statute enacted for a peculiar, temporary purpose. It was not the restraints upon governmental interferences with civil rights which were given an enlarged meaning. So far as these guarantees were invoked it was almost entirely for assistance in hampering the attempt of the government to carry on what Madison called "the principal task of modern legislation": the "regulation of these various and interfering interests." [19] And by "interests" Madison here meant those produced by the "various and unequal distribution of property." He very well knew, and said, that not all factional differences were economic in origin. But he was also of the opinion that the most difficult tasks confronting executives and legislators would ordinarily be those produced by pressures emanating from economic interests.

Toward the close of his argument in the income tax case James C. Carter said to the Court:

---

[16] J. B. Thayer, *Legal Essays* (1908), 158.
[17] McCulloch v. Maryland, 4 Wheaton 316, 407 (1819).
[18] Hurtado v. California, 110 U.S. 516, 530-531 (1884).
[19] *Federalist*, No. 10 (Ford ed.), p. 57.

> "Nothing could be more unwise or dangerous—nothing more foreign to the spirit of the Constitution—than an attempt to baffle and defeat a popular determination by a judgment in a law suit. When the opposing forces of sixty millions of people have become arrayed in hostile political ranks upon a question which all men feel is not a question of law, but of legislation, the only path of safety is to accept the voice of the majority as final." [20]

But the majority of the Justices unwisely listened instead to the plea of Joseph H. Choate to stop "the communist march . . . now or never." [21] There was, of course, no communist march. Had there been one the Court would have been as powerless to stop it as it was, in the long run, to stop those regulatory measures which the conservatives, and many of the liberals, of the nineties regarded as socialistic legislation.

THE CONSERVATION OF CONSTITUTIONALISM

Undoubtedly judicial review was intended to be a conservative device, but it was intended to conserve the Constitution, not a particular economic philosophy. The attempt to make the two into one very nearly succeeded, but that success could only be temporary. The forces which conditioned the very life of the nation in the twentieth century made impossible the continued existence of this union. In the dramatic Court fight of 1937 the plan of President Roosevelt was defeated, but the Court too was forced to retreat. On the judicial record that retreat was from certain decisions, certain juridical doctrines, of the past few years. The more basic change was the retreat from the judicially created and expressed principles of *laissez faire*.

A journalistic commentator recently wrote that the Court no longer (since 1937, that is) gives to the Constitution a literal interpretation. Such a view is based upon the assump-

---

[20] 157 U.S. 429, 531-532 (1895). [21] *Ibid.*, 533.

tion, astonishing in its implications, that the men of 1787 intended that the general clauses of the Constitution be given the interpretations placed upon them in 1935 and 1936. The constitutional theory of Justice McReynolds has been changed in many ways, but the Constitution of James Madison is unimpaired. Indeed, the law of that Constitution is today in a healthier condition than it has been for half a century. To say that is not to say that the doctrines of today will or should be in all respects the doctrines of day after tomorrow, any more than it is to say that the statutes recently sustained reflect in all instances the highest legislative wisdom. It is to say that the stature of American constitutional law is not to be measured by the number of judicial restraints or by the height of the statutory mortality rate. That stature is to be judged by the strength, which is, in large part, the flexibility of constitutional government. Flexibility can, it is true, degenerate into flabbiness and not all constitutional government has exhibited strength. But surely the history of constitutional government in the United States, including in that history the record of the Articles of Confederation and of the state constitutions, proves both that flexibility need not mean weakness and that a constitution cannot long endure which is not adaptable to the needs of a growing nation. Considered in the light of the intent of the framers—"to form a more perfect union, establish justice, . . . promote the general welfare"—the constitutional law of today is far stronger than the frozen intransigence of 1935-1936. And once more the doctrines of the Court are in substantial accord with the main currents of national life.

In terms of present circumstances constitutional law is better suited to deal with the problems of war time and with that period of post-war readjustment which will produce in the future, as they have produced in the past, many difficult and acute problems for adjudication. We can not foresee the exact nature of those problems, although we can probably detect the vague outlines of some of them. But we can have confidence that they will be dealt with in the method of constitutional government. And to that method the courts have made one contribution of unchallengeable value in their emphasis upon the importance of rational debate and justification. It is this method which enables us to hold before the whole people, majority and minorities alike, the ideal of discussion rather than violence as the only proper reliance in politics.

TABLE OF CASES

TABLE OF CASES

INDEX